E·S·S·E·N
ISR

ALSO AVAILABLE IN THE *ESSENTIALLY* SERIES

Essentially Turkey
Carole and Chris Stewart

Essentially Yugoslavia
Celia Irving

Forthcoming:

Essentially Cyprus
Pamela Westland

Essentially Hungary
Nicholas Parsons

Essentially Egypt
Carole Stewart and Andrew Hogg

E·S·S·E·N·T·I·A·L·Y
ISRAEL

CAROLE & CHRIS STEWART

CHRISTOPHER HELM
London

© 1989 Chris and Carole Stewart

Line drawings by Lorna Turpin
Christopher Helm (Publishers) Ltd, Imperial House
21–25 North Street, Bromley, Kent BR1 1SD

ISBN 0-7470-3011-1

A CIP catalogue record for this book is available from the British Library.

All rights reserved. No reproduction, copy or transmission of this publication may be made without written permission.

No paragraph of this publication may be reproduced, copied or transmitted save with written permission or in accordance with the provisions of the Copyright Act 1956 (as amended), or under the terms of any licence permitting limited copying issued by the Copyright Licensing Agency, 7 Ridgmount Street, London WC1E 7AE.

Any person who does any authorised act in relation to this publication may be liable to criminal prosecution and civil claims for damages.

Typeset by Opus, Oxford
Printed and bound in Great Britain by Billing and Sons Ltd, Worcester.

C·O·N·T·E·N·T·S

Map **vi**
Introduction **1**
1. History **5**
2. Jerusalem **27**
3. West Bank **89**
4. The Coast **103**
5. Galilee **129**
6. The Dead Sea, Northern and Central Negev **165**
7. Eilat, Southern Negev and Sinai **179**
8. General Information **189**
Bibliography **203**
Index **207**

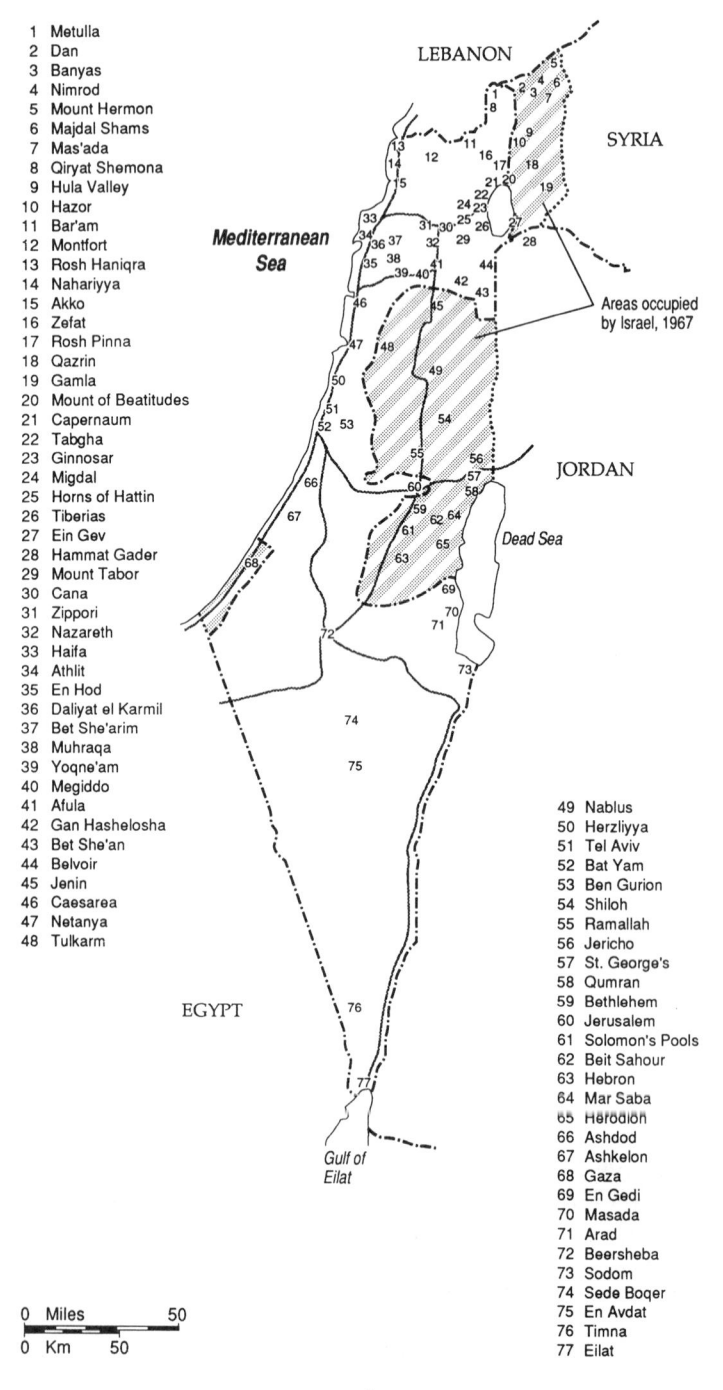

1 Metulla
2 Dan
3 Banyas
4 Nimrod
5 Mount Hermon
6 Majdal Shams
7 Mas'ada
8 Qiryat Shemona
9 Hula Valley
10 Hazor
11 Bar'am
12 Montfort
13 Rosh Haniqra
14 Nahariyya
15 Akko
16 Zefat
17 Rosh Pinna
18 Qazrin
19 Gamla
20 Mount of Beatitudes
21 Capernaum
22 Tabgha
23 Ginnosar
24 Migdal
25 Horns of Hattin
26 Tiberias
27 Ein Gev
28 Hammat Gader
29 Mount Tabor
30 Cana
31 Zippori
32 Nazareth
33 Haifa
34 Athlit
35 En Hod
36 Daliyat el Karmil
37 Bet She'arim
38 Muhraqa
39 Yoqne'am
40 Megiddo
41 Afula
42 Gan Hashelosha
43 Bet She'an
44 Belvoir
45 Jenin
46 Caesarea
47 Netanya
48 Tulkarm
49 Nablus
50 Herzliyya
51 Tel Aviv
52 Bat Yam
53 Ben Gurion
54 Shiloh
55 Ramallah
56 Jericho
57 St. George's
58 Qumran
59 Bethlehem
60 Jerusalem
61 Solomon's Pools
62 Beit Sahour
63 Hebron
64 Mar Saba
65 Herodion
66 Ashdod
67 Ashkelon
68 Gaza
69 En Gedi
70 Masada
71 Arad
72 Beersheba
73 Sodom
74 Sede Boqer
75 En Avdat
76 Timna
77 Eilat

LEBANON

SYRIA

Mediterranean Sea

Areas occupied by Israel, 1967

JORDAN

Dead Sea

EGYPT

Gulf of Eilat

0 Miles 50
0 Km 50

I·N·T·R·O·D·U·C·T·I·O·N

Israel is a land of striking contrasts. You may see it in the gleaming Mercedes, crawling impatiently behind a donkey on the roads to Jerusalem; in the imposing modern hospital and university at Beersheba, only minutes from the well where Abraham watered his flocks. The frenetic bustle of the Arab *Souk* in Old Jerusalem is as much a part of today's Israel as the brash, traffic-congested avenues of Tel Aviv. Elderly White Russian nuns go about their devotions, oblivious of coach-loads of tourists taking their turn on a camel at the summit of the Mount of Olives. Stark modern sculpture, beloved of the Israelis, stands sentinel over the wilderness of ageless deserts.

In such a small country, you might expect a degree of uniformity, at least in topography. Even here though, there is nothing typical, unless it is in contradictions. You will find impossibly dry and harsh deserts (with tracts miraculously coaxed to fertility by the Israelis), valleys, mountains, ravines and canyons, flat coastal plains, golden beaches, lakes, oases, lush hills and pastures, orange, olive groves and vineyards, and the lowest point on earth where the Dead Sea lies, choked to an unearthly stillness by a saturation of minerals.

Scattered over this varied landscape are the remains of civilisations and conquerors long since dead. Shadows of the ancient worlds of the Canaanites, the Israelites, Nabataeans

INTRODUCTION

and Hittites are discernible among the more tangible remains left by the Greeks, Romans and Byzantines. The intricate art and architecture of the Arabs still stand cheek by jowl, but peacefully now, with the heavy beauty of Crusader ruins; here and there, evidence of 400 years of Ottoman rule shows itself in an elegant portal or a splendid mosque.

With the discovery that the earth was round, Jerusalem lost in the eyes of the scientists, its position as the centre of the world. But far from losing its eminence, Palestine had, and still has, a significance wholly out of proportion to its tiny size, in the eyes of almost half the population of the world. The country might have declined into an unimportant middle eastern backwater, had it not been for the fact that it was in this land that God chose to reveal himself to the Jews, the Christians and the Moslems. The Holy Land was to become the focus and cradle of belief for almost half the world's population.

History is still in the making here. Rarely a day passes when we don't hear something about this country in the news. This tiny land was, and still is, the fulfilment of the passionate dream of an ancient people scattered over the globe for 2,000 years and more. Certainly Jews have always lived here, but the great majority was exiled in ancient times and they have only been returning in significant numbers since the late 18th century. The 20th century saw the biggest immigration, gathered from 100 different countries and cultures. In fact, Palestine only became the State of Israel 40 years ago, and with it came the problems that divide the Middle East today. Whatever your views on Israel and the 'Palestinian problem', a visit is likely to change your perspective and confuse you still further. There are no simple answers. But there's no shortage of people willing to talk about it and you will be surprised at how much normality and even conviviality exists where you may have expected nothing but bitterness and strife.

Above all this book is not intended to move you one way or another in your views and affiliations on the Middle-Eastern question. In so far as is possible we steer clear of political statements, while tacitly upholding a peaceful and humanitarian solution that would offer a life of dignity and fulfilment for all who call this land their home. For the sake of brevity, the title of this book is *Essentially Israel,* but this also includes the occupied territories.

We cannot within the limited pages of this book answer all the questions you are likely to have, but if you only have a few days or a few weeks to spare, we have endeavoured to give you a flavour. Browse through the descriptions; they will help

INTRODUCTION

you to decide in advance how you might wish to spend your time and give you an idea of what to expect. The 'guide' chapters are divided into geographical areas for ease of identification. Bear in mind that distances in Israel are small: if you want to visit Galilee as well as the Negev desert and the Dead Sea area, this won't mean a great amount of travelling.

We have given Jerusalem a seemingly disproportionate amount of space. It cannot be otherwise. The city is hardly more than a large town, but it's a fascinating and diverse microcosm of the whole country. It is a melting pot of cultures and beliefs, the 'eternal city'. History too has been given a long chapter. It is impossible to make sense of this extraordinary country without at least a general understanding of the turbulent sequence of events. We hope we have made it interesting and entertaining.

Finally, Israel is, like any country in the world, sometimes extraordinary beautiful, sometimes disappointingly mundane. Often delightful but frequently infuriating. We have tried to be honest and tell it as it is – warts and all. But such judgements are always subjective and, in the final analysis, you must make up your own mind. We are confident that your visit here will be a unique and memorable experience. *Shalom. Salam.*

C·H·A·P·T·E·R·1
History

Pre-Biblical

The most ancient bones found in the Holy Land may be 600,000 years old; primitive man had found his way here as long ago as the early Stone Age. The climate would have been very different; more reliable rainfall watered the thickly forested mountains, plains and valleys, and the whole land teemed with wildlife. But by 14,000 BC the climate had changed to resemble more nearly what we know today; it became hotter and drier and the desolation of stones and dust that we see now in the deserts and wilderness of Israel was created. By 10,000 BC the Stone Age hunter-gatherers had settled in villages to grow basic crops and raise domestic animals.

From 4000 BC the Stone Age made way for copper and bronze, bringing about trade and exchanges of culture between the hitherto isolated groups. Civilisation and culture began to make its appearance in the separate city-states of the plains.

The great empires of the ancient world developed where favourable conditions for agriculture existed, where abundant water for irrigation and easily tilled soil created conditions for supporting a large population, a proportion of which was not engaged in the production of food. Thus the great delta of the Nile gave birth to the Egyptian Empire, while further north, between the rivers of the Tigris and Euphrates – in the 'Cradle of Civilisation' – flourished the Empire of Mesopotamia.

In the world of 2000 BC these two empires stood virtually alone: there was nobody else to war against or to trade with. The roads between Mesopotamia and Egypt were worn deep by the constant passing of armies, of merchant caravans, of prophets and priests and the occasional diplomatic mission.

The route between the two great empires lay through a country that formed a land bridge between the deserts of Arabia and the 'Great Sea' (Mediterranean). This was the LAND OF CANAAN, inhabited by disparate groups of Canaanites, Amorites, Jebusites and others, living in independent city-states under the control of Egypt. The mounds or *Tels* of these cities are still visible today – Hazor, Megiddo, Gezer, Shechem, Jerusalem, Hebron, Beth Sh'an and others.

THE TRIBES OF ISRAEL

It was in this insignificant little country, a mere stop on the road between empires, that God chose to reveal himself to man. Round about 1800 BC, Abraham, leader of a tribe of nomads, arrived in Canaan, pasturing his flocks in the hills. As he was travelling in the desert, he was visited by God, who told him that he would be the father of two great nations, and that one of them would be God's chosen people, whose interests He would look after. Despite his great age, Abraham subsequently produced two sons; by Hagar, an Egyptian serving-maid, he had Ishmael, who was to be the father of the Arabs; and by his wife, Sarah, he had Isaac (literally 'The Laugh' because of the great age of Abraham and Sarah). Isaac was to be the father of the Jews.

Abraham's wandering tribes grazed their flocks in Canaan for many years before famine drove them south to Egypt. There they settled, at first seduced by the ease and plenty of the land, but later, as the Egyptians came to fear their influence and cleverness, persecuted and enslaved. They stayed, leaderless and undecided, for 430 years until the arrival of Moses.

MOSES, one of the Children of Israel from Abraham's tribes, had achieved a high position in Egyptian society. However he grew tired of the life and, drawn by the call of the wilderness, he wandered into the desert of Sinai. There he met and befriended a nomad leader, Jethro, and soon married his daughter, Zipporah. While away in the hills near Mount Sinai, looking after Jethro's sheep, Moses was called by God to lead the Israelites out of Egypt and back to the Promised Land.

Back in Egypt, Moses reminded the Israelites that they were the chosen people of God, and mobilised them for the flight to come. Then by trickery and with considerable assistance from God, he managed to wrest the tribes away from their captors.

They fled across the Red Sea, and spent 40 years (a biblical term denoting a long time) in the wilderness of Sinai. Here Moses received from God the Ten Commandments. This was the re-affirmation of the Covenant which God had made with the Israelites earlier through Abraham, Isaac and Jacob. Through this Covenant He would look after the interests of His people if they would obey the laws He prescribed. The early history of the Jews can be seen as an ebbing and flowing of God's favour as the tribes follow or depart from the Law.

The Conquest

Despite the 40 years of hardship that Moses had endured as leader, God was not to grant him a sight of the Promised Land. It was JOSHUA who presided over the fording of the Jordan and the taking of Canaan from its indigenous peoples – the Canaanites, Hittites, Perizzites, Amorites, Hivites and Jebusites. Joshua, a disagreeable character who showed mercy to neither women nor children as he massacred the populations of city after city, butchered and burned his way through the land.

When archaeologists are excavating a *tel* it is easy for them to identify the stratum that corresponds to the period of Joshua's conquests – it is a blackened and scorched layer. In fact though, the conquest of Canaan by the Israelites was a process that lasted many years, and probably came about as much by assimilation as by bloody conquest. In particular the religion of the Israelites – a God who cared for the individual and loved all men as equal – must have appealed to the common people of the city-states. The religion that held sway in Canaan was little more than a device for maintaining the power and privilege of the priesthood and the élite. It is likely that the ordinary people, warmly embracing this new religion, would have risen and overthrown their oppressors, opening the city gates to the Israelites.

On the coastal plain, meanwhile, Israel's arch enemy had arrived, establishing city-states at Ashdod, Ascalon, Gaza, Ekron and Gath. These were the PHILISTINES, the 'Sea Peoples' who had come from Crete and the Aegean. Their iron technology gave them an advantage over the less sophisticated Israelites, who used only bronze. The Philistines gave their name to the coastal plain of southern Canaan, Philistia, from which came the later name for the whole land – Palestine.

By about 1050 BC the Israelites, now a loosely-knit confederation of twelve tribes, had consolidated their position throughout the land of Canaan. The focal point of their worship, the ARK OF THE COVENANT resided at SHILOH. Constant pressure from the Philistines and the Canaanites pushed the Israelites into uniting as a single kingdom under King SAUL.

Saul, who had been an ordinary farmer before being called to kingship, did a great deal for his people, but towards the end of his reign he began to turn from the ways of God's prophet, Samuel, who had put him in power. He finally became deranged with jealousy and hatred for the young shepherd, David, who had so spectacularly put the Philistines to flight. Saul was finally defeated by the Philistines at Mount Gilboa. He took his own life, and the Philistines, finding his body and those of his sons, impaled them on the walls of Beth She'an. David became king.

King David

David reigned from 1012 to 972 BC. During this period he further welded his people together by taking the hitherto impregnable Jerusalem from the Jebusites. By setting up the Ark of the Covenant there, he made Jerusalem the capital and religious focus of his kingdom. Under his rule the territory occupied by the Israelites reached its greatest extent.

David is remembered as a romantic figure: shepherd-boy, hero, king, lover, poet and musician – a man of wild passions and troubled conscience. Arab legend says of him 'At the sound of his voice wild beasts left their lairs, water ceased to flow, and men and women followed him into the desert, there to die in ecstasy.' But he was also a great conqueror and administrator, the very ideal of kingship and the prototype of the expected Messiah. He died in 972 BC, and the kingship passed to one of his sons, Solomon.

Solomon

Arab legend enthuses even more lyrically over Solomon, crediting him with power over the winds, knowledge of the speech of animals and command over *djinns*. 'He would shelter from the sun beneath a canopy made by all the birds, and the sun itself would stand still while he said his evening prayers.' He too was a lover and a poet, author of 'Song of

Songs', one of the most beautiful love-poems in the literature of the world. He it was who finally built the Temple at Jerusalem, using the wealth of materials gathered by his father, David; it was unsurpassed in splendour in its time, and perhaps one of the most magnificent buildings the world has ever seen.

The truth about Solomon is that he came to power by having the other contenders murdered. He probably was the wisest of men, and a great administrator, but the main achievement of his reign was to strengthen the apparatus of government and bolster the privilege of the élite, by taxing the poor to maintain an immense private army. Even so he lost much of David's hard-won territory.

On Solomon's death the land of Israel, now shrunken and internally divided, split into two kingdoms. The northern kingdom, Israel, elected the district governor JEROBOAM as king; the southern kingdom, Judah, was ruled by Solomon's son REHOBOAM. In the northern kingdom, golden idols were set up at Dan. The people of both kingdoms began to forget the covenant with God, despite the earnest protestations of the prophets.

The Assyrian Conquest

In 721 BC, after years of turmoil, the Israelites paid the price of their inconstancy to God. The empire of Assyria had been aggressively expanding to the East, and with the accession to the throne of SARGON, Israel was cruelly laid to waste. The southern kingdom of Judah preferred to pay tribute and come to terms with her bloodthirsty neighbour. Assyrian policy was to deport the population of the conquered lands and to replace them with captives from elsewhere. From this mixture of populations came the SAMARITANS. The rest of the Israelites of the northern kingdom were carried off into captivity.

King HEZEKIAH of Judah, harkening to his prophets and sensitive to the threat of being overwhelmed by Assyria, instigated thoroughgoing religious reforms – but he also fortified Jerusalem and engineered a water-supply for time of siege, just in case. His fears were well founded. In 701 BC the Assyrians, under SENNACHERIB, stormed through Judah. Jerusalem itself was miraculously saved: as the defenders looked glumly from their towers at the hordes on the surrounding hills, Sennacherib's army 'melted like frost at the glance of the Lord'. Or, to put it more prosaically, the attackers were virtually wiped out by plague. For the prestige of

HISTORY

Jerusalem as the City of God, and for the confidence of the tribes of Judah in the love of their God, it is not hard to imagine how important this event was.

Babylon

Despite some creditable improvements – wise prophets and good kings – the tribes of Judah, now known as the Jews, soon deviated again from the way of God. In 586 BC the new empire of BABYLON succeeded where the Assyrians had failed and took Jerusalem. The city was ravaged, the Temple utterly destroyed and the sacred objects stolen, and the Jews of Jerusalem led into captivity at Babylon.

Not all exiled Jews found life in Babylon that disagreeable, however; many carved out comfortable niches for themselves, setting up businesses and rising to positions of high official rank. From here dates the beginning of the 'DIASPORA'.

The Persian Empire

The ascendancy of Babylon was not to last for long: gathering to the east was a powerful new empire. In 539 BC CYRUS swept the Assyrians before him as he established the first Persian Empire. His policy was to populate the distant borders of his dominions with people who could be relied upon to be loyal to him. Accordingly he freed the Jews, and sent those who wished back to Jerusalem. There, with a certain amount of autonomy and religious freedom, they set about reconstructing the Temple. By 515 BC a new Temple stood in Jerusalem, a shadow of its former glory perhaps, but still a focus for the Jewish faith. A brief age of comparative peace and security reigned in the calm between the rise and fall of empires.

Alexander the Great

Nearly 200 years after the completion of the second Temple, one of the most remarkable empires in world history appeared on the scene. On the plains of Issos in Syria, ALEXANDER THE GREAT defeated the Persians and rolled them back as he forged the empire that within 20 years would encompass virtually all the known world. Jerusalem surrendered and paid tribute without a fight, and in return Alexander granted her privileges. The peace continued.

History

The Disputed Inheritance

In 323 BC Alexander died, leaving his generals to quarrel over the vast empire he had left. Alexander's most important legacy was the influence of Hellenism – the 'breadth and harmony of a new mind' – the civilising art and ideas of Greek culture which, allied with the mysticism and monotheism of the Jews, have so shaped the modern world. The soldiers, tribute collectors and all the trappings of conquest soon faded away, but the culture endured. The Ptolemies and the Seleucids, who were the two major factions warring for control of the empire, were both equally earnest in their promulgation of Hellenism.

The land of Israel suffered the brunt of their fighting; the years of peace were over. Judaism and Hellenism had been eyeing one another warily for many years; each found in the other a phenomenon both intriguing and attractive, yet repellent. The Orthodox Jews held that there was no compatibility between godless Hellenism and the Law. The masses, however, were enjoying the new influences on what must at times have been rather a suffocating creed. They were taking part in athletic contests, secular debate, going to the theatre – but they were also neglecting Jewish ceremonies and failing to keep the Sabbath.

The Hellenes, for their part, were intrigued by the religion of the strange ascetic race they had conquered. Under Ptolemy II Philadelphos, the Hebrew Old Testament was translated into Greek – the SEPTUAGINT. The legend goes that 70 translators, fluent in Hebrew and Greek, were sent to Alexandria where they were locked in 70 cells to complete their work. At the end of their labours they emerged with 70 identical translations – word for word. This understandably impressed the Greeks.

By 175 BC Antiochus Epiphanes of the Seleucids was on the throne. He was certainly unbalanced, and he hated the exclusivity and asceticism of the Orthodox Jews, doing all in his power to provoke them. Hellenisation was enforced; circumcision was banned, worship in the Temple and the keeping of the Jewish festivals were forbidden, and pagan ceremonies were instituted in their stead. The final blow came when the Temple was defiled by the sacrifice of sows upon the altar.

Maccabean Revolt

This proved too much for the devout. When, in 167 BC, the priest Judas Mattathias was ordered to perform a pagan sacrifice at Lydda, he refused. Another priest stepped forward to do the work. Mattathias killed him together with the presiding Seleucid officer. Then he and his five sons fled to the hills where they waged a highly successful guerrilla war against the Seleucids. Judas Mattathias was nicknamed *Maccabi* – the Hammer. Within a short time thousands had flocked to the banner of his revolt, and the Maccabees were pushing the Seleucids back on all fronts. Finally they took Jerusalem itself, and established the HASMONAEAN dynasty. Israel was again its own master, and under the Hasmonaeans, her territory reached its greatest extent since the time of David. In 165 BC the defiled Temple was rededicated and a tenuous peace reigned for a time.

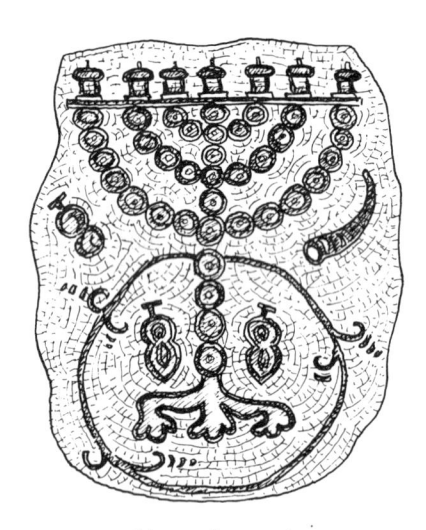

Menorah mosaic

The Romans

As empires tend to do, the Hellenic Empire declined. Rome swiftly filled the vacuum, soon dominating all the lands surrounding Israel. The unity of the Hasmonaeans in Jerusalem was soon torn by wars of succession. In 63 BC POMPEY, who had been summoned to the area to quell disturbances in the Roman province of Syria, moved south and laid siege to Jerusalem. After three months he entered the city with a bloody massacre.

Now began centuries of misunderstanding between the Romans and the Jews. Israel became a vassal-state to the Romans, the most troublesome of all the lands within the *Pax*

Romana. In 37 BC Rome appointed as governor a native of the land, with strong Roman affiliations – HEROD THE GREAT.

Herod is remembered for his cruelty, his madness and his prodigious building works. All over the country today one can see the remains of his monuments – layers of huge, beautifully cut and dressed stone blocks, surmounted by the lesser blocks of the Mamelukes and the Ottomans. To win the favour of the Jews, who hated him, he rebuilt the Temple, making it as magnificent an edifice as it had been at the time of Solomon; only this time he incorporated the vast fortress of the Antonia into the structure. Paranoic and power-maddened, his rule became ever more intolerable to the Jews, until he died raving and mutilated by disease in 4 BC. As a parting shot he incarcerated 1,000 of the most prominent Jews of Jerusalem in the Hippodrome, with orders that they should be slaughtered at the moment of his death; thus Jerusalem would weep at the hour of his passing.

Herod's successor was the procurator PONTIUS PILATE, who took command of Jerusalem in 26 AD. Under Pilate, Roman treatment of the Jews became harsher still. Meanwhile, in the hills and valleys surrounding Lake Tiberias, a tiny but tumultuous event was taking place. JESUS OF NAZARETH had announced that He was the son of God. At the time the Romans were not too concerned, for the Jews had split into many eccentric sects since the tempestuous years of the Hasmonaeans. Rome had no idea of the consequences of this brief ministry of three years in the pastoral hills of Galilee.

About 30 AD, Christ was tried and crucified; three days later He rose from the Sepulchre. Upon these events are based the religion of Christianity.

The First Revolt

By the year 66 AD, Roman oppression of the Jews became intolerable and the Jews rose in the FIRST REVOLT. Astonishingly enough they succeeded in throwing off Roman rule, and there followed three heady years of Jewish independence. But the Romans returned, hungry to avenge this humiliation. In 70 AD TITUS laid waste the land surrounding Jerusalem. It took him three years to take the city, and when he finally entered, he slaughtered 100,000 Jews, wrecked the city and destroyed the Temple. Those Jews who survived were taken into captivity.

Despite the destruction, some Jewish survivors remained in the city, and life continued as near normal as possible while part of the city was reconstructed. But Rome gave no quarter to the troublesome Jews this time, and the oppression continued unabated. When HADRIAN announced his intention of flattening the old city and using it as a foundation for a new pagan city, Aelia Capitolina, another suicidal revolt was born.

Bar Kochba Revolt

Led by the Jewish 'Messiah', SHIMON BAR KOCHBA, the revolt had spectacular successes and for three years succeeded in holding the Romans at bay. In the end though, Roman might prevailed, and after the inevitable slaughter, Hadrian went ahead and built his pagan city with its temples to Jupiter and Venus. The sites of the Crucifixion and the Sepulchre were covered over, and the ruins of the Temple were excluded from the new city. The Roman historian Dio Cassius called this a 'major war'; he reported that the Romans had had to capture 50 fortresses, destroy 985 villages and kill a million people before victory came.

Now the Jews were banished altogether from Aelia Capitolina, on pain of death. The Jewish people were reduced to a dispersed nation without a centre in its own land, while Christianity launched a programme of expansion probably unparalleled in the history of the world.

Rome Adopts Christianity

In 313 the emperor CONSTANTINE adopted Christianity as the official religion of the Roman Empire, now transforming into the Byzantine Empire centred on Constantinople. Churches sprang up all over the Holy Land and the wilderness and deserts became cities of hermits and monks. Constantine's mother HELENA, visiting the Holy Land in 320, gave the movement new impetus when she discovered the True Cross. Pilgrims flocked to the Holy Land in thousands. The Byzantine emperors, and the Christians who remained in the Holy Land, persecuted the Jews more and more harshly. Jerusalem was now a Christian city and Jews were only permitted to enter on one day of the year, to bewail the loss of their Temple.

2nd Persian Empire

Peace reigned during the strong years of Byzantium, while the Holy Land took on a distinctly Christian veneer. The persecution of Jews continued unabated. But in 614 the Jews were able to repay some debts; a new Persian empire under

HISTORY

CHOSROES rose in the east and, with the help of the Jews, drove the Byzantines from the land. All Christian monuments were destroyed except the church at Bethlehem; the Christian population was massacred and tens of thousands of monks were butchered in their caves and monasteries. By 629 however, HERAKLIUS had re-taken the Holy Land for the Byzantine Empire; the Persians were driven out and so were the Jews.

Islam

In 570 the PROPHET MOHAMMED was born near Mecca in Arabia; with him was born the great world religion of Islam. By 636, the Arabs, newly united under Islam, had swept from the deserts through the Holy Land. In 638 the Caliph OMAR took Jerusalem. The Moslem conquest and triumphal entry was almost unique in the history of the Holy City; there was no massacre, no looting and no defiling of sacred places. This marked the start of the longest period of religious tolerance the city had ever known. The Jews were finally allowed to return to Jerusalem; everyone was free to worship as he pleased.

But this period of harmony could not last; as power shifted back and forth within the empire of Islam, the liberal and statesmanlike regime of Omar was superseded by the influence of less enlightened rulers. In 1009 the Fatimid Caliph HAKIM, in a fit of madness and hatred, destroyed all Christian monuments throughout the Holy Land, and killed all the Christians he could lay hands on. Jerusalem sank into decline amid the warring of the three religions.

In 1071 the SELJUK TURKS defeated the withering Byzantine Empire at Manzikert. Within a year the Seljuks were upon Jerusalem. They desecrated what was left of the holy sites and murdered pilgrims. The stirrings of anger which had moved Christian Europe since the time of 'Mad Hakim', finally erupted in a cry for a Christian force to free the Holy Land from the tyranny of the Seljuks. In 1095 Pope URBAN II called for the FIRST CRUSADE.

The Crusades

In 1099 the Crusaders took Jerusalem. There followed the bloodiest massacre the city had ever witnessed – Jews and Moslems, women and children, the aged and infirm, all cut down until 'the streets of the city were washed in blood'. 'From such unthinking fanaticism was born the inflexibility of Islam.

The memory of this massacre for ever stood in the way of a permanent *modus vivendi*' (J. O'Connor).

Having perpetrated this atrocity the Crusaders settled down to a frenetic programme of building, imposing their European system of feudalism on their new dominions, and absorbing the relative luxury and sophistication of their new eastern home. 'The Holy Land flourished like a garden, with many regular clergy, religious persons, hermits, monks, canons, nuns, cloistered virgins and chaste and holy widows', wrote the Bishop of Acre.

The Latin Kingdom lasted about 200 years, years in which harmony and exchanges of courtesy and trade alternated with ferocious hostilities between the Christians and the Moslems. The fortunes of the Latin Kingdom began their decline with the decisive defeat inflicted upon them by SALADIN at the 'Horns of Hattin' in 1187. Thoroughly beaten, they handed Jerusalem over to the victors and retired to Acre.

The Mamelukes

By 1291 the Mamelukes, who had seized power in Egypt and were now striving for dominance in the Moslem world, forced the Latins from Acre, whence they retired from the Holy Land for good, establishing communities of knights in Cyprus and Malta. The Mamelukes took over in Palestine, but they were too busy consolidating their power elsewhere to pay the country the attention it required.

The Mamelukes were an unlovable dynasty who had achieved power by treachery and viciousness. Apart from some ambitious building work, still standing to this day at Acre and Jerusalem, the land fell into decline. By 1517 the Mamelukes were finished , and Palestine was like a ripe fruit which the burgeoning Ottoman empire, having dislodged the Byzantines from Constantinople, was ready to pluck.

The Ottomans

Ottoman rule started well, with an energetic revival under SELIM I and SULEYMAN THE MAGNIFICENT. But the flowering was brief, and with the death of Süleyman, the empire started its long, slow decline. Denuded and depopulated, Palestine fell into neglect, nothing more than a tax farm for the treasuries of the Sultans in Istanbul.

In 1700 an exodus of Ashkenazi Jews arrived, fleeing from persecution in northern Europe. They swelled the ranks of the Sephardic Jews who had been banished from Spain by the

HISTORY

Catholic Kings in 1492. Over the years more and more Jews trickled into Palestine, fleeing repression and persecution. Their numbers were composed of poor peasants and artisans, but also revolutionaries, intellectuals and professional people. In common they had their faith and their idealism, and together they attempted to create an ideal community based upon the land and on their common faith. In 1882 came the FIRST ALIYAH.

As the Ottoman Empire reached the depths of its decline, dragging Palestine with it, events in Europe were leading up to the First World War. Its aftermath was to have a momentous effect upon the wretched little country of Palestine.

Mezuzah modelled on Hurva Synagogue

HISTORY

BRITISH MANDATE

During the First World War Palestine acquired considerable strategic importance. The British, in the interest of undermining the power of the Ottomans, eagerly fostered the beginnings of Arab nationalism. A bewildering array of contradictory agreements was signed, promising everyone as much independence as they could desire. To confuse the issue still further, Britain and France clandestinely entered into the infamous SYKES–PICOT AGREEMENT, by which the conquered lands of the Ottoman Empire were to be divided exclusively between these two countries.

To make matters still worse, the British also wanted the support of the Jews. As a result, the hitherto improbable dream of a Zionist state started to crystallise into a real possibility when Lloyd George's Foreign Secretary, BALFOUR, published the following declaration:

> His Majesty's Government view with favour the establishment in Palestine of a national home for the Jewish people, and will use their best endeavours to facilitate the achievement of this object, it being clearly understood that nothing shall be done which may prejudice the civil and religious rights of existing non-Jewish communities in Palestine, or the rights and political status enjoyed by Jews in any other country.

After the First World War, Britain took over the rule of Palestine from the defeated Ottomans, and the British Mandate was ratified by the League of Nations, along with the Balfour Declaration. In 1917 the British GENERAL ALLENBY entered Jerusalem and officially accepted the surrender of the Turks. Whereas the Balfour Declaration was made by politicians, it was Allenby and his troops who had to cope with reality. At the time, the total population of Palestine was 600,000, mainly Arab, with less than 100,000 Jews. Arab nationalism started to find a voice, albeit a disorganised one. The Palestinian Arabs, though, had no real diplomatic representation to combat the pressure of Zionism.

By 1920 Jewish immigration was markedly increasing. The Palestinian Arabs became increasingly nervous, their discontent erupting into riots and attacks on Jewish settlements. The British were in an impossible situation. Supporting the basic tenets of the Balfour Declaration and looking after the interests of the Arab population, they tried to keep control, imprisoning offenders from both sides.

The British then made a blunder whose ramifications were in no small way responsible for the conflict that seems so insoluble to this day. To settle the Arab/Jewish question the British needed an official Arab leader with whom to negotiate. In a move which was to have fatal consequences for Jews, Palestinians and eventually for the world, the British granted a general amnesty for all involved in the 1920 unrest, allowing one of the Arab agitators, HAJ AMIN AL-HUSSEIN, to become Grand Mufti of Jerusalem. Hussein was rabidly anti-semitic, anti-British and had a long record of violence. A reign of terror followed, during which the Mufti ruthlessly removed any moderate Palestinian voices that might, in these early days, have helped to negotiate an acceptable and lasting peace with the Jews.

Hussein's reign of terror at times reduced the flow of Jewish immigrants. By the 1930s, however, the rise of Nazism prompted a substantial and sustained increase in immigration. By 1936 the Arabs had become alarmed and a serious uprising gave Britain cause to review her stance; as a result the Balfour Declaration was repudiated.

At the outbreak of the Second World War, DAVID BEN GURION pressed for a Jewish force to fight alongside the allies. Mindful of the problem that could be created, once the war was over, by a trained, armed Jewish force in Palestine, which might later turn against the Mandate in pursuit of a Zionist state, there was considerable resistance in Britain, not least from the army. The JEWISH BRIGADE was formed primarily as a result of pressure and support from CHURCHILL who said, 'I like the idea of the Jews trying to get at the murderers of their fellow countrymen in central Europe. It is with the Germans they have their quarrel – I cannot conceive why this martyred race scattered about the world and suffering as no other race has done should be denied the satisfaction of a flag.'

In spite of this, after the war the British still refused to return to the earlier promise of the Balfour Declaration. The lure of Arab oilfields to a country impoverished by six years of war in Europe was too strong. Allowing immigration to increase to an extent where the political balance tipped in favour of the Jews was guaranteed to inflame Arab hostility. And so began the pitiful episode of immigration controls whereby thousands of desperate Jewish refugees, rendered destitute and homeless by the Holocaust, headed for the promise of Zion, only to be turned away, often with tragic results, or interned by the British.

But many of the illegal immigrants did succeed in getting into

Palestine, largely assisted by the *HAGANAH* and the *IRGUN*. Both these organisations were covert Jewish defence forces: the *Haganah* was the 'official' arm of the *Yishuv* (the Jewish community in Palestine before the state was created); the *Irgun,* led by the future Prime Minister MENACHIM BEGIN, was a right-wing, hard-line splinter group of the *Haganah*.

With the growth of the Jewish population, Arab unrest mounted and with both the Arabs and the Jews committing acts of terrorism, either against each other or the British, the situation in Palestine became impossible. In 1947 the British handed the problem over to the United Nations.

On 29 November 1947 both Arabs and Jews waited for the results of the vote from the United Nations General Assembly in New York. The delegates were asked to decide whether or not Palestine should be split into two separate states with 57 per cent of the land going to the Jews, and Jerusalem coming under international control.

To the Arabs the whole affair was a monstrous injustice. The Arab peoples had generally welcomed and lived side by side with Jews, in a spirit of co-operation – and now it would seem that the Palestinian Arabs were having to give up their land to accommodate Jews who could no longer live in Europe. If the partition vote succeeded, the Arabs had already decided that they would mount a full-scale war against the Jews once the British withdrew.

For the Jews, too, partition was far from ideal. To begin with, it didn't include Jerusalem, which for Jews represented the spiritual focus of their faith. Secondly, the borders they would receive for their state would be so long and tortuous as to be indefensible. None the less, an affirmative vote would be a start. Few Jews were under any illusions though; they knew that whatever the UN might decide, the territory would still have to be fought for. In the process, a better territorial arrangement might be won.

There were 33 votes for partition, 13 against and 10 abstentions; the motion was carried and for the first time in over 2,000 years the Jews had their own state.

The result drove the Arab world into a fury. Riots broke out all over Palestine and Jewish settlements were attacked. From Beirut, Cairo, Baghdad and Damascus the cry went up for a 'holy war' to drive the Jews into the sea. The British planned to stay in Palestine to supervise and enforce partition but in the face of terrorist acts against the British Army by the *Irgun*, public opinion in Britain clamoured for withdrawal and the date was set for 15 May.

THE STATE OF ISRAEL

At 4.00 on 14 May 1948, David Ben Gurion proclaimed independence for the new state of Israel. The ceremony took less than half an hour, during which time the massed armies of Syria, Lebanon, Iraq, Jordan and Egypt gathered along the length of the new state's borders. A few hours later, Egyptian planes started to bomb Tel Aviv. The moment it was born, Israel was at war.

WAR OF INDEPENDENCE

Against what seemed like overwhelming odds the new state was victorious, although at a cost of more than 6,000 lives. Covert preparations long before the British withdrawal had helped give the Jews an edge, and a lack of any kind of unified organisation or agreement between the invading Arab forces diluted their impact considerably. The fighting lasted until the beginning of 1949 and Israel managed to expand the territory granted to her by partition, although she lost east Jerusalem in the process. The new state now constituted the Negev, the coastal Plain, Galilee and a corridor leading to west Jerusalem. Jordan took Samaria, Judea and East Jerusalem.

PALESTINIAN REFUGEES

Following the announcement of partition, and during the war, many Palestinian Arabs had fled the country, some out of genuine fear, some persuaded to go by the Arab forces themselves, who assured them that their return was guaranteed once their inevitable victory was secured. There was to be no return. Israel couldn't afford to upset the balance of the new state by allowing a stream of Palestinians to return, and so the hapless refugees were 'temporarily' housed in camps in Lebanon, Jordan and Gaza. The Arab world showed no desire to absorb their fellow Arabs into their own countries and so the refugees stayed in the camps, at the mercy of international charity.

The War of Independence may have been officially over, but as far as the Arab states were concerned they were still at war, and the Israelis had to cope with regular Arab raids over the new borders. To add to the problems the Arab countries imposed economic sanctions; Egypt denied Israeli shipping use of the Suez Canal and blockaded the Gulf of Akaba/Eilat on the Red Sea.

The Suez Crisis and Sinai Campaign

By 1956, instances of Arab terrorist attacks were increasing, particularly from Egypt and Jordan. Egypt's President NASSER had already upset Britain and France by nationalising the Suez Canal. Tension increased still further as the Soviets firmly allied themselves with Egypt. As Nasser's troops started to amass in the Sinai, poised for an attack on Israel, France and Britain, seeing a way to gain control of the Suez Canal, persuaded Israel to attack from the Sinai while they moved in from the north. Moving rapidly, Israel routed the Egyptian troops, taking control of the Gaza Strip and the whole of the Sinai in the process.

Their occupation was to be short lived. In the face of vociferous condemnation from the United States, the Soviets and the United Nations, Britain and France withdrew, and the Israelis handed over their newly-won territory to a United Nations peacekeeping force.

The Six-Day War

The Israeli victory in the Six Day War, eleven years later, must have staggered the Arab forces as much as it astonished the world. This time, Israel faced attack from Egypt in the south, Syria in the north and Jordan to the east. Led by General MOSHE DAYAN, the Israelis attacked on all fronts. Almost before the Arabs knew what had hit them, Israel was in possession of the Golan Heights, the Sinai, the Gaza Strip, the West Bank and, to their joy, east Jerusalem. Israel was indisputably the superior military force in the Middle East.

With this decisive victory came a new confidence and an atmosphere of euphoria. Israel had greatly increased her borders. The Syrians no longer had the strategically dominant position over the plains of Galilee, the Sinai provided a vast buffer against Egypt and above all, the whole of Jerusalem and the territory to the east, south and north was in Israeli hands.

But victory brought its problems. The new borders had to be defended at a crippling cost, and the state now had to contend with a large and hostile Palestinian population in the occupied territories. Israel agreed to return the territories only if the Arab world would officially recognise her right to exist within secure boundaries. This recognition was not forthcoming and Arab bitterness increased as the Israelis set about settling Jewish communities in the newly occupied West Bank.

HISTORY

Yom Kippur War

Yom Kippur, the Day of Atonement, is the holiest day in the whole Jewish calendar. This was the day that the Egyptians and Syrians chose in 1973 to invade Israel, the Egyptians crossing the Suez Canal and the Syrians storming the Golan Heights. Israel was at prayer and paid dearly with heavy losses for her lack of alertness. But, yet again, after a desperate scramble to mobilise, her military superiority won the day, driving the invaders back behind the original lines. Nineteen days later, the UN ordered a cease-fire and the war came to an end.

In 1977 Israel's Labour Government, which had held power since the state came into being, lost to the right wing *Likud* Party led by Menachim Begin, known for his hard line towards the Arabs; it would have seemed that the climate was unlikely to improve. But this equation didn't take into account Egypt's President SADAT who, in the face of overwhelming hostility from the Arab world, visited Jerusalem and addressed the *Knesset* on the question of a Middle East settlement. His action was eventually to cost him his life at the hands of Islamic fundamentalist assassins in 1981. But his initiative led to the CAMP DAVID AGREEMENT, signed in 1979. Certainly the agreement went some way to relieve tension. The Israelis agreed to hand back the Sinai to Egypt, to halt the settlement of the occupied West Bank and the Gaza Strip, and in these two areas, after a period of no more than five years, Israeli troops were to be withdrawn and a measure of autonomy granted to the Palestinian inhabitants.

But where progress may have been made with Egypt the rest of the Arab world condemned the agreement, as they would condemn anything that fell short of a complete return of all the occupied territories and a settlement of the Palestinian refugee problem. Within Israel too, there was dissent. Hard-liners felt that no concessions at all should be made to the Arabs and that Israel should not give back any of the territory it had won in the Six Day War. Sinai has been handed back to Egypt, but Israeli troops still occupy the West Bank and Gaza.

Lebanon

The situation in Lebanon is far too complicated to cover here. Suffice it to say that the Lebanese civil war had given the PALESTINIAN LIBERATION ORGANISATION the opportunity to move into a position in Southern Lebanon where it began a

HISTORY

regular bombardment of northern Galilee. In 1982 the Israelis invaded Lebanon with the aim of driving out the PLO guerrilla bases. Having achieved this aim, the Israelis moved onwards towards Beirut. The initiative proved hugely unpopular with the majority of the Israeli people and in spite of their military superiority, it became increasingly obvious that there was to be no victory on the ever shifting sands of Lebanon's volatile political map. Casualties were high, the cost was even higher and Israel was condemned by the mass of world opinion.

Israel eventually withdrew from Lebanon. The Prime Minister, Menachim Begin, resigned his position and a year later in 1984, a general election was held. The result was inconclusive. Labour had a slim majority, the *Likud* came a close second but the smaller parties, thirteen in all, secured 13 seats in the 120-strong *Knesset*. The leader of the Labour Party SHIMON PERES, attempted to form a government but was forced to agree to a National Unity Government with the leader of the *Likud*, YITZAK SHAMIR, as Prime Minister and himself as Deputy Prime Minister and Defence Minister. The two leaders were to swop roles after the first 25 months.

And so the uneasy co-existence continues. Occasionally guarded hopes arise for a peaceful settlement, only to be dashed by the intransigence of one side or the other.

Not all Jews and Israelis live in hatred and fear of the Palestinians and the Arabs, however – or vice versa. Time and again in Israel one comes across initiatives started by the Arab and Jewish people, settlements where the two races, embracing three religions – for there are Christian Arabs too – live together in harmony and peace. Aggression comes naturally to neither the Jews nor the Palestinians; they are both peace-loving peoples. When the groundswell of moderate opinion is in a position to smother the unyielding fanaticism, then there may be peace.

We'll leave the last lines to Louis Golding, writing about the new university on Mount Scopus in Jerusalem.

> It is too audacious to dream that Scopus might bring back again the two splendours so long faded from these shores of the Mediterranean, the splendours of the Arabs, who persist without splendour, and the Greeks who are dead? It was the Jews and the Arabs in the earlier Dark Ages – when Europe was distracted by wars of creed as she is today by wars of commerce – it was the Jews and the Arabs who held high the torch on the northern littoral of Africa, and illumined the darkness of the plateaux of Spain. What a sodality might be restored between Jews and Arabs, housed

in intricate philosophies and shadowy courts, taking equal delight in the fretting of logic and cedarwood, the interweaving of rhymes and embroideries.

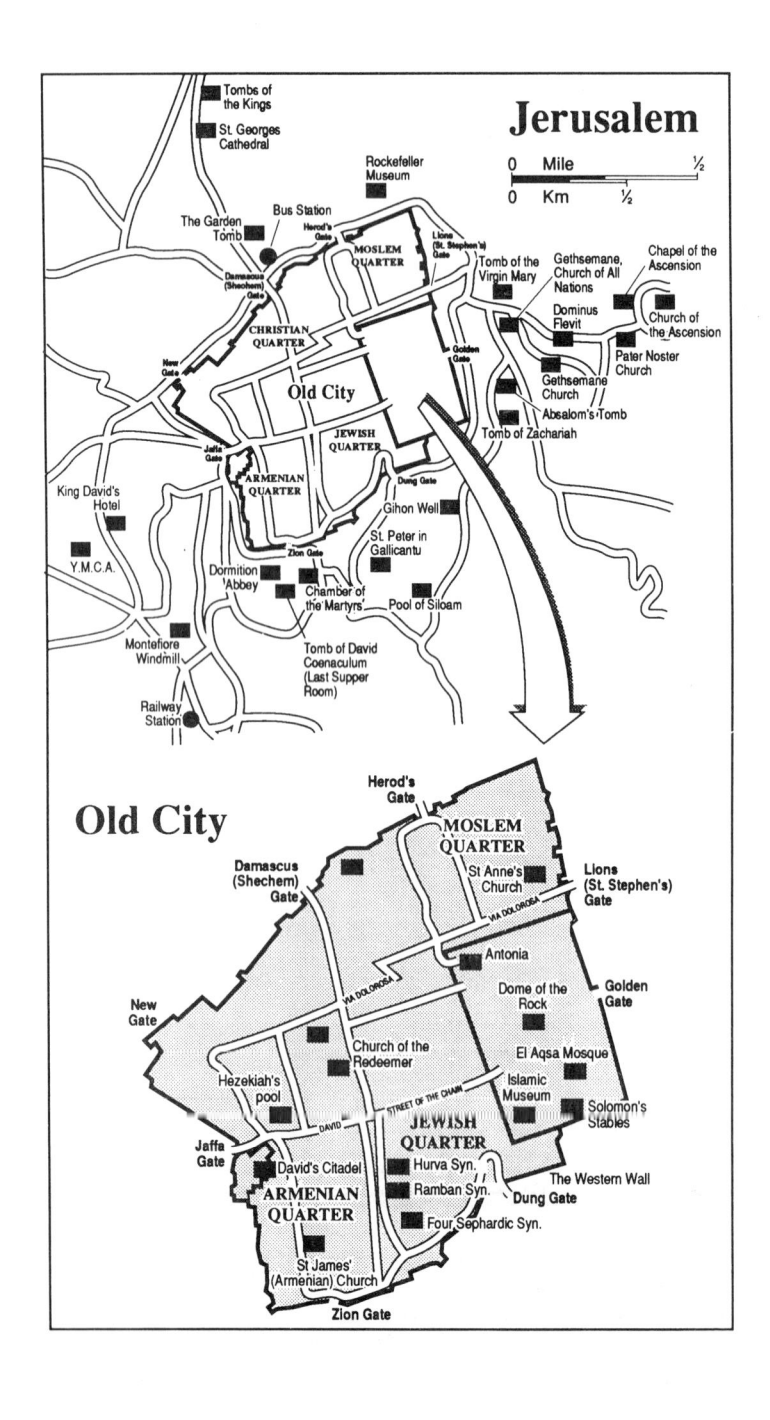

Jerusalem

Old City

C·H·A·P·T·E·R·2
JERUSALEM

INTRODUCTION

For 40 days each year, a great city with towers, domes and golden spires was said to hang suspended in the air, hovering over the misty blue hills of Judaea. This singular phenomenon would be apparent early in the morning, and the fabulous city would linger until it faded and was extinguished by the heat haze, as the sun climbed above the wilderness of dust and stones.

Even today this timeless city exercises an almost mythical fascination for the tens of thousands who are drawn to her as pilgrims or tourists. For even if Jerusalem is not the geographical hub of the world, as the Crusaders and many before them believed, it is surely the hub of the spiritual world, the focal point of three of the great religions, and thus holy to 1,000 million Christians, 750 million Moslems, and the physical and spiritual centre of history and worship for 15 million Jews.

The name, *Yerushalayim* in Hebrew, means city of peace; Jerusalem has been called the 'City of Peace' since it was founded in the gloom of pre-history over 3,000 years ago. During those thousands of years the city has known more of siege and massacre, of pillage, pestilence and destruction than of peace; and still they call her 'The Shadow of Paradise', Ariel, the 'Hearth of God's Home', *El Quds* 'The Sanctuary',

'Gazelle among Nations'; still she is bewailed by distant Jews, longing to see her, 'Next year in Jerusalem'.

This adoration of the city from near and far has inspired some of the world's most moving poetry. The yearning of the Jews for Jerusalem is as enduring as the city itself thoughout its long and turbulent history. Today the city is still there, built again from golden stone, adorned with the monumental paraphernalia of worship, ringing with the pealing of church-bells, the plangent call of the *muezzin*, and the devout murmuring of Orthodox Jews studying in their *Yeshivas*. Today the Jews still worship at the Western Wall, the last tangible remains of their vastly beautiful Temple of antiquity.

What has made this spot so holy? When David brought the God of the Israelites to the city, and Solomon constructed the first Temple, the city was sanctified for ever. But even before that auspicious event, there was an air of holiness about the place, for it is said that it was upon the Threshing Floor of Araunah, which stood on Mount Moriah, that Abraham set about the sacrifice of his son.

The Arabs have a legend that explains it: There were once two brothers, poor farmers, working identical plots of land adjoining one another on a hillside. The elder brother was married with two small children; the younger brother was a bachelor. Harvest time came, and the two brothers laboured all day in their separate fields to cut and tie the corn into sheaves. At the end of a long hot day's work they each had an identical stack of sheaves.

In the cool of the evening the younger brother strolled out to the fields to enjoy the air and the moonlight. He stopped and looked at the stacks of corn. 'It's not right', he thought. 'My brother works as hard as I do, and grows the same amount of corn on his field. But he has a wife and little ones to feed; they need this corn much more than I do.' And he took half of his stack and added it to his brother's stack. Then he went home to bed.

Later that night the elder brother walked out to take the evening air. As he looked at the two stacks he thought 'It seems unfair that I should have as much corn as my brother. After all, I have all the comforts of a family, and my life is a great pleasure to me. He has nobody, and his life is one of constant toil.' And so he moved half of the sheaves back onto his brother's stack.

In the morning, as they came out to the fields and greeted one another, they were both a little confused as to what had happened. But neither said anything. The next night exactly the same thing happened – and the next. But on the fourth

Mosaic

night, they both arrived together, and roared with joyous laughter when they realised what had happened.

God had been watching these proceedings, and he was so struck by the simplicity and goodness of what he had just witnessed, that he made that spot his holy place on earth from that day. And there they built Jerusalem.

History

The city of Jerusalem was one of the few settlements in the Promised Land that Joshua failed to take. In those days (1400 BC) there was no magnificent city but a rude pile of stones, roughly assembled into towers, walls and earthy dwellings, by the primitive Jebusites who lived there. But the city was strong, due to its position on a promontory between the valleys of Hinnom and Kidron. Smug in their unassailable position, the Jebusites taunted David that their lame and blind alone would be sufficient to defend the city from the Israelites.

But with skill and cunning, David took the city, and driving the Jebusites out, made it the capital of his kingdom. Jerusalem is one of the few capital cities in the world that is not built on a major river or sea-port, or at the crossing of important trade-routes. David chose it partly because he knew of its sacred reputation, and partly for political motives. It was right in the centre of the two halves of his kingdom, and the city belonged to none of his tribes.

About 975 BC David brought the Ark of the Covenant – the portable temple in which the Israelites carried their God – to Jerusalem. Solomon built the First Temple and God was installed in suitable splendour in the city. It was the duty of every Jew in the land to visit Jerusalem and worship at the Temple three times a year. When the kingdom split in two, the northern tribes, who no longer had access to the Temple, made graven images to worship instead, which saved them the trips to Jerusalem, but was acceptable neither in the eyes of the prophets, nor of God.

The result was that the Israelites lost the protection of God, and the city was taken by the Babylonians (587 BC). The Jews were exiled and the Temple torn down. In captivity at Babylon they languished, lamenting the loss of their beloved city.

In 539 BC, when the Persians defeated the empire of Babylon, the Jews were allowed to return. They reconstructed the city and built the Second Temple. For many years Jerusalem became an autonomous Jewish city under the benevolent control of Persia. When Alexander conquered the world in 332 BC, Jerusalem was sensible enough to capitulate; during the short years of Alexander's empire, things continued as normal.

After the death of Alexander, as Ptolemy and Seleucus fought for control of the empire and Palestine, the influence of Greece made itself strongly felt at Jerusalem; a Hippodrome was built for public spectacles, athletic events became a regular feature, and pagan temples appeared all over the town. What started as a harmonious exchange of culture became intolerable when Antiochus Epiphanes had the Temple re-dedicated to Olympian Zeus and sacrificed pigs on the altar. The Jews rose under the Maccabees and swept the Seleucids from the land.

The first euphoric years of Jewish independence soon became a time of turmoil as the Maccabees established the secular Hasmonaean dynasty. The constant feuding for the throne of Jerusalem finally brought the Romans – now the sovereign power in the region – onto the scene. In 63 BC Pompey successfully laid siege to the city, and installed the Roman puppet, John Hyrcanus, as governor.

Rome was vast and powerful, with all the knowledge and science of the known world at her fingertips; but she was never wise enough to know how to come to terms with the

Jews. She never realised the significance of their theology, and, failing to understand their cohesion and devotion, she persecuted them. Persecution, however, made the Jews even stronger in their resolve. They would not settle under the *Pax Romana* and they would neither deny their God nor acknowledge the superiority of Rome and the Caesars.

Thus the Roman years in Jerusalem were characterised by a mutual incomprehension and hatred. The reign of Herod the Great (37–34 BC) was typical; his brutality to his subjects became legendary. His sobriquet 'The Great' has survived only because of his vision as a builder. The remains of his work, the Herodion, the Tomb of Abraham at Hebron, the Winter Palace at Jericho, the Temple and the Antonia Fortress, and his countless water storage and distribution projects, have earned him a place among the great builders of the world.

Round about 30 AD, Jesus of Nazareth travelled from the pastoral world of Galilee to the seething hubbub of the Holy City. He was familiar with the city, as He had been there many times before with Joseph and Mary. He knew Herod's Temple well, for there He had astounded the Elders in debate when He was twelve years old. He also knew that at Jerusalem was His destiny. So He went to the city at Passover with His disciples, and there He was arrested, tried and crucified.

After his death and resurrection some of His disciples remained underground in Jerusalem; others set forth on the dusty white roads of Palestine to spread the word of the Son of God to the corners of the world.

In 66 AD Roman oppression in Jerusalem, had become intolerable for the Jews, and they rose up in the First Revolt. It seems incredible that this tiny nation was able to hold at bay the might of Imperial Rome for four years, but it did. The Emperor Vespasian sent his son, Titus, to sort things out. Titus besieged Jerusalem for three terrible years. When his soldiers finally entered the city in AD 70 they massacred the population and destroyed the Temple, tearing it down stone by stone – an incredible feat when you look at the size of the remaining blocks.

But the Jews of Jerusalem were nothing if not tenacious. Those who survived and stayed on partially reconstructed their city and tried to live their lives as near normally as possible. When the Emperor Hadrian announced that he intended to flatten the old city and build a new one along Roman lines, another successful revolt was sparked off – the Bar Kochba Revolt. They captured Jerusalem, and again held the Romans off for three years. But again the revolt was put down. Hadrian went ahead with his new city of Aelia

Capitolina anyway, and no Jew was allowed to set foot in it, on pain of death.

After 200 years of varying degrees of tolerance, the draconian restrictions were lifted so that the Jews could visit the city, where they were permitted only to stand on the seventh step of the ruined Temple gate, on one day a year – the anniversary of the Temple's destruction.

Under the Emperor Constantine, Rome accepted Christianity, and the power base of the Roman Empire shifted to Byzantium. Constantine's mother, Helena, visited the Holy Land in 328 and discovered the True Cross. Her son wrote to her: 'No words can express how good the Saviour has been to us. That the monument of His Holy Passion, hidden for so many years, has at last been restored to the faithful, is indeed a miracle. My great wish is, after freeing the site of impious idols, to adorn it with splendid buildings.' And thus started the great age of church-building in the Holy Land. From this date too, the roads of Europe and the Near East were worn by the feet of countless pilgrims, making the arduous and dangerous journey to the land where the mysteries of Christianity were born. The Jews were again permitted to live at Jerusalem, but there was no end to the persecution.

In 614 the new Persian Empire swept through the Holy Land, and with the connivance of the Jews, destroyed all the churches and most of the Christian inhabitants. The Jews then enjoyed a brief domination of the Holy City until the Byzantines regained their strength, under Heraklius. The Persians were pushed out of Palestine, and the Jews were driven from Jerusalem once more.

Jerusalem was now the focal point for two world religions, a city of peace and sanctity, but a city where hundreds of thousands had been slaughtered over the years, for their adherence to one creed or the other. In the year 570 the Prophet Mohammed was born in Mecca. At some time during the years of his ministry, he made a journey by night from Mecca to Jerusalem, and from the stone on Mount Moriah where Abraham nearly sacrificed his son, he ascended into heaven. Jerusalem was now holy to a third great religion.

Mohammed's revelations welded the tribes of the Arabian deserts together under the banner of Islam. In 638 the Moslems took Jerusalem, under Caliph Omar. This time there was no bloodshed, no pillaging, no defilement of holy places. Omar himself refused to worship in the Church of the Holy Sepulchre, lest his followers should turn it into a mosque. There followed that rarest of things for Jerusalem, a period of religious tolerance. Jews were allowed back into the city,

Christians were free to worship as they pleased. Mount Moriah was declared as the holy precinct of Islam.

But such a state of affairs could not last long, and as power shifted within the empire of Islam, the Caliphs became less magnanimous. In 1009 'Mad' Caliph Hakim, of the Fatimid dynasty of North Africa, destroyed all the Christian monuments in the Holy Land, and massacred the Christians. The Seljuk Turks defeated the Byzantine Empire at the battle of Manzikert, and continued south to take Jerusalem from the Arabs. Seljuk occupation of Jerusalem was brutal, and, with the constant murdering of pilgrims and the defilement of the Holy Places, word reached Europe and fired the anger of western Christians. The result was the First Crusade.

It took the Crusaders three years to reach Jerusalem, taking the odd Christian city on the way. The motley army consisted of the flower of European chivalry, monks, devout pilgrims and thousands of the wretched rabble for whom any misery was better than conditions in the dark ages of Europe. They took the city after a siege lasting a month. Then Jerusalem witnessed the most appalling carnage in its whole blood-soaked history. No one was spared, in one of the blackest days that ever besmirched the history of Christianity.

When the Crusaders had taken Jerusalem, they were not really sure what to do with it; nobody wanted to be king, and many of the knights and most of the rabble, having reached the Holy City and taken it, set off for home. But a king was found in Baldwin I and the Latin Kingdom shakily rose to its feet. For nearly 100 years the Franks, as they were called, ruled from Jerusalem, running the Holy Land on the feudal lines they were familiar with from Europe.

Most of the excesses of the Crusaders are best forgotten, but they will always be remembered for their building. It is interesting to compare the beautiful earthy simplicity of the Crusader churches and fortresses, with the highly ornate and technically more sophisticated building that had been going on in the east for hundreds of years. The Crusaders built with a vengeance during their short tenancy of the Holy Land, and because of its solid quality, much of it remains to delight us today.

In 1187 the Crusaders were decisively defeated by Saladin, and two years later he took Jerusalem. Saladin's entry into the city was remarkable for its moderation. Again there was no orgy of killing.

By 1250 ascendancy in the Islamic world had fallen to the Mamelukes from Egypt. The 250 years of their rule in Palestine were notable for a steady decline in the country's fortunes; the

Mamelukes were too busy guarding their rear to do much more than extract taxes from Palestine, though they too have left some fine architecture.

In 1520 the Mamelukes fell to the inexorable spread of the Ottoman Empire. Sultan Süleyman the Magnificent built the impressive walls that surround Jerusalem to this day. Under his brilliant and enlightened rule the city flourished and was richly embellished with schools, mosques, hospitals and monuments. Unfortunately later Sultans, who ruled Palestine almost uninterruptedly for 400 years, failed to live up to Süleyman's example, and Palestine and Jerusalem declined, soon to become an impoverished backwater – little more than a tax-farm, run by venal and self-seeking administrators.

In the 1830s Mohammed Ali, an officer in the Egyptian army, masterminded a successful Egyptian rebellion against Turkish suzerainty, ousting the Turks from Palestine in the process. Compared to the corrupt misrule of the Turkish Pashas, Mohammed Ali and his son Ibrahim Pasha made an enlightened contribution to the development of Jerusalem. In a climate of benevolent tolerance Jews began to flood back to the city, Christians gained many privileges and pilgrimage increased significantly. But Mohammed Ali's day was not to last. The European powers grew increasingly concerned as Ali turned his gaze acquisitively towards the Ottoman capital of Istanbul. Whilst the Ottoman Empire was still the 'sick man of Europe' it was controllable. Ali had already demonstrated a remarkable ability to strengthen the lands he controlled, and the possibility that the balance of the sprawling Ottoman Empire might also come under his firm hand was too much of a risk. Pressure was brought to bear by the European powers. Ali was 'returned' to Egypt and Jerusalem was once again under Ottoman control.

But Ali had to all intents and purposes written the first important chapter in the development of modern Jerusalem. The Ottomans were back, with European connivance, but they had to agree to adopt Ali's reforms. From now on European influence in the city was established.

While Jews continued to pour into the city, building and re-building synagogues, the world's churches, championed by their various prestige-seeking governments, moved into Jerusalem to stake their claim to a piece of the Holy City. The building boom that followed brought all manner of anachronisms to the Jerusalem skyline; the onion domes of the Russian Church of Mary Magdalene, the austere steeple of the Lutheran Church of the Redeemer, and English Gothic-style Cathedral that looks for all the world as though it has been plucked straight from the 'dreaming spires' of Oxford's skyline.

But the powers were not content with building new manifestations of their love of the Holy City. They also indulged in squabbles over the rights of various denominations to the existing churches and Holy Places, squabbles that frequently became violent and often involved bribes to the Ottomans to find in favour of one power or another.

Jerusalem was now beginning to sprawl beyond the boundaries of Süleyman's magnificent old walls. Sir Moses Montefiore, a Jewish philanthropist, effected the building of the first suburb outside the Jewish quarter, to persuade the Jews to leave the impossibly crowded confines of the old city. As the century drew to a close, more and more Jews arrived, many settling either in the old city or in the new suburbs springing up outside the old city walls.

As the First World War came to a close, Britain took control of Palestine from the tottering Ottoman Empire and Jerusalem surrendered to General Allenby. The British had assumed an intolerable burden. With promises to Arabs and Jews alike, the British dug themselves in for 30 years, ruling at first through a military government and then through a civil administration based in Jerusalem. The Jewish population grew rapidly.

Even before the British withdrew from Palestine in 1948, Jerusalem had become a battleground. Trapped in a pincer of Arab armies, with water supplies cut, the *Haganah* fought bravely and with immense ingenuity, against overwhelming odds, to keep a corridor open for supplies from Tel Aviv to feed the 85,000-strong Jewish population. When the British finally left in May 1948, the Jewish forces scrambled to take control of the administration buildings. Any idea that Jerusalem was to be internationalised, as had been stated by the Partition Vote, was so much straw in the wind. The city would be the passionately desired prize of whoever won the war; the vastly outnumbered and ill-equipped Jews or the joint forces of the Arab countries that now threatened the city – Egypt, Iraq and the Jordanian Legion.

By June, East Jerusalem was firmly in Arab hands, the Jewish Quarter of the Old City had surrendered to the Jordanians, and much of the area was destroyed. By the time of the ceasefire in 1949, the Jews had lost the one prize that mattered above all. Whilst they still retained control of West Jerusalem, the Holy City itself was lost, annexed, together with the West Bank, to the Kingdom of Jordan. Jerusalem was partitioned.

The years between the partitioning of the city and the

reunification after the Six Day War brought problems for both sides. East Jerusalem was cut off from some of the basic supplies it had hitherto shared with West Jerusalem, such as a reliable supply of electricity, while West Jerusalem was virtually an island isolated in the midst of hostile Arabs. In 1949 when the United Nations made moves to put the internationalisation clause of the partition plan into practice, the Israelis hurriedly transferred all their government institutions, including the *Knesset*, from Tel Aviv to West Jerusalem. In the face of considerable worldwide opposition, Jerusalem was declared the capital of Israel.

In 1967, during the Six Day War, the Israelis took East Jerusalem and the Jewish Quarter from the Jordanians. While the rest of the territories that had been won in the war were only to be occupied, Jerusalem was declared a unified city and the newly-won areas of the city were annexed.

The city may be unified, but today there is evidence everywhere of the years of partition. There are, for instance, two bus stations and two very distinct commercial areas. The atmosphere of East Jerusalem, its streets, hotels, cafés and restaurants, a short stroll from West Jerusalem, is so totally different that you feel you could almost be in another country.

But although there are signs all too frequently of the tension that exists here, generally speaking you will be surprised at the way the Arabs and Jews mix together and go about their business during the daylight hours.

Walls and Gates of the Old City

The Old City of Jerusalem is one of the finest surviving examples of a medieval walled city. In 1540, shortly after the Ottomans took Jerusalem, Süleyman the Magnificent wanted the city beautified, so he built the walls that still stand, patched and restored, to this day. Although they look fairly substantial to the casual observer, they are more decorative than effective from a military point of view.

One of the best ways to get to know Old Jerusalem is to walk round the top of the walls — entrances at Jaffa, Damascus and Lions' Gates. From here you have a privileged view of the city's secret places.

The most magnificent gate, still looking much like it did when Süleyman built it, is certainly the DAMASCUS GATE, the very hub of the Moslem quarter. From here the important trade route north to Damascus left the city. Just within the gate is a recently excavated ROMAN COURTYARD, now adorned with a couple of open-air cafés. On the street just inside the gate are

Damascus Gate

some good Arab coffee-houses where you can sit and watch the frenetic activity which swirls around the neighbourhood, for the gate itself is a busy centre of commerce, the funnel between Arab East Jerusalem and the bazaars of the Old City.

On the west wall of the city is the JAFFA GATE. Here you will find the TOURIST INFORMATION OFFICE, MONEYCHANGERS,

The Old City Wall, Jaffa Gate and the Citadel

CHEAP HOTELS AND RESTAURANTS, TAXIS and the CITADEL OF DAVID. The gate is massive and austere, with a breezy angled entry for pedestrians, originally to make things difficult for attackers. There is a belief among the orthodox Jews of Jerusalem that within the gate is a *Mezuzah*, such as that found in the doorways of Jewish houses; this one is said to contain texts written by the hand of God Himself. You may see the pious touching the stones of the gate with reverence and kissing their fingers.

Jaffa Gate is the only point at which the walls of Jerusalem are broken; for this, history will remember Kaiser Wilhelm II, whose imperial dignity during his state visit to Palestine in 1898 would not permit him to dismount from his coach and pass the gate on foot. The gate was accordingly knocked down and a road put through. History will take a different view of the entry into the city of General Allenby in 1917. After a victorious campaign against the Germans and the Turks, he dismounted and entered the Holy City on foot as a pilgrim.

Inside the Jaffa Gate is DAVID'S CITADEL. Despite the name none of the buildings here has anything to do with the Shepherd King. The oldest part of the complex is easily recognisable as the work of Herod; on the lower levels are huge unmistakable blocks of limestone. This was once a great square tower, one of the three built by Herod as part of the city's defences. They were called 'Phasael', after his brother; 'Hippicus', in honour of his friend, and 'Mariamne', after his wife. This is the only one surviving today. As usual the upper levels were built by the Mamelukes and Ottomans.

David's Citadel

Today the interior of the citadel has been landscaped and the archaeologists' finds beautifully displayed to public view. There is a MUSEUM in the tower, and you can climb to the top for magnificent views of Jerusalem. Also in the tower is a wonderful little MUSEUM OF DOLLS, representing in typical dress each of the dozens of races, types and denominations that people this cosmopolitan city. On summer evenings a *son et lumière* gives the history of the citadel and the city – this should not be missed; neither should the MODEL OF THE CITY in the cellar below the west wall of the citadel.

The DUNG GATE, which enters the city at the beautiful square between the Jewish Quarter and the Western Wall, is so called because the city tannery used to be here. Dung,

Minaret from Haram es-Sharif

collected from the animals and drains of the city, was an important ingredient in this process.

It was through the GOLDEN GATE that Jesus passed when He entered the city on Palm Sunday, riding a donkey. It is a gate to which many legends and much holiness are attached. It was blocked up when the Moslems took Jerusalem, as it led directly into *Haram es-Sharif*, which was closed to all but the faithful, and it remains blocked to this day.

Through the LIONS' GATE, or ST STEPHEN'S GATE, St Stephen is supposed to have been led before he was stoned to death. The lions above the gate were adopted by Süleyman from the coat of arms of the Mameluke Sultan Baybars.

St Stephen's Gate or Lions' Gate

Christian Quarter (Including the Via Dolorosa)

The CHRISTIAN QUARTER is quieter, the streets tucked away from the main tourist routes; almost serene compared to the hustle, bustle and stridency of the adjoining Moslem Quarter. Here you can stroll along the steep, honey-coloured streets without fear of being sent flying by bands of boisterous schoolchildren.

There are around 32 Christian denominations in this city; the variety well evidenced by the confusing array of clerical 'costumes'. Humble brown robes (with the occasional glimpse of blue jeans at the hem), nuns in long or short robes, some black, some white, some grey. There are priests with a variety of headgear, magnificent beards and robes of purple and black. You might get a glimpse of the occasional patriarch sporting a lavishly embroidered mitre, as he glides by in the back seat of the diocesan Mercedes.

Strictly speaking, the VIA DOLOROSA or WAY OF THE CROSS does not lie entirely within the confines of the Christian Quarter. But pilgrims and tourists usually follow the Via Dolorosa from its start in the Moslem Quarter, through the various stations of the cross, to its culmination in and around the Church of the Holy Sepulchre. We will therefore start our tour of the sites of the Christian Quarter at the start of the Via Dolorosa. We will detail the stations themselves and the various sites en route that are connected in some way with Christ's life and death.

Via Dolorosa

You would be hard put to find more tourists and pilgrims concentrated in one area than here. Following the Way of the Cross, and ensuring you get a good picture of what is traditionally held to have happened at each stage isn't easy – especially when your nose is intermittently buried in a guide book.

The route is not, as you might have imagined, one road leading to Calvary (Golgotha), punctuated at intervals with the traditional Stations of the Cross. It was not until the Middle Ages that the route was actually called the Via Dolorosa, and the stations, effectively spiritual reminders to the pilgrims of the details of Christ's final journey, began to be 'set'. The precise route, if it were known, would have to penetrate a maze of buildings which have fused together as the city has contracted and expanded since the time of Christ. The result is a rather confusing route which almost doubles back on itself, runs through the heart of the noisy Arab *souk*, over the roof of the Church of the Holy Sepulchre and into Calvary.

It is quite probable that Jesus wasn't tried at the Antonia Fortress (the first Station on the Via Dolorosa) but at Herod's Palace – the site of today's Citadel of David by the Jaffa Gate. This would mean that the traditional Way of the Cross is likely to be wholly inaccurate. None the less, centuries of tradition and millions of devout pilgrims from all over the globe have trod this path, their firmly held beliefs stamping on the sites an air of authenticity. It will take a great deal more than archaeologists and modern historians to change the beliefs of hundreds of years.

The logical place to start is ST STEPHEN'S GATE (Lions' Gate) in the eastern wall of the Old City. Although the first station is some way further on from the gate, you can take in ST ANNE'S CHURCH – the entrance is a short way from the gate on the right – and the site of the POOL OF BETHESDA first.

This 12th C Crusader church, while rather austere, is the most beautiful church in Jerusalem. Traditionally, the site is believed to be the home of the Virgin Mary's parents – Anne and Joachim – and her birthplace. The church is now under the care of *Les Pères Blancs* and has been since the Ottoman Turks gave the site to the French in 1856, in acknowledgement of French support in the Crimean War.

The history of St Anne's is inextricably linked with that of the adjacent ruins of the Pools of Bethesda. The pools were created around 200 BC to supply the constant demand for water from the nearby Temple. It is here that Jesus is believed to have cured a man who had been sick for 38 years. John describes the pool as a place where 'the blind, lame and paralysed' gathered in the hope of gaining relief from the waters. It was a popularly held belief that when the waters 'stirred', the angels were present and the waters took on special curative powers.

The Romans turned the pools into a healing sanctuary, complete with temple dedicated to the God Serapis. The Byzantines replaced the temple with a church, dedicated to the Virgin Mary, but it was destroyed in the early 11th C by the Arabs. The Crusaders built their church on the present site beside today's excavated ruins. With the arrival of the triumphant Saladin, the church was turned into a Moslem *Medrese* (Theological School) which flourished for a while and then fell to ruin until the coming of the French in the mid 19th C.

Walk through the beautiful, shady CLOISTERED GARDEN to the EXCAVATIONS past the church itself at the far end of the site. Walkways have been erected over the site. The corrugated iron canopy covers a well preserved MOSAIC.

If you're lucky there may be a group of pilgrims singing inside the church. Sit at the back and marvel at the superb acoustics; the simplest offerings can sound like heavenly choirs. The interior is simple and unadorned except for basic wooden pews and a white stone altar. The light, reflected from the creamy white walls, is soft and diffused and there is a remarkable atmosphere of peace and tranquillity – a rare commodity in a city which, in spite of its name, has little of it to offer anywhere.

Leave St Anne's and turn right up the street. After a short distance look down at the PAVEMENT, inauspiciously sited outside the public lavatories. The stones date from the 2nd Temple Period. A little further up the street you will see a flight of stairs doubling back on the left hand side. This is the entrance to the UMARIYE SCHOOL and STATION 1 on the Way of the Cross.

Today the school covers just part of the site of the huge Antonia Fortress, and from the school courtyard there is an excellent view of the Temple Mount. It is here that Jesus may have been brought in front of Pontius Pilate for trial. Later, as you move up the Via Dolorosa, you can take two detours; one to view the ECCE HOMO ARCH, probably constructed in 2 AD, but traditionally held to be the arch where Pilate displayed Jesus to the mob, and the LITHOSTRATOS – a huge, subterranean chamber with the impressive remains of a great courtyard. Both of these sites would have been within the confines of the Antonia Fortress.

Now go back down the steps for STATION II, outside the entrance to the FRANCISCAN BIBLICAL SCHOOL. Here, Jesus took up the cross. At either end of the attractive garden courtyard are two modern chapels – to the right, is the CHAPEL OF THE FLAGELLATION and to the left, the CHAPEL OF CONDEMNATION.

Continue up the street and note the ECCE HOMO ARCH. Here, you can step into the entrance of a simple chapel within The CONVENT OF THE SISTERS OF SION. The chapel itself is glassed off.

Make sure you take a detour now to see the previously mentioned LITHOSTRATOS. As well as a view of the vast STRUTHION POOL, there are displays of jewellery, ceramics and pottery and the Lithostratos itself; the paving-stones worn to a satin finish with age. The whole affair is well laid out and atmospherically lit with a soft background of haunting music. There is even a silent slide show, with pictures of old Jerusalem and its varied inhabitants dissolving silently into pictures of Christ, projected onto the ancient stone walls.

Note within the railed off area, the games scratched onto part of the pavement. These would have been played by Roman soldiers using animal knuckle bones or sticks – the forerunners of dice. It could well have been here that Pilate's guard taunted Jesus: 'they plaited a Crown of Thorns and put it on his head and arrayed him in a purple robe. They came up to him saying "Hail King of the Jews" ' (John 19:2–3).

You can take another detour from tracing the stations and visit the Greek Orthodox 'PRISON OF CHRIST'. In an atmosphere heavily laden with incense and sputtering candles you climb a short flight of stairs to the prison itself. A larger room is claimed as the prison of Barabbas and the thieves.

Return to the Via Dolorosa and turn left at the junction. You are now leaving the Via Dolorosa for a short distance. On the right-hand corner of the junction is the Austrian Hospice and on the left is a little Polish Chapel. Look up and you will see carved in relief into the wall, Jesus staggering under the weight of the cross – STATION III. Right next door is the ARMENIAN CATHOLIC CHURCH. Over the door of the chapel at the entrance is another relief carving, depicting Jesus greeting his mother – STATION IV. Just past Station IV turn to the right to rejoin the Via Dolorosa. Immediately on the left you will see STATION V, where Simon of Cyrene took the weight of the cross. STATION VI is next; marked on a wooden door on the left – The CHURCH OF THE HOLY FACE OF VERONICA. Tradition has it, although there is no support for this in the gospels, that Veronica wiped Jesus' face as He passed by on the way to Calvary. An imprint of Jesus' face was left on the napkin. The name Veronica actually means true image – *vera icon*. At the top of the street at the busy junction you will find STATION VII. Here, beside the wall on which the death sentence was posted, Jesus fell for the second time. The station is marked by a plaque on the wall of the *souk*. At this point He would have passed through the old city gate.

At Station VIII, marked by a cross on the wall of the Orthodox Monastery of St Charalambos, Jesus spoke to the weeping women of Jerusalem, saying 'Daughters of Jerusalem, weep not for me; weep for yourselves and for your children. For the time will come when you will say "Blessed are the barren women, the wombs that never bore and the breasts that never nursed" ' (Luke 23:27).

At Station IX, Jesus fell again, now in sight of the place of His Crucifixion; the spot is marked by a Roman column.

The Church of the Holy Sepulchre and the Final Stations of the Cross

The remaining four stations are inside the CHURCH OF THE HOLY SEPULCHRE. Down through the ages, millions have come from all over the world, facing incredible hardship and danger, to reach Jerusalem. Many perished or were taken into slavery before they even set foot in the Holy Land; thousands beggared themselves; thousands more, with blood on their hands, have fought their way here in the name of the Crusades. And, of all the sights they came to see, this is the one that drew them, and still draws them, like a magnet. You

Church of the Holy Sepulchre

have arrived at one of the most venerated sites in the world and undoubtedly the holiest shrine in all of Christendom.

There is much uncertainty and dissension about many of the Jerusalem sites connected with Jesus' life and death. But there is sufficient evidence for archaeologists and historians to be sure that this is the place where he was crucified, buried and raised from the dead. With the exception of the Garden Tomb, claimed by the Protestants and discussed later, there is no disagreement.

It doesn't really matter which guide book you read – the consensus is generally the same. Your first sight of the exterior of the church is likely to be something of a disappointment and your feelings are unlikely to change when you step inside. None the less there is a great deal of interest here and your attitude, whether you're a pilgrim or a curious tourist, is likely to change if you give the site more than a cursory look, especially if you make the effort to visit the church very early in the morning before most of the tourists arrive. Take some time to read the following history too. It will go some way to explaining why the church appears as it does today.

Jesus was crucified and buried outside the walls of the city in a 'place called Golgotha (which means the Skull)'. Golgotha, or Calvary, was part of a quarry, and investigations during the 1960s have shown that the area in and around the Holy Sepulchre was indeed a stone quarry. It was not until the 4th C that a church was actually built to mark the site. So what had happened in the interim?

In the years following the crucifixion, there was a marked rise in civil unrest and disobedience against Rome. By AD 66 the increasing dissaffection found its voice in a revolt savagely suppressed by Titus; 65 years later another revolt, the Bar Kochba uprising, brought the wrath of Hadrian on the heads of the unruly Jewish population. Jerusalem was almost completely destroyed and Rome, determined to eradicate the Jewish problem, rebuilt the city on Roman lines, renaming it *Aelia Capitolina* and re-establishing pagan worship. By this time, the walls of the city encompassed Calvary, but the site had not been built on, although it is more than likely that Christians had continued to worship here. Hadrian, seeing Christianity as simply another troublesome Jewish sect, ordered a pagan temple, dedicated to Aphrodite, to be built over the site. The quarry was filled in and levelled off to provide the foundations. The temple itself was built over the tomb, and a statue of Jove placed over the hill of Calvary. From this point until the conversion to Christianity of the Emperor Constantine some 200 years later, the site, although covered over, was revered by the small but tenacious Christian population of Jerusalem and an ever increasing stream of pilgrims – the holy sites ironically clearly delineated for them by the pagan temple and statue; and so the tradition lived on.

In 326, Constantine's mother, Helena, supervising the demolition of Hadrian's pagan shrine, uncovered the tomb itself, well preserved beneath Hadrian's concrete foundations, the hill of Calvary, and in a nearby cistern, the remains of what was believed to be the True Cross.

Now two churches were built on the site. One covered the tomb itself, which was cut away to make it free standing, and the other, separated by a courtyard, encompassed the hill of Calvary, to the east of the site. Over the years of Byzantine rule the churches were enlarged and embellished.

The early part of the 7th C saw a struggle for ascendancy

between the Byzantines and the Persians – a struggle that was to weaken both empires fatally. In 614 AD the churches were put to the torch by the invading Persians, and the True Cross was carried off. But Persian ascendancy was not to last for long, and when Heraklius took Jerusalem again for the Christians, he ordered the construction of a new church, finally consecrated in 628.

The enfeebled Byzantine and Persian empires were easy prey to the Arabs, now beginning to unite into a formidable force under the common banner of Islam. From 633 onwards the Arabs began their conquest of Palestine. Led by the Caliphs, the guardians of Islam after Mohammed's death, Jerusalem fell to their rule in 638.

The church remained relatively unscathed during the enlightened and tolerant rule of Caliph Omar. It is said that he was invited to pray in the church, but refused on the grounds that his presence inside the holy building would be enough for his followers to turn it into a Mosque – he chose instead to pray in the courtyard outside. But, under the rule of the Caliphs, Christian persecution began to grow, reaching an all time low under the 'mad' Caliph Hakim in 1009. Hakim systematically destroyed both the church and the tomb itself.

The Christian community in Jerusalem was poor, Europe was preoccupied with its own problems, and the Byzantine Empire was beginning to crack at the seams. In the mid 11th C the Byzantine Emperor Monomachus found the means to commence systematic reconstruction. There was little in the way of resources to rebuild the church, and what efforts were made were hampered by earthquakes and continual raids.

Meanwhile, to complicate matters still further, a new force to be reckoned with was gathering momentum in the Middle East – the Seljuk Turks. Defeating the Byzantines and reaching Jerusalem in 1071 this regime started to persecute and harass Christian pilgrims and to profane holy shrines, which eventually moved an outraged Europe to dispatch the first of the Crusades.

The Crusaders captured Jerusalem in 1099 and after a horrendous massacre, set about altering and rebuilding the church. The new church, vastly extended to encompass the whole Golgotha site and bring under one roof all the various chapels and shrines that had over the years sprung up around the original Byzantine churches, was completed in 1149. The structure you see today is essentially that built by the first Crusaders.

The Crusader hold over Jerusalem was to be short lived. Only 38 years after the completion of the church, Saladin established a power base in Egypt and launched an attack on the Crusaders, taking Jerusalem from them in 1187. Under Saladin the control of the church was handed over to Moslems and all but closed to visiting pilgrims except on payment of a crippling fee.

From now on Jerusalem passed from Arab, briefly back to Crusader, to Turk, again to Arab, to Mameluke, and eventually to Ottoman Turk.

Europe, having long given up crusading as a bad job, determined to protect the Holy sites, and especially the Church of the Holy Sepulchre, by peaceful means. Over the years different powers negotiated for different rights to parts of the church. The various rulers of Jerusalem effectively sold parts of the church off piecemeal, often for very handsome prices for the exclusive use of this or that Christian sect.

But it was the ascendancy of the Ottomans that set the seal on the future of one of the decidedly less than Christian aspects of the Church's history. The ups and downs of the Ottoman Empire's relationships with the rest of the world, and their notorious fondness for bribery, were the deciding factors in the likelihood of a Christian sect being granted the right to build altars, chapels or restore parts of the church. Once granted the Ottomans could, and did, change their minds frequently, transferring the rights to and fro.

The lack of continuity began to take its toll. It took so long for any one sect to gain permission to restore and renovate that the fabric of the church began to collapse, and the hostile relationships between the sects often broke out into brawls and violent occupations of each other's territory. When work was successfully carried out it was frequently conceived in isolation and often seriously undermined any semblance of a harmonious whole.

In 1852 the Ottomans passed the Law of the 'Status Quo' designed to put an end to the un-Christian squabbling. The law, which dictated who was allowed to officiate where and at what time, which parts were solely owned by one sect and which were jointly owned, who should be responsible for the cleaning and repairing of which part of the church, who was responsible for ringing the bells, etc. was fairly arbitrary. However a number of grey areas were still left, whose future was to be determined by joint committees and over which the rights of ownership are still contested. Earthquakes and fires began to take a serious toll but the squabbling continued, and in 1935, with Palestine under the British Mandate, the British authorities intervened and propped the edifice up with such hideous scaffolding that the sects forced themselves into a measure of co-operation. Gradually they arrived at an uneasy and by no means comprehensive agreement, allowing for much-needed restoration work to proceed. It continues to this day, and a visit to the church involves dodging the little tractors that frequently buzz around inside, and putting up with the noise of constant reconstruction work.

Today six different Christian denominations occupy their designated places in states of varying hostility within the unequal hierarchy of this church. The Greek Orthodox and the Franciscan Catholics head the list, followed by the Armenians, with the Copts, the Syrians and the Ethiopians very much in third place.

The interior of the church is large and disorienting. There are all sorts of ways to tour it, but as it is likely that you will visit it after having followed the stations of the cross, we will start our tour by continuing through stations X – XIV in as logical a sequence as possible.

Immediately you enter the door of the church, turn to your right and climb the stairs which lead to CALVARY. Here you will find two chapels. At the entrance to the first, the Franciscan CHAPEL OF THE CRUCIFIXION, is STATION X where Jesus was stripped of His clothes. The chapel's altar marks STATION XI, where Jesus was nailed to the cross. Note the elaborate mosaics that decorate the chapel walls. Right next door is the GREEK ORTHODOX CHAPEL that marks the spot where the cross was raised – STATION XII. The elaborate altar, decorated with huge candles and festooned with votive lamps, has a distinctly Eastern atmosphere. STATION XIII is to be found between the two chapels and is marked by a statue of the Virgin Mary. This is the spot where tradition holds that Mary received the body of Jesus after He was taken down from the cross.

Leave Calvary by the steep stairs at the rear of the Greek Orthodox Chapel, back down into the main body of the church itself. Turning immediately to your left at the foot of the stairs, opposite the entrance to the church, you will pass the STONE OF UNCTION. The painting on the wall behind the stone depicts Jesus' body being laid out and prepared for burial. Flanked with candles and overhung with eight elaborate lamps, the pinkish slab was laid in 1810 to cover the remains of the stone which originally marked the site and had been hacked about by zealous pilgrims eager for a relic to carry home with them.

Pass the Stone of Unction and head for the ROTUNDA and the holiest spot in the whole of Christendom – the XIVth and final station, THE TOMB, where Jesus is believed by millions to have been buried. The tomb is enclosed in an ornate marble 'kiosk'. Inside are two chambers. The first, known as the CHAPEL OF THE ANGELS, is so called after the angel who informed Mary Magdalene that Christ was risen, and the second, which you have to bend low to enter, is the tomb itself. On the right hand side of this tiny space is a slab of marble, concealing the rock tomb where Christ was laid to rest before his resurrection. As you can imagine, this is the focal point for thousands of pilgrims and there is almost always a queue.

Notice on the outside of the ornate Sepulchre the sooty apertures. An extraordinary ceremony is performed in and around the tomb at Easter – the 'miracle' of the 'Holy Fire'. Hundreds of the faithful, mainly from the Eastern branch of the church, gather overnight around the tomb, which is sealed off. The following day the Greek Orthodox Patriarch and an Armenian priest enter the tomb and after an interval of prayer thrust flaming torches through the apertures. The crowds press forward to light their candles from the 'holy' flame, theirs in turn serving to light the candles of hundreds of other worshippers. It's a very old ceremony which caused some consternation amongst such early travel writers as Henry Maundrell, who wrote this description after visiting Jerusalem in 1697.

> Coming to the Church of the Holy Sepulchre, we found it crowded with a numerous and distracted mob, making a hideous clamour very unfit for that sacred place, and better becoming bacchanals than Christians. They began their disorders by running round the Holy Sepulchre with all their might and swiftness crying out 'this is he'. After they had by these vertiginous circulations turned their heads and inflamed their madness, they began to at the most antick tricks and postures in a thousand shapes of distraction. Sometimes they dragged one another along the floor all round the Sepulchre, sometimes they sat one man upright on another's shoulders, sometimes they took men with their heels upwards, and hurried them about in such an indecent manner as to expose their nudities. Nothing can be imagined more rude and extravagant.

Meanwhile...
> the two Miracle-Mongers had not been above a minute in the Holy Sepulchre when the gleaming of Holy Fire was seen. Those that got the fire applied it immediately to their beards, faces and bosoms pretending it would not burn like

earthly flame. But I plainly saw, none of them could endure this experience long enough to make good that pretention.

Opposite the entrance to the Chapel of the Angels is the Greek Orthodox CATHOLICON, the largest chapel in the whole, sprawling building. The church once had some semblance of architectural harmony but the Greeks, eager for their own separate area, enclosed the Catholicon amidst considerable protest from all the other denominations, and to the detriment of the rest of the building. The most interesting feature of the chapel is the 'NAVEL OF THE WORLD' – a stone receptacle which can be seen from the entrance of the Chapel – more often than not closed off to visitors by a chain.

Follow the Rotunda round to the rear of the Sepulchre to find the tiny, COPTIC CHAPEL. Here you will find an aged, white-bearded, black robed Copt crouched in the glow of lamp and candlelight. He will beckon to you to enter and having lifted a curtain for you to kiss or touch a corner of Christ's tomb (believed by the Copts to be where Christ's head lay) will press a plastic cross into your hands, murmur a prayer and indicate that a donation would not go amiss. Frankly, it is highly unlikely that the stone is part of the tomb at all but the Copts have such a humble stake in the Church, and so many of the other Christian sites in the city are based on years of belief and tradition rather than fact, that it seems churlish in the extreme not to oblige.

Opposite the little Coptic chapel is the SYRIAN CHAPEL. After the rather gaudy display of lamps, candles and icons, this little room is bare and neglected. Its ownership, and therefore the right to renovate it, are disputed by the Armenians and Syrians. Leading from the chapel is the TOMB OF JOSEPH OF ARAMATHAEA. You can usually find a quiet moment by yourself in the Syrian Chapel as many of the tourists and pilgrims don't find their way in here, or are discouraged by the lack of colourful, religious paraphernalia.

Leaving the Syrian Chapel follow the Rotunda round to your left for the ALTAR OF MARY MAGDALEN. This area, with its black and white floor, and the adjoining CHAPEL OF THE APPARITION, are both administered by the Franciscans. There is no gospel support for the event, but tradition holds that Christ appeared to His mother on this spot after His resurrection.

Leaving the Chapel of the Apparition, turn eastwards down the left hand side of the colonnaded AMBULATORIUM. At the end you will come to the first of a succession of chapels – this one, owned by the Greeks, is known, with no foundation whatsoever, as yet another 'PRISON OF CHRIST'.

Follow the ambulatorium further eastwards for the CHAPEL OF ST LONGINUS. There are two traditions here. One holds that Longinus was the Roman soldier who is recorded as having stabbed the crucified Christ in the side to ensure He was dead; the second is that he was the Centurion who cried out in acknowledgement that Jesus was the Son of God.

A wide stone staircase now leads down, first to the CHAPEL OF ST HELENA and thence to the CHAPEL OF THE TRUE CROSS. The walls of the stairway are covered with religious graffiti – tiny crosses gouged out of the stone by centuries of pilgrims. St Helena was the mother of the Emperor Constantine who first adopted Christianity as the official religion of the Roman Empire. Tradition has it that it was here that St Helena discovered the cross on which Christ was crucified.

The excavations below the Chapel of St Helena, not usually accessible to the public, show the depths of the original quarry on which the church was built, and its later use as a cistern. Here, the Armenians, who own the chapel, found a fascinating painting dating from 330 AD depicting a pilgrim vessel. It is now clear that pilgrims came from far afield to visit this spot as long ago as the 4th C.

Note the mosaic on the floor of the Chapel of St Helena. It depicts the shocking genocide of the Armenians by the Turks before the First World War.

Back up the steps to continue round the Ambulatorium. The first chapel is known as the CHAPEL OF THE MOCKING or the 'Oratory of the Insults'. A little further on, behind protective glass, you can see a portion of the ROCK OF CALVARY. The next and final chapel is the CHAPEL OF ADAM. Byzantine tradition has it that Adam is buried here. Behind the chapel more of the Rock of Calvary is visible. There is a fissure in the rock face which gives credence to the Gospel description – 'when Jesus died the earth quaked and the rock split' (Matthew 27:51).

And now you are back to the start of your tour and the Stone of Unction. Leaving the church, turn sharply left before you cross the courtyard and through a small doorway into the Ethiopian domain – known as DEIR ES SULTAN. Before you reach the roof, where the monks live in tiny, hutchlike cells, you will pass through two charmingly simple chapels. The upper chapel has a vivid painting of Solomon greeting Sheba. As you emerge into the hot Jerusalem sunshine, you will find yourself on the roof of the church, in a kind of courtyard with the dome of the Chapel of St Helena protruding in the centre.

In the MURISTAN, reached by crossing the Church of the

Holy Sepulchre's courtyard and exiting via the left-hand corner, you'll find the modern LUTHERAN CHURCH OF THE REDEEMER. A stiff climb up a narrow winding staircase to the belltower will give you a fantastic view of the city. There are shops and cafés around this area so you can take a rest from sightseeing and get badgered into buying a souvenir or rest over a cool drink.

There are numerous other places of interest in this quarter, but only those with plenty of time to spare will be able to do justice to the major sights and still have time left over. One of the pleasures of Jerusalem is in just strolling around the streets and exploring, with no particular purpose and destination. This is how to get a feel for the atmosphere of the place and to find your bearings in this maze.

Near the Church of the Redeemer is the CHURCH OF ST JOHN, traditionally held to be the home of Zebedee who was the father of the apostles, James and John. The Church dates from the 5th C with later 7th and 11th C additions. If you have time, pay a visit to the GREEK ORTHODOX PATRIARCHATE MUSEUM, to be found in the street of the same name. Here, there is an interesting collection of religious paraphernalia, a lovely garden and a beautifully restored Crusader building.

Moslem Quarter

From *Omar ibn-Khattab* Square, inside the Jaffa Gate, take the narrow stepped David Street and follow it as it descends into the ARAB BAZAAR. By an arcade decked with colourful vegetables and hung with the carcasses of kids and lambs, the street kinks a little, right and left, and then becomes the 'STREET OF THE CHAIN'. At the bottom of the street is the *Bab el-Silsileh*, the GATE OF THE CHAIN, leading into *Haram es Sharif*, or the TEMPLE MOUNT.

In times gone by there was a golden chain suspended from heaven which had its end near here. The people of Jerusalem would settle disputes by means of this chain, for if anyone spoke anything but the truth in the presence of the chain, it would swing with great violence, as if moved by an unseen hand. The story goes that a cunning old trader borrowed a large sum of money from a gullible acquaintance. Having got his hands on the money, he refused to give it back despite threats and entreaties. Finally after a year, the case was taken to the chain. Now the trader, well versed in the art of deception, had converted the money to precious gems, and these he inserted in a hollow stick which he took to the

Moslem Quarter, Jerusalem

hearing. Asking his accuser to hold the stick while he composed himself for the dignity of the occasion, he declared loudly and clearly that he was not in possession of the sum of money lent him, and that he had returned it to his accuser. The chain was still, and then after a pause, withdrew up to Heaven in disgust at the depth of man's duplicity. It has never reappeared.

Through the *Bab el-Silsileh* you can enter the Temple Mount. As you pass the tiny door in the gate, you and your bags are searched, for this is a holy but highly contentious place; on several occasions fanatics have attempted to burn the mosque. Before you stretches the vast enclosure that was once the site of Solomon's Temple. This is one of the Holy Places of the world, a huge expanse of shining white stone, surrounded by galleries and minarets, and set with magnificent buildings, arches, tombs and trees. But above all it is light, peaceful and spacious, a striking contrast to the murky labyrinth of the Bazaar.

Before it was so magnificently adorned, this was MOUNT MORIAH. It may have been the site of Abraham's near sacrifice of his son. David knew it as a holy place and bought from its owner, Araunah, who had his threshing-floor here. This was to be the final resting place of the Ark of the Covenant, the chosen site of God for His Temple on earth. Centuries later, after the site had been sanctified and then defiled and ravaged by the Romans, the rock became holy to the Moslems as the place from which Mohammed made his night journey to Heaven. Pious Jews will not enter the Temple Mount, for the exact position of the Temple and the Holy of Holies, forbidden to all Jews except the High Priest, is not known, and thus they might inadvertently tread on hallowed ground.

There are eight flights of steps up from the great pavement, leading to the platform in the centre of which stands the DOME OF THE ROCK. At the head of each flight is a triple arch, built by the Crusaders. The Moslems believe that the Scales of Justice, in which each human soul will be judged on the Last Day, will be suspended from these arches. Walk round the Dome and admire each of its sides, and the exquisite blue tiling, for this is one of the glories of world architecture, built in 691, under the great Caliph Abd-el-Malik.

Temple Mount, Jerusalem

Although the dome has collapsed and been restored several times and the tiling on the façade has been replaced, the main building is almost entirely original. The burnished dome is modern; it is not gold but an alloy of bronze and aluminium. The shrine is octagonal and perfectly symmetrical in every way, the dome iteself soaring over 100' above the floor.

In the centre is the rock from which Mohammed ascended to heaven. One night, as Mohammed was asleep, he was awakened by the Angel Gabriel, who led him on a white winged beast from Mecca to the 'Distant Mosque', *al Aqsa*, at Jerusalem. Here Mohammed met Abraham, Moses and Jesus, whom he led in prayer before ascending with the angel into heaven. There he passed through the various levels until he reached the presence of God. From God he received detailed instructions for the observances of the faithful. He descended again, and mounting his steed, *al Buraq*, returned to the *Ka'ba* at Mecca before daybreak. It is this event which makes the rock on Mount Moriah sacred to the Moslems. The Prophet's footprint in the rock proves the point. This shrine – *Qubbat as-Sakhra* – is the third holiest shrine of Islam, after the Ka'ba and the Tomb of the Prophet at Medina. At one time Moslems prayed facing Jerusalem, until Mecca was granted the most holy status.

The style and proportions of the dome are a result of the Moslems' admiration for the architecture of the Church of the Holy Sepulchre, which they copied in many respects. When the Crusaders took Jerusalem, they believed that the Dome of the Rock was the Temple of Solomon, so apart from setting up an altar over the rock, and surmounting the dome with a golden cross, they left it intact. The churches built later by the Knights Templar – who took their name from the Temple of Solomon – have the same form as the Dome of the Rock. Ironically, it was this unusual form of church, with the altar in the middle of a circular space beneath a dome, and the form of service that developed round it, that caused the Templars to be branded as heretics. (See the Templar churches in London – Chancery Lane – and Cambridge.)

When Saladin took Jerusalem in 1187, he removed the cross and the altar, and restored the shrine to its former glory. Some 350 years later Süleyman the Magnificent had the whole façade re-covered with the blue faience from Persia. Along with everything else during the later Ottoman years, the dome fell into disrepair. The restoration that makes it what it is today was carried out between 1958 and 1962 – notably the replacing of the old lead sheeting of the dome, and the restoration of much of the tilework.

Enshrined within the dome are some hairs from the beard of the Prophet. The shrine is not a mosque; no public prayers are held here, but many Moslems come here for private devotions. Non-Moslems are free to stroll around the Temple Mount and to visit the shrines and mosques, except during noon-day prayer on Fridays. But it is a holy place, so 'modest dress' is required.

A few paces to the east of the dome of the Rock is the *Qubbat al-Silsileh* – the DOME OF THE CHAIN, which marks the spot where the chain previously alluded to was suspended. This is a small cupola mounted on pillars, with no walls except for a rudimentary *Mihrab* to indicated the *qibla*, or direction of prayer. The whole enclosure of *Haram es-Sharif* (Noble Sanctuary) is dotted with these small, lesser shrines: the DOME OF THE ASCENSION, where Mohammed prayed before his journey to heaven, was restored, according to the inscription, in 1220 by one *Asphah Salar 'Iz-ud-Din Said as Sa'ad Abu 'Omar 'Uthman Ibn 'Ali-az-Zanjeeli.* There are also shrines to Solomon, Moses, Joseph and St George.

Al Aqsa

Against the southern wall of the enclosure is the *Al-Aqsa* Mosque. Al-Aqsa means 'the far mosque', where the *Ka'ba* at Mecca is the near mosque. Caliph Omar built the first mosque on the site, near the rock, when he took the city in 635. In those days the Arabs had not had time to attain the splendour that their empire was later to achieve, so the mosque was a simple insubstantial affair of wood and sun-dried bricks, although it was big enough to hold 3,000 of the faithful. It collapsed within 50 years. In 690 Abd al-Malik built a great stone mosque on the site, but that too was destroyed by an earthquake 50 years later. Another mosque was built, only to collapse again in another earthquake. A new mosque was built by Caliph al-Mahdi in 780, and this one survived until 1033 when the mosque was rebuilt in its present form by the Fatimid Caliph az-Zahir.

The Knights Templar converted this mosque into a church and armoury, stabling their horses in the vaults beneath – a perfect arrangement for the warrior-monks. In 1187 Saladin re-consecrated the building as a mosque, and that it has remained until the present. What you see today is the result of extensive renovations carried out in the 1940s. The magnificent wooden gilded ceiling was a gift from Egypt. It's a beautiful mosque with seven spacious aisles and a great wooden roof, high above, supported on rows of marble columns and arches. The wooden *Minber*, or pulpit, was a gift from Saladin. The colonnades beneath the silver dome are the same as they were when the mosque was built over 900 years ago.

Islamic Museum

Just to the west of *al-Aqsa* is the ISLAMIC MUSEUM. Here, in a building mostly constructed by the Crusaders, is a fine collection of tiles, wood-carving, carpets, illuminated Korans, manuscripts and ornate weaponry. In the 12th C this vaulted hall was the living quarters of the Knights Templar.

Mosque of Omar

Just to the east of the Church of the Holy Sepulchre is the 12th C MOSQUE OF OMAR. This mosque commemorates the event which took place here when the Arabs first took Jerusalem from the Byzantines in 635. The Patriarch of the city, Sophronius, refused to surrender the city to anyone but the Caliph himself. So Omar, who was then at Mecca, made the journey to Jerusalem and received the keys of the city from the Patriarch. Omar was the first Caliph, the first successor to the Prophet (See page 32). He was a simple pious man who possessed but one shirt and lived a life of austerity.

The Western Wall and the Temple

When the Children of Israel were a nomadic tribe, wandering with their flocks in the deserts and hills of the Middle East, they carried their God with them. The portable temple in which He dwelt was known as the 'Ark of the Covenant'. The Ark took the form of a beautifully crafted oblong chest of acacia wood, lined inside and out with beaten gold, and borne on a litter by the priests or Levites. Where the tribes camped, the Ark would be placed in a 'Tabernacle', a sophisticated tent made of several layers of rich drapes, with two chambers. In the inner chamber, the 'Holy of Holies', rested the Ark itself, while the outer chamber was for the observances of the priests.

In the time of Samuel, the Israelites suffered a defeat at the hands of the Philistines, and the Philistines stole the Ark. They took it to Ashdod and placed it in the temple of Dagon, their fish- or grain-god. The following day the statue of Dagon was found shattered into a thousand pieces before the Ark, and the people of Ashdod were sorely smitten with 'boils upon their secret and hindmost parts'. The Ark was accordingly moved to the other Philistine cities of Gath, and Ekron, with the same results in both places. Finally the Philistines realised that there was more to this box than they had thought, and they returned it to the Israelites. When David made his capital at Hebron, the Ark found a more permanent resting place for seven and a half years.

Finally Jerusalem fell to the Israelites, and the Ark of the Covenant was transported there to be set up for ever on Mount Moriah. In the last years of his reign King David gathered the materials for the construction of a fitting House of the Lord. King Hiram of Tyre furnished the timber for the Temple: Cedars of Lebanon and cypresses. It is said that 30,000 men were engaged in the hewing and transport of wood, and that Hiram's payment took the form of wheat, oil, wine and 20 frontier towns.

The massive limestone blocks were quarried deep underground and away from the Temple precinct, so that the rude sounds of work should not disturb the repose of the Lord. Some 1,000 priests were trained in the art of masonry so that the coarse banter and oaths of ordinary workmen would not defile the House of God.

It was Solomon who presided over the building of the Temple. He was reputed to have power over *djinns*, hellish spirits, whom he employed in the more menial and heavier labours of the building. On the eastern wall of the Temple Mount is a dome which marks the spot where he would have sat on his throne and kept the fiery *djinns* in order.

The Temple was completed in seven and a half years. According to the story in Kings, after the opening celebrations, a curious cloud descended upon the Holy of Holies, and thus God established the Temple as his dwelling-place on earth.

Like the Tabernacle of the wilderness, the Temple was divided into two parts, the Holy Place, an outer chamber where the priests performed their offices, and the inner sanctum, or 'Holy of Holies', where the Ark stood, and which the High Priest entered only once a year, on the Day of Atonement. Little more is known about the appearance of the Temple of Solomon.

In 587 BC the Temple was razed to the ground by the Babylonians, and the Jews taken into exile. Fifty years later they returned and started work on the Second Temple. Work was completed in the spring of 515 BC, but the Temple was a pale shadow of the original. During the next 500 years it was defiled by the Ptolemies and the Romans, and even consecrated as a pagan shrine to Zeus. When Herod the Great became governor of Jerusalem under the Romans, the Temple was battered and decayed; in order to ingratiate himself with the Jews, Herod undertook to renovate it. In fact he virtually rebuilt it, and it is the remains of Herod's Temple that are visible today in the Western Wall.

Herod's Temple, built over a period of 18 years from 20 BC, was the greatest of the temples in magnificence as well as in size. But dominating the great court around the Holy Places, the Antonia Fortress was built, a heavy-handed symbol of Roman power and oppression. Even the Talmudists, who hated Herod, had to admit to the magnificence of the Temple. 'He who has not seen the structure of Herod has not seen a structure of beauty in his life.'

After the Great Revolt, Titus destroyed the Temple utterly; not a stone of the actual structure was left standing. There is a legend that each part of the Temple was built by a separate class of citizens; it was the paupers who raised the foundation walls. While the city was being ravaged and sacked, and the courts and palaces were falling in flames, Angels touched the Wailing Wall with their wings, proclaiming: 'This the work of the poor, shall never be destroyed.

And so it is today. The great stone wall, that is so deeply loved by the Jewish people, is nothing more than the foundations of Herod's vast Temple. What you see of the Wailing Wall today is less than half of its full height, for the massive blockwork extends below the pavement rather more than above it.

There is not a building in the history of the world that is so deeply beloved by a nation as the remains of the Temple of the Jews. The wall is open for worship 24 hours a day, and it is never unattended; there is always someone, man, woman, or child, quietly praying, weeping over the loss of the Temple, or bewailing the hard lot of the Chosen People. Prayers and entreaties to God are written on slips of paper and pushed into the cracks between the stones. Anyone may approach the Wall, Jewish or non-Jewish, and many non-Jews find the experience deeply moving. The Wall has the status of a synagogue, so there are separate sections for men and women. Late on a warm summer night, when the Wall is peopled with just a few quiet worshippers, you may find it one of the most moving and beautiful sights in the Holy City.

Jewish Quarter

The JEWISH QUARTER of the Old City was all but destroyed in the 1948 War of Independence, and it wasn't until 1967, when all of Jerusalem came under Israeli control, that any real restoration work was undertaken.

The destruction carried with it a degree of blessing. During the clearance of the rubble and the preparation work for new foundations, some of the finest archaeological discoveries were made, and although the archaeologists may not always have prevailed over the developers, much has been preserved and the old sits surprisingly happily alongside the new.

Coming from the picturesque but shabby Moslem area, the squeaky clean, golden-hued Jewish domain comes as something of a jolt. The quarter is a network of narrow, staggered streets, open squares, artists' shops and galleries, cafés, restaurants, chic apartment blocks and synagogues. The noise of boisterous Israeli children mingles with the chanting from the *yeshivas* and the *muezzin* drifting over from the *Al Aqsa* Mosque and the Moslem Quarter.

The area is quite well signposted to all the major places of interest, but as with all of old Jerusalem, the maze of streets can still become confusing. If you want to make a systematic tour of the area you can't do better than to arm yourself with a copy of *Quartertour Jerusalem – Walking Tour of the Jewish Quarter*.

One of the best places to start your tour and to get an idea of what life in the Jewish Quarter was like before it was destroyed, is at the OLD YISHUV COURT MUSEUM. From the Jaffa Gate turn right, passing the entrance to the Citadel on your right, and continue down the road towards the Armenian Quarter. Look out for St James Street on your left. The street becomes *Rehov Or Hahayyim* and here you will find a restored house, now a museum arranged to reflect the way of life of both *Sephardi* and *Ashkenazi* Jews in the 19th C. The structure of the complex is typical of the building style prevalent at this time, and consists of two courtyards around which the living accommodation and the synagogues of groups of families were arranged. The courtyards served as a meeting area for the little community, but also as a place where the women shared facilities for such household tasks as cooking and washing. The synagogue on the ground level is *Sephardic* and named for Rabbi 'Ari' (*Itzak ben Shlomo Luria*), a famous mystic, who was born here in the 16th C. On the upper floor you will find a synagogue dedicated to a Moroccan rabbi, *Haim ben Attar*, also a *Sephardi*, although the synagogue was later adapted to *Ashkenazi* rituals. Note the two 'guest' rooms in the complex. The *Sephardic* room has the chairs lined round the walls, whilst the *Ashkenazis* preferred to congregate in the middle of the room. Well worth looking at are the collections of clothing, household utensils, furniture and wonderful old photographs. But the most interesting displays are the tools of the various trades – apothecaries, tailors, shoemakers and hatters, etc.

Head next for the CARDO – one of the most important archaeological finds in Jerusalem. The Cardo was the main thoroughfare for Byzantine Jerusalem. The original Roman processional street started at the Damascus Gate and stretched across to David Street. The Byzantines extended it to the NEA CHURCH built by Justinian in the 6th C AD and later destroyed in an earthquake.

Steps lead down to the uncovered section of the Cardo. From here turn left into the covered area for a look at a reproduction of the MADABA MAP. This mosaic was discovered on the floor of a Byzantine church in Jordan, and shows how Jerusalem was laid out in the 6th C BC. It confirms the mammoth proportions of the Cardo; the street was 73 feet wide, the roofing to protect the citizens from the elements was supported by huge 16 feet high columns. You'll find a rather erratic AUDIO VISUAL DISPLAY in this section, which, if it's working properly, will tell you more about the excavations and the history of the Cardo. Further on you'll find the area where Crusader restorations to turn the Cardo into a market have now been updated and converted to rows of expensive boutiques. From here you can walk down to examine the EXCAVATIONS dating from the First Temple Period – an example of happy compromise between developers and archaeologists; modern apartment blocks are built on stilts over the site.

Nearby on *Plugat Hakotel* Street are the excavations of the foundations of ancient Jerusalem's city walls, known as the BROAD WALL and built by King Hezekiah in 701 BC.

For more archaeological gems make for BURNT HOUSE. In 70 AD the Jews revolted against their Roman overlords, only to be severely defeated. Jerusalem was razed to the ground by Titus and the Temple was destroyed. This remarkable find is a house belonging to a wealthy temple priest. An AUDIO VISUAL PRESENTATION (there are plenty of showings in English) shown inside the excavations themselves will give you all the details; it's a truly fascinating experience.

Near the Burnt House, with its entrance on *Misgave Ladach* Street, are some interesting CRUSADER RUINS now designated as an archaeological garden. When the Crusaders conquered Jerusalem the Holy Sites became accessible to thousands of pilgrims. The official language of the city, the *lingua franca*, was French and as the many German pilgrims who came here had no knowledge of the language a German-speaking hospice was founded by German members of the Knights Hospitaller to cater for their needs. The ruined structure you are standing in was the Church of the Holy Mary of the German Knights which served the complex. The site is well provided with explanatory signs.

As you would expect there are plenty of SYNAGOGUES in this quarter. If you've never visited one before, don't expect the ornate grandeur of the churches you may have already seen in the city. The synagogue may be the forerunner of the church, the chapel and the Mosque, but simplicity more often than not prevails.

Near the southern end of the Cardo (the open section) you'll find the HURVA. The HURVA SYNAGOGUE, which lies ruined below, was built in the 1700s, destroyed by the Moslems, rebuilt in 1857, only to be destroyed again after the Jews surrendered the quarter to the Jordanians in 1948. Once its graceful 18th C parabola was one of the dominant landmarks on Jerusalem's skyline; now only a sweeping, stone arch over the ruins commemorates its beauty. Hurva literally means 'ruin' – the name stuck after the synagogue was first destroyed.

Here, too, you will find the RAMBAN SYNAGOGUE, named for the famous 13th C scholar Rabbi *Moshe Ben Nahman* (also known as *Nahmanides*) who came to Jerusalem from Spain. Finding that the Jewish population had dwindled alarmingly, he set about encouraging the establishment of a new Jewish community. The little mosque next door was built by Jewish converts to Islam. The proximity of the two religious 'houses' proved too inflammatory, and in 1474 the Moslems destroyed the synagogue. Rebuilt again, the Ramban needed to be expanded to accommodate the growing numbers of immigrant Jews moving to Ottoman-controlled Jerusalem in the 16th C. The plans caused a further furore and eventually the Jews were forbidden the use of the synagogue altogether. It only started to function again as a synagogue when the Israelis retook the quarter from the Jordanians in 1967.

Head south from Hurva Synagogue Square down *Mishmerot Hakehuna* Street. Look out on the left for steps leading down to the SEPHARDIC SYNAGOGUES – a complex built below ground level in the 17th C to meet the needs of the growing *Sephardic* community. The 'sunken' complex circumnavigated a decree by the Moslem rulers that no synagogue should stand higher than any Moslem building. There are four interconnecting synagogues; the first is called after a rabbi from the Second Temple Period, YOHANAN BEN ZAKKAI. The second is the ELIJAH SYNAGOGUE. To proceed with prayer, there should, according to Jewish tradition, always be a quorum (*minyan*) of ten men. A legend relates that once, on *Yom Kippur*, when the congregation was one man short, the prophet Elijah appeared to make up the numbers. In the little room at the back of the synagogue you will see a chair, apparently kept here in the event that Elijah should ever need to make up a shortfall again. Before you leave, take note of the elaborate Holy Ark, brought here from a destroyed Italian synagogue after the Second World War.

The other two synagogues are reached by going back through the *Yohanan Ben Zakkai* Synagogue. The first is the CENTRAL SYNAGOGUE, originally a courtyard serving as the women's section of the *Yohanan Ben Zakkai.* Next door is the ISTAMBULI SYNAGOGUE. During the War of Independence, this complex housed families sheltering from Arab attacks as the advance gradually moved through the quarter – leading to eventual surrender by the Jewish residents and the exhausted *Haganah* defenders.

Leaving the *Sephardic* synagogues, continue down *Mishmerot Hakehuna* Street and turn left into *HaHazozrot* Street, a narrow alleyway running between the SEPHARDIC EDUCATIONAL CENTRE buildings. Turn left at the end and look out for a gate in the wall on the right, leading into BATEI MAHSE (SHELTER HOUSE SQUARE). This place is more interesting for its history than for any architectural merit, but it's worth a look en route for the RUINED APSE OF THE NEA CHURCH – more about this later. The square is flanked on the western side by the long, low ROTHSCHILD HOUSE, built along with other houses in the square, most now destroyed, to shelter the influx of new immigrants in the 19th C and to attempt to relieve the desperate overcrowding of the rest of the Jewish Quarter. The idea was that the newcomers would have a chance to find their feet and establish themselves, and would then be expected to move on and make way for new occupants. In practice the inhabitants generally stayed put, as the housing on offer was rather better and more modern than anything else in the quarter. It was here that the inhabitants of the quarter congregated after the surrender to the Arabs at the end of the War of Independence, clutching the few belongings they could rescue and ending an almost continuous Jewish occupation of the area for nearly 2,000 years.

Take flights of steps to the south-east of the Rothschild Building where you will find the little metal door that will lead you down into a basement. Here you can view the ruined apse of the Nea Church, built by Justinian in 543 AD. The site displays photographs and comprehensive details of the excavations of what was once the greatest church in Christendom.

There are many more synagogues, archaeological finds and other places of interest within the Jewish Quarter, but it is not within the scope of this book to cover them all. Indeed, excavations are constantly in progress and new discoveries are being opened to the public every year. If this area is of particular interest, you would be well advised to take a walking tour of the quarter.

The Armenian Quarter

The Armenian Quarter of Jerusalem, home to some 3,000 of this tenacious and oppressed people, stands on the old Western Hill, a walled city within a walled city. Under the long years of Ottoman domination the Armenians who had settled here were as much under threat from the ruling power within the city walls, as from without; accordingly they surrounded their cathedral, convent and town with a further wall. The wall still stands, making the Armenian Quarter the most inaccessible of all the city's quarters to the stroller. But now, for the first time in some 500 years, they are lowering their guard, and in their new-found security they are spreading outside their old walls with the construction of a new seminary.

Within the quarter are a library, a convent, school, meeting houses, beautiful gardens with stately Cypress trees, and above all, the homes of the inhabitants, all within a beautiful walled town which, in appearance, has scarcely changed since the Middle Ages.

The focus of the Armenian quarter is the CATHEDRAL OF ST JAMES, considered by many to be the most beautiful church in Jerusalem. James, the son of the fisherman Zebedee, was the first of the Apostles to die, executed by Herod. He was the first bishop of the early Christian Church, the headquarters of which were here on the Western Hill. The Armenian Church and nation, the first to accept Christianity as a state religion, in 301, has been established in Palestine since the 4th C. The cathedral dates from the 12th C and with the Patriarchate, stands on the site of Herod's citadel gardens.

Within the cathedral porch are two ancient knockers or gongs, with which the Christians were summoned to prayer. When the Moslems, under Omar, took Jerusalem in 637, the pealing of bells was forbidden to the Christians; the *nakus* (Arabic, perhaps borrowed from 'knockers') were acceptable because Noah, on the command of Allah, had used one thrice a day to call the workmen employed on the ark, and to attract people to hear his warnings of an approaching judgement. Bells have always been abhorrent to the Moslems. In 1823, a traveller stated that the only bell in Jerusalem was a hand-bell in the Latin convent. Much more recently there was a riot amongst the Moslems of Nablus because a bell had been put up in the mission school. One of these knockers in the cathedral porch, enormous planks suspended on chains, was of iron, the other of wood. Today, now that the bells are in use again, the knockers are used to mark the beginning of the service.

The lofty cathedral, which is considered to be one of the five principal sites of pilgrimage in the Holy City, is decorated with glorious blue tiling. On the north side is the shrine of St James, the brother of John. This is an exquisite little chapel of tortoiseshell inlaid with mother-of-pearl, below whose altar is said to be preserved the head of St James, the first Apostle-martyr, beheaded by Herod in 44 AD. Before the high altar of the cathedral is the traditional throne of St James, but the Patriarchs, who are entitled to use this throne, always take the chair beside it as a mark of humility. The treasure of the Armenian convent is reputed to be a fabulous collection of gold and silver plate, jewelled vestments and priceless manuscripts. The Gregorian music and ceremonial of this church are profoundly beautiful.

As you walk around the cathedral and the compound, take time to admire the *Khatchkars*. These are the decorative crosses engraved in the stone walls over the ages by priests, monks and pilgrims. Each one is unique, though there are literally hundreds of them in the cathedral precincts. The oldest ones are on the western wall of the church and date from 1151. These crosses have been used in Armenia since the 9th C and are reckoned to be the origin of the Crusader Cross, the 'Cross of Jerusalem'.

The church itself is a perfect example of fine medieval Armenian workmanship.

A characteristic of Armenian churches is the great number of lamps. The hundreds of lamps which glow in the quiet shadows of St James are the work of Armenian goldsmiths of Persia, Istanbul and the old Armenian community of Van.

Queen Melisende, who was Armenian, the wife of Foulques of Anjou and daughter of Baldwin II and Queen Morphia, was responsible for the building of the Bazaar in Jerusalem and for much of the building of Nablus, her dower town. She was crowned in 1129. She also built St Anne's Church, to many the finest church in the city. The Armenian/Crusader style of her architecture displays that harmonious blend of East and West for which Armenia is justly celebrated.

Within the walls of the quarter the Armenians have their own tiny *Yad Vashem*, a small and humble MUSEUM devoted to the massacres that the Armenians suffered at the hands of the Turks at the beginning of this century.

The Cathedral of St James is only open from 3:00 pm, and even then not every day of the week, so check before you go. Outside the walls are a number of Armenian tea-shops and shops selling books, paintings and the ceramics for which the Armenians are famous. There are also several Armenian ceramic businesses in the *Souk*.

Mount Zion

Mount Zion, just outside the Zion Gate and opposite the Armenian Quarter, is dominated by the imposing CHURCH OF THE DORMITION, whose huge conical roof can be seen from almost any point in the city. In this area you will find the traditional site of both the LAST SUPPER (the Cenacle), DAVID'S TOMB and, just over the road, the CHURCH OF PETER IN GALICANTU.

The Church of the Dormition was built by the German Kaiser Wilhelm II in the early 19th C, marking the spot where the Virgin Mary is believed by some to have 'fallen into eternal sleep'. The church was constructed over part of the site of the Byzantine Church of Zion, one of the most important churches for early Christians. The interior is decorated with an elaborate golden mosaic whilst the floor is highly decorated with concentric rings depicting the prophets, the twelve apostles and the zodiac. Concerts are frequently held here, and it's worth making enquiries to see if you can get seats – the acoustics and the atmosphere are superb. Downstairs in the crypt a central shrine covers a statue of Mary reclining in her eternal sleep. All round the walls are chapels donated by individual countries.

Zion was the name of the Jebusite fortress conquered by David, and for many years it was erroneously believed that it was also the site of David's city. Historical and archaeological knowledge has long proved otherwise but tradition dies hard and DAVID'S TOMB is still, and probably always will be, a holy site for Jews and Moslems alike. Although the place is hardly a magnificent shrine, this tomb is a very holy place for Jews. Men will be requested to cover their heads (suitable head-covering is provided) and behaviour is expected to be suitably subdued.

Above the Tomb is the CENACLE (LAST SUPPER ROOM). Once again the authenticity of this site is dubious. The room dates from around the 12th C, and aside from its associations with the Last Supper, it is also traditionally believed to have been the place of the descent of the Holy Spirit at Pentecost.

You can climb up to the roof of this complex. It is often quiet up there so it can be a good spot for a moment's respite away from the throng. As an added bonus, the view of the old city is excellent.

Before you leave the area you might want to see the CHAMBER OF THE HOLOCAUST, dedicated to the memory of the 6 million Jews slaughtered by the Nazis. It has none of the stirring grandeur of YAD VASHEM (see West Jerusalem), but it is an intensely moving experience. The displays are simply laid out in a series of low lit rooms. Some of the photographs and exhibits are extremely harrowing, but none so much as the exhibition of anti-semitic and racist propoganda collected *since* the war; some of the exhibits show how efforts have been made to debunk the Holocaust as Jewish propaganda.

The Church of St Peter in Galicantu, another of the Italian architect Barluzzi's gems, built in 1931, commemorates St Peter's threefold denial of Christ following the crucifixion. Galicantu literally means 'cock-crow'. In a lovely setting on the eastern slope of Mount Zion the church is also claimed by some to have been the site of the house of the High Priest Caiaphas, where Christ was imprisoned before being taken before Pontius Pilate; interesting excavations in the crypt of the church help to support their claim.

Mount of Olives

There are more tombs, churches and shrines than there are olive trees on this barren hill over to the east of Jerusalem. It's sacred to Jews, Moslems and Christians alike. For the Jews it has associations with King David and with the Day of Redemption, when the Messiah will lead the faithful from here through the Golden Gates of the Holy City; for Christians and Moslems, there are powerful links here with the last days of Christ. It's a good place to go first if you've never been to the city before. The Mount rises to some 350 feet. On the eastern side are the velvet undulations of the Judean hills, and on the west a stunning view of the city and the Temple Mount, especially early in the morning or at dusk.

You can get to the summit, the Arab Village of *Et Tur*, four ways. By bus from the Arab bus station opposite Damascus Gate, by Bus No: 99, by taxi (agree the price beforehand or make sure he turns on the meter) or Shank's pony via St Stephen's Gate – it's a stiff climb.

The highest point on the Mount is the tower of the White Russian Orthodox CHURCH AND CONVENT OF THE ASCENSION; a closed order who rarely allow any visitors into their incense-laden, prayer-filled world. Many of the aged nuns here fled the Russian revolution; the novitiates are mainly orphaned Arab girls.

Leaving *Et Tur*, walk down the hill for the Dome or CHAPEL OF THE ASCENSION, marking the spot where Christ traditionally ascended to heaven. This little shrine, dating from the 4th C, was reconstructed by the Crusaders after the 614 Persian destruction, and eventually taken over by the Moslems in the 12th C. It is still in Moslem hands today. Entrance is free unless you fall prey to one of the unofficial 'guides', often local children, who will give you a brief tour with an inaccurate history and then demand *baksheesh*. Inside the chapel, which functions as a mosque, you will see a footprint claimed to be left by Christ. This building was one of the architectural inspirations for the magnificent Dome of the Rock.

Carry on downhill for the PATER NOSTER CHURCH. Here, in a beautiful courtyard cloistered on three sides and planted with palm trees, is a grotto excavated in 1911 and firmly believed to be the spot where Christ taught the Lord's Prayer to his disciples. There was originally a church on this spot, built by Helena, the mother of Constantine. The church came to be known as the Eleoni – Church of the Olive Grove. In 614 the building was destroyed by the Persians. The ruins were discovered in the 19th C by a French princess who dedicated 17 years of her life and the best part of her fortune to building the cloister and the Carmelite nunnery so that 'the grotto would always be surrounded by veneration and prayer'.

The walls of the cloisters are decorated with over 64 versions of the Lord's Prayer on colourful glazed tiles. The nuns run a little bookshop, difficult to bypass on your way out, selling amongst other things icons, books and postcard versions of the multilingual Lord's Prayer.

Keep walking down the hill in the direction of the monstrous Hotel Intercontinental. Whilst the view from inside might be the best in Jerusalem, it does not afford the rest of the city the same compliment. Just past the hotel is the best OBSERVATION POINT. You can't possibly miss it. In season it swarms with tourists, souvenir touts and bad-tempered camels who spend their miserable days getting up and down, up and down with interminable loads of tourists. In spite of all this, it really is the best place to take photographs of the whole city and to try to get Jerusalem into perspective.

As you look down into the valley below, remember that many adherents of all three faiths, Moslem, Jewish and Christian, believe that all humanity will be judged here at the 'end of days'. The valley is known as the Valley of Kidron, but also as the Valley of Jehoshaphat (meaning 'the Lord Judges'). As you look over to the walls of the city, you can see the GOLDEN GATE (sometimes known as the Mercy Gate), long since sealed up. Through this gate the Messiah will lead the resurrected. In between and alongside the churches dotting the Mount of Olives, there is a huge JEWISH CEMETERY; with its proximity to the Seat of Judgement, it has for centuries been a coveted spot for interment.

Follow the road back along the ridge until you see an orange sign and a steep path leading downwards to the left. A short way down is the entrance to the TOMBS OF THE PROPHETS. The site is flagged by a homemade sign in black felt tip pen, which solemnly informs you that this is the last resting place of the prophets Haggai, Zachariah and Malachia. More than likely a small Arab boy will pop up from nowhere and charge you an entrance fee. Don't bother with this unless you've got plenty of time to spare and are carrying a torch. The tombs are certainly not old enough to be authentic and unless tombs in general interest you, give this a miss.

Further down on the left hand side is the mass grave of 48 Israeli soldiers who died fighting in the Jewish Quarter in 1948. A little further on, another gate leads you into the JEWISH CEMETERY – one of the oldest and largest in the world.

As you walk down the road you will see, on the right hand side, the entrance to DOMINUS FLEVIT. This lovely little church was built by the Franciscan pilgrim/architect Antonio Barluzzi in 1953. The new church incorporates the ruins of a 5th C Byzantine church, built on a spot with a magnificent view of the Holy City, where tradition has it that Jesus stood and wept over the fate of Jerusalem. The church is unashamedly modern – built to resemble a tear-drop, and dispensing with tradition to the extent that the apse is on the west end rather than on the east. This is so that worshippers can gaze upon Jerusalem over the altar from the body of the church, for the east wall is made of plate glass.

Next, the baroque RUSSIAN CHURCH OF MARY MAGDALENE. With its golden onion domes, it's one of the most striking buildings in Jerusalem. The church was built in 1885 on the orders of Tsar Alexander III in memory of his mother.

Church of Mary Magdalen, on the Mount of Olives

You won't be allowed in unless you are properly dressed – i.e. no shorts, bare shoulders or trousers for women. The Arab guardians at the gate will provide a flowered coverall for the immodest. The church is only open on Tuesdays and Thursdays and if you can't combine it with a general tour of the Mount of Olives it would probably be better to miss it out. Aside from the lovely view it commands and the attractive shady gardens in which it is set, it is not particularly remarkable inside.

At the foot of the hill is the site that draws millions of visitors; the GARDEN OF GETHSEMANE. *Gethsemane* – meaning olive press in Aramaic – is traditionally where Jesus spent the night with his disciples before his betrayal by Judas and subsequent arrest. The garden is filled with very ancient, gnarled olive trees, though it's unlikely that these are the same trees that witnessed the agony of Christ.

Ancient olive trees in the Garden of Gethsemane

Next to the garden is the CHURCH OF ALL NATIONS or BASILICA OF THE AGONY. Another triumph of the Italian architect Barluzzi, the church was built with donations from 12 nations on the site of two previous churches – the 4th C Byzantine *Egreria* Church (Elegant) and a later 12th C Crusader edifice. The façade of the church is decorated with a magnificent mural, whilst inside heavily-stained glass windows impart a sombre, gloomy atmosphere. The paucity of light makes it difficult to see the beautiful blue and gold mosaics which decorate the inside of the 12 cupolas. But light there is enough, to see the mosaics in the apse surrounding the altar. The theme of the three murals is Christ praying in His Agony whilst the disciples sleep – Judas betraying Him with a kiss – and Jesus' surrender to the Roman guard. Directly in front of the altar is the Rock of Agony itself, surrounded by a wrought iron 'crown' of thorns.

Traces of the MOSAIC FLOOR of the original *Egreria* Church can be seen beneath the present-day floor level.

On the other side of the road a little further down from the Church of All Nations and the garden, you plunge through an impressive Crusader doorway down a wide flight of stairs to the CHURCH OF THE ASSUMPTION, and the crypt which holds the TOMB OF THE VIRGIN MARY. There are a number of last resting places claimed for Mary, one in the Church of the Dormition just over the way on Mount Zion, and yet another outside Ephesus in Turkey. This particular site is connected with the belief that Mary requested the apostles to be present at her death. They were there, wafted on clouds to witness her assumption into heaven in the arms of Jesus.

The site is unmistakably Eastern; the interior sombre, festooned with lamps and candles and heavy with incense. As you descend the stairs, the first chapel on your right is dedicated to the Virgin's parents – Anne and Joachim. It is in fact the burial place of the Crusader Queen Melisende. The chapel on the left is dedicated to Joseph. In the crypt, part hewn out of the rock, is the tiny sepulchre itself. Note the *Mihrab* on one of the walls opposite the tomb. This spot is also sacred to Moslems: Mohammed is believed to have seen a gleaming light marking the spot where his 'sister' was buried, when he 'flew' over the tomb on his magical horse on his journey from Medina to Jerusalem.

Return to the courtyard at the top of the stairs and turn left

Church of All Nations

for the CAVE OF GETHSEMANE. Traditionally, this is where the disciples slept while Jesus prayed on the night of his arrest. Here too was the scene of Judas' betrayal. It is now a simple chapel with nothing but traces of the mosaic floors of a Byzantine chapel, and faded Crusader murals to catch the eye. For all that, its very simplicity is conducive to contemplation and if you manage to dodge the crowds, can provide a quiet place for thought and prayer.

Bethany

A few minutes' bus ride from Jerusalem, on the eastern slope of the Mount of Olives (it's easiest to take a bus from the bus station nearest the Damascus gate) – is the dusty little village of BETHANY. The village has strong associations with Jesus: it was here, in the house of either Simon the Leper or Mary, Martha and their brother Lazarus, that He stayed when He was in the Jerusalem area. It was in this village that Jesus brought Lazarus back to life after he had lain dead for four days. This miracle gives the village its Arabic name – *el Azariyeh* – the place of Lazarus.

The Byzantines, whose Christian zeal led them to search out and mark with churches and sanctuaries so many of the sites associated with the life of Christ, identified Lazarus' tomb in the late 3rd or early 4th C. A church was built soon afterwards to mark the spot. Earthquakes and the passage of time took their toll and further churches were subsequently built, notably by the Crusaders in the 12th C. Under Moslem control, the churches fell into disrepair. The sanctuary over the tomb of Lazarus itself was abandoned and the crypt was turned into a mosque (the miracle of Lazarus is venerated by Moslems as well as Christians). The modern church, dedicated to Mary and Martha, was designed by Barluzzi and built in the 1950s.

The steps down to LAZARUS' tomb, now under Arab control, are steep and uneven and can be slippery, so take care and hold on to the rails. This is not the entrance through which Jesus would have passed but you will see a bricked off section just above the tomb itself which would have been the original entrance. A set of tiny steps leads into the tomb proper – you have to stoop almost to a crawl to enter. Be warned that you need to keep a sense of humour about you – both your fellow tourists and the ubiquitous unofficial Arab guides may well welcome your re-emergence from the tomb with 'Behold, Lazarus is risen!'

Leaving the tomb, turn left and head up the dirt track, turning left again by the tiny, modern Greek Orthodox Church, for the ruins of what is claimed to be the HOUSE OF SIMON THE LEPER. Stand on the bank opposite for the best observation point.

Back to the Tomb of Lazarus and head downhill for the entrance on your right of the CHURCH OF MARY AND MARTHA. Just inside the church courtyard on your right-hand side, you'll see a recess in the wall. This was the original entrance to Lazarus' Tomb. Opposite are extant remains of a 4th C church. Next, on the right hand side, is a niche commemorating Pope Paul VI's visit to the church in 1964. A little further along you can see the remains of CRUSADER TOMBS and, if you turn right at the extreme end of the courtyard, you will find at the end of the passageway on your left, a door which leads down into a Crusader Crypt. Here you will find a perfectly reconstructed MILL AND OIL PRESS and the remains of earlier church walls dating from the 5th C.

The church itself is decorated with four murals that bring to life the associations of Jesus with this tiny village. Over the altar, the mural depicts Mary telling Jesus that Lazarus has died; to the left of the altar, Jesus finding Mary and Martha weeping, and to the right a depiction of the resurrection. Over the entrance door Jesus is shown feasting with the resurrected Lazarus in the House of Simon the Leper.

Mount Scopus

Mount Scopus is situated to the north-east of Jerusalem. Scopus means 'observation' and if you go up there you'll see why – there is an excellent view of the city itself and, on the opposite side, vistas of the hazy folds of the Judaean hills. On a clear day you can see the Dead Sea.

If you are short of time, you could get your fill of Jerusalem views from the Mount of Olives and give this one a miss.

At the summit of Mount Scopus is the impressive HEBREW UNIVERSITY and the HADASSAH HOSPITAL. The Israelis managed to hang on to the hospital and university in the aftermath of the War of Independence, although both institutions were cut off from West Jerusalem. The difficulties faced in reaching them led to a new university and hospital being built elsewhere in West Jerusalem. None the less, throughout the 19 years between the end of the War of Independence and the Six Day War, the Israelis managed to keep a toehold in this demilitarised territory, relieving the small garrison posted there with the help of a UN escort every two weeks. Both the university and the hospital are functioning again today. You can tour the campus on your own, or there is a guided tour every day except Saturdays. Don't miss the impressive modern amphitheatre located on the north-east side of the campus. It was here, in 1925, that the university was opened in the presence of such dignitaries as General Alenby, Lord Balfour and Chaim Weizmann.

Further down the mount are the graves of many British soldiers and members of the Jewish Legion, who died in the First World War.

East Jerusalem

Located between the Damascus Gate and Herod's Gate, almost opposite the East Jerusalem Bus Station, you'll find ZEDEKIAH'S CAVES. Tradition has it that these caves were originally quarries, and that the vast stones hewn out of the rock were used to build Solomon's magnificent temple. King Solomon's masons were reputedly the founders (or at least the inspiration) for the Freemasons – explaining why a vast, natural cavern, some distance into the labyrinth, is still used for yearly Freemason get-togethers. So why Zedekiah's Caves? Tradition has it that in 586 BC King Zedekiah fled through these caves, which were believed to have run all the way to Jericho, to escape the triumphant forces of Nebuchadnezzar's Babylonian army. The caves run over 200 metres under the Old City.

A little further down Süleyman Street you'll find the ROCKEFELLER ARCHAEOLOGICAL MUSEUM. If you haven't the time to visit the Israel Museum, this is an excellent, and more manageable, second best. If you can possibly take advantage of one of the free guided tours here, you will be well rewarded. The guides are voluntary, very knowledgeable, and impart their enthusiasm for their subject to all who listen. A session here will add greatly to your knowledge of the history of the Holy Land and to the enjoyment of your visit.

Return along Süleyman Street and turn right up *Salah ed Din* Street. Just before you reach the intersection with Nablus Road you'll find the entrance to the TOMB OF THE KINGS on your right. The catacomb of tombs cut into the rock here are actually those of Queen Helen of Adiabene and her son, Izates. The Queen converted to Judaism in the 1st C AD, and came from Adiabene, a small kingdom on the Persian border, to live in Jerusalem. She arrived about 48 AD during a time of famine, endearing herself to the people of the city by her valiant efforts to relieve their distress. She returned to her kingdom before her death, but her bones were sent to lie in a sarcophagus in the tomb at Jerusalem.

The huge enclosure you see today was used as a quarry. The great caverns and catacombs were hewn from solid rock and would have been closed by a stone rolled across the mouth, just as in the tomb of Christ. Queen Helen's sarcophagus is in the Louvre today.

A little further along is the AMERICAN COLONY HOTEL. It is not within the scope of this book to describe specific establishments, but this hotel is worthy of mention. Once a Turkish Pasha's Palace, its public rooms, and some of its more expensive suites, have been restored in the original style. The central courtyard is a delightful place for a drink or a light meal amongst the flowers and the little central fountain. Certainly one of the most pleasant places to stay in Jerusalem.

Head back towards the Old City down the Nablus road. Make a detour to have a look at the Anglican CATHEDRAL OF ST GEORGE. The complex consists of, besides the Gothic-style cathedral, a college, residences, a pleasant garden and a small hostel for pilgrims.

Further down the Nablus Road you will find the GARDEN TOMB. In 1883, General Gordon (of Khartoum), while looking at the curious hill just north of the Damascus Gate in East Jerusalem, noticed a marked resemblance to a skull, as others had done before him. '*Golgotha*, the Place of the Skull', he thought. Thereupon, he wrote a paper arguing that this place was the true site of the Holy Sepulchre, and not the church to the west. Subsequent excavations revealed a very ancient tomb on the site, a coincidence too striking to be ignored. The spot was then adopted by the Protestant Church who had hitherto been rather left out in the matter of custodianship of the Holy Places.

The argument was shaky, but none the less the Garden Tomb, as it is now known, has an air of sanctity about it. The site is no less genuine than 100 other 'holy sites' in Israel, and the care and devotion that have been lavished on the garden and the tomb make it a perfect retreat from the frenetic bustle of the other holy sites. The enthusiastic and charming custodians of the site are always ready to give the visitor guidance.

From the Damascus Gate take *Hanevi'im* Street and look out just before the first intersection for the small HOUSE-CHAPEL, dedicated to St Polyeuctus, an Armenian soldier who was martyred in the 3rd C for his adherence to Christianity. This little chapel houses what is arguably the most beautiful MOSAIC in the Holy Land. The Armenians were past-masters at the art of mosaic and this beautifully preserved example shows storks, partridges, geese, ibis, eagles and ostriches interspersed amongst vines and flowers. The colours are still remarkably vivid for a mosaic that is over 1,300 years old. At the apse end the inscription reads – 'For the memory and salvation of all the Armenians, whose names the Lord knows'.

Turn up *Chail Hadassa* Street for the TOURJEMAN POST MUSEUM. If you are interested in the history of Jerusalem from 1948 to 1967, when the city was divided between the Israelis and the Arabs, this place will fascinate you. The museum overlooks the Mandelbaum Gate area – a frontier post during the frequent skirmishes throughout the eleven years of partition. The museum offers, in addition to permanent exhibits, an audio visual display.

KIDRON VALLEY TOMBS

Below the Arab village of SILWAN, just to the east of the walled city, lies the KIDRON VALLEY. Traced with dozens of dusty paths, stony and dry as a bone, it winds its way down to the Dead Sea. Looking rather forlorn on the eastern side of the valley are the KIDRON VALLEY TOMBS – battered and cracked

'Absalom's Tomb', Kidron Valley

by earthquakes and the ravages of age, they are still intact, virtually as they were when Jesus knew them. They are thought to be the tombs of wealthy Jews who had developed a taste for the Hellenistic style that mingled with Judaism after the death of Alexander the Great. That makes them over 2,200 years old, perhaps the only buildings in Jerusalem today which survive exactly as they were in the time of Jesus.

The free-standing construction with the conical roof, rising to a tulip, is most interesting, and perhaps unique. The lower part is carved straight from the rock, while the upper half is of masonry. It is known as ABSALOM'S TOMB, but it is unlikely to be the tomb of David's son. The others are cut straight into the rock, and are more like the rock-cut tombs left by the Hellenic communities on the shores of Asia Minor. As with the Jewish Cemetery, above on the slope of the Mount of Olives, this is a particularly fortuitous place to be buried as it is here that the Day of Judgement will take place.

Hezekiah's Tunnel

After the death of Solomon, King Hezekiah succeeded to the throne of the southern kingdom of Judah at Jerusalem. His city and his people were under threat from the looming shadow of Assyria to the east; so Hezekiah strengthened the fortifications of the city. The most vulnerable part of an ancient city under siege was the water supply. Hezekiah lived long before the time of Solomon's Pools, the Mamilla Pool and the later water supplies of Jerusalem; in his day the only source of water for the city was the GIHON SPRING outside the city walls, in the Kidron Valley. So Hezekiah, who was not daunted by the immensity of the undertaking, had a tunnel bored to take the waters of the spring from their source to the POOL OF SILOAM, beneath today's village of SILWAN. The tunnel channelled the water to a point that was within the city walls of the period, and also deprived the besiegers themselves of water.

As an engineering work of the ancient world, it ranks as a remarkable feat. The tunnel, which was started from both ends simultaneously, winds in a somewhat erratic fashion for 580 yds deep in the bedrock of the city. It still runs to this day, and the more adventurous can walk through it in knee-deep flowing water and utter darkness, from Gihon to Siloam. Apart from the fact that the coolness of the tunnel makes it a delicious respite from the heat of the summer sun, it's well worth the effort. Take a torch to see the work of the pickaxes of 3,000 years ago.

The POOL OF SILOAM is a holy place too, for Jesus healed the eyes of a blind man by washing them in its waters.

Warren's Shaft

Joshua's bloody campaign to wrest the Land of Canaan from its inhabitants to provide a homeland for the Chosen People was ruthless and highly successful. With the help of God and some astute military tactics, he was able to take even the most formidable cities of the land – the 'Cities fortified up to Heaven'. But Jerusalem, the cunningly sited city of the Jebusites, fortified by thick walls and the deep clefts of Kidron and Hinnom, was too strong for him. The Jebusites remained safe behind their walls.

Years later, when David set up his capital at Hebron, he was only biding his time for the moment to take the coveted city between the valleys. The Jebusites taunted him from their impregnable walls, rousing the warrior-king to a fury. 'Our lame and blind will suffice to defend the city', they cried. But David was more subtle than Joshua and he sent his scouts to find the city's weak spot. At this time, long before Hezekiah built his tunnel, Jerusalem took its water supply from a deep shaft where buckets were lowered down a vertical funnel into a well.

'Whosoever getteth up to the gutter and smiteth the Jebusites and their lame and their blind that are hated of David's soul, he shall be chief and captain.' And one by one, led by Joab, David's soldiers climbed up the shaft and took the city from within. Looking at the shaft today, this feat seems impossible, but in 1910 a group of British soldiers proved the theory by climbing the shaft without ladders.

The shaft was discovered in 1867 by Charles Warren, an engineer in the British army. Today you can descend through an illuminated cave to just above the vertical part of the well. The entrance is just below the CITY OF DAVID.

City of David

When David first took Jerusalem and made it his capital, his city was just a small enclosure on the promontory south of the Temple Mount. Archaeologists have recently been working on this site, discovering a number of houses, steps and a sewage system. You can visit David's City now, but it's not easy to imagine how it would have looked 1,000 years before Christ. Hopefully this deficiency will soon be rectified with a display or a museum.

West Jerusalem

Since the reunification of Jerusalem in 1967, the west and northwest of the city has erupted with massive housing developments and the skyline of 'downtown' West Jerusalem is now punctured with the monoliths of huge modern hotels. Looking at the sprawl, it's hard to believe that only 120 years ago there were no settlements to speak of in this area. That is, until the Jewish philanthropist, Sir Moses Montefiore, built housing a little to the south-west of the Old City to coax some of the Jewish inhabitants to live outside the city walls.

By no stretch of the imagination could WEST JERUSALEM be called beautiful. But the mandatory use of the golden Jerusalem stone for all buildings has helped to produce a degree of harmony. If you are short of time the old City must be your priority, but West Jerusalem contains many interesting sites as well as some of the best SHOPS and more RESTAURANTS, CAFÉS, PUBS and FAST FOOD JOINTS than you can wave a bagel at. You'll find the greatest concentration of eateries around the roads leading off, or near to, Zion Square. *Ben Yehuda* Street, for instance, is a pedestrian precinct and one of the liveliest spots in West Jerusalem. Try Rivlin Street or George V Street as well.

Yemin Moshe

Below the west wall of the old city lies the suburb of *Yemin Moshe*. Today it is a pretty village of flower-lined alleys and traditional flat-roofed Jewish homes, inhabited exclusively by Jerusalem's super rich. But it wasn't always like that. Built by Sir Moses Montefiore as the first settlement outside the walls, it was intended as a self-supporting community of artisans – with its own WINDMILL, which is still there. During the period of Jordan's occupation of the Old City, *Yemin Moshe*, lying within rifle-shot beneath the walls, was constantly raked with fire. As a result it became a dangerous slum where only those with no alternative would make their homes. When Jerusalem was reunited the incumbents were evicted to make way for the modern development. Along with the new Jewish Quarter in the Old City, *Yemin Moshe* is a fine example of contemporary Jewish building and planning.

King David Hotel and the YMCA

This 1930s hotel is located on King David Street within walking distance of the Jaffa Gate. The King David is a truly beautiful hotel in the grand tradition and worth a visit, if only for a drink. The hotel was the headquarters of the British Mandate in Palestine and a wing was devastated in an infamous bombing attack carried out by the *Irgun* and the Stern Gang in 1946.

On the opposite side of the street is the YMCA. This wonderful building somehow combines the full flavour of middle-eastern architecture with a distinctive 1930s feel. It was constructed in 1933 by the same architects who designed the Empire State Building. You can get a good view of the city from its 120 ft high observation tower and eat very well in its excellent restaurant or cafe.

Mea She'arim

Just a short walk north of the Old City is the Orthodox Jewish quarter of *Mea She'arim*. A stroll through the streets of this quarter takes you back to the Jewish enclaves in the towns and cities of the 19th C Europe. In the evening it is quiet and strangely beautiful. Black-clad figures, pale and bearded, flit quietly to and fro in the dimly lit alleys, or stroll in pairs, deep in earnest discussion. Through open windows wafts the murmur of boys reading the Torah as they study in their *Yeshivas*. The women are scarved, thick-stockinged and demure. Battered shops sell holy books, writing and illuminating materials, prayer-shawls, Judaica and all the paraphernalia of earnest devotion.

But should strollers in this pious domain inflame the sensibilities of its denizens, they will see a dramatic change. The inhabitants are roused to fury by any show of immodesty in anyone passing through their quarter. Shorts and short skirts, low necklines and even uncovered heads, can and will provoke both verbal and physical abuse – even to spitting, stoning and rough handling. Everywhere there are notices imploring visitors to respect the customs and sensibilities of the inhabitants. Not much to ask, you would think, but visitors still persist in flouting the rules.

Mea She'arim is the very heart of Judaism. Many Israelis see the inhabitants as a burden to the state, for they are non-productive, spending their lives in study and prayer, making their meagre living by copying sacred texts or praying on behalf of distant Jews unable to get to the Wall. They are also volatile, extremely reactionary and not above going to extreme lengths to ensure their minority views are respected. But most Jews appreciate the fact that it is this very repository of devotion, faith and zeal that has maintained the purity and strength of Judaism through the vicissitudes and persecution of 3,000 years.

Biblical Zoo

The Biblical Zoo in the north-west of the city is worth a visit, especially if you've got the kids in tow. On a hot day, the zoo park provides plenty of opportunity for shade, and the concept of the whole animal 'collection' is rather interesting. Each of the species of animals is mentioned in the Old Testament and was once indigenous to the Holy Land. An apt quotation from the Scriptures is displayed on a placard in front of each cage. You will see Roebuck, Lemur, Cranes, Shelducks, Lions, Tigers, Swans (including magnificent black ones), porcupines, gazelles and all sorts of other fauna. The admission fee is a bit steep but you might think it's worth it to get away from the dust and noise of the city on a hot afternoon.

Knesset

If you forget to bring your passport with you, you won't be allowed in to join the twice weekly tour of the KNESSET, Israel's Parliament, or to sit in the visitors' gallery and listen to some of the heated debates.

Israel Museum

Below the *Knesset* on the hill of *Givat Ram*, lies the huge complex of the Israel Museum. This is not a museum that should be visited lightly, with just an hour or so to spare before rushing off somewhere else. The museum is vast and the number and variety of its exhibits is quite overwhelming. The constantly changing exhibitions of painting and sculpture alone are worth a good day's visit, and then there is hall after hall of archaeological finds, of religious relics of the world, of ancient and modern Judaica, of costumes and weaponry, etc. Outside the museum is the garden of modern sculpture, and the magnificent SHRINE OF THE BOOK.

The Shrine of the Book, built to house the Dead Sea Scrolls (see Qumran), is one of the masterpieces of modern world architecture. The beautiful white roof was inspired by the lids on the urns in which the scrolls were discovered. The massive dark basalt monolith, against which the shrine gleams starkly, represents the powers of darkness in conflict with the powers of light.

Mount Herzl

About 5 km to the west of the Old City is the forested park of Mount Herzl. Here lie the remains of Theodore Herzl, the prophet and founder of Zionism. In the MUSEUM on the site are replicas of Herzl's study and library, as well as many of his books and works, and documents pertaining to the early years of Zionism.

Nearby is a cemetery for Israeli soldiers killed during the establishment of the state of Israel. This is a beautiful spot with lovely views over the hills of Judea.

Yad Vashem

YAD VASHEM is the official National Memorial Shrine dedicated to the memory of the six million Jews annihilated by the Nazis during the Second World War. The scope of *Yad Vashem* was laid down in a law passed in 1953. Aside from providing a permanent memorial to the victims, 'the task of *Yad Vashem* is to gather in to the Homeland material regarding all those members of the Jewish people who laid down their lives, who fought and rebelled against the Nazi enemy and his collaborators, and to perpetuate their memory and that of communities, organisations and institutions that were destroyed because they were Jewish'.

A visit here should be high on the agenda of anyone visiting Jerusalem. Even if you only spend a short time at the memorial you cannot fail to be deeply moved, so it's best not to go on a day when you've planned a heavy schedule of sightseeing afterwards.

From the car park the memorial is approached down the AVENUE OF THE RIGHTEOUS AMONG NATIONS. The trees planted here are in honour of non-Jews who risked their lives to save Jews during the Holocaust.

Visit the HISTORICAL MUSEUM first. It documents the story of the systematic destruction of European Jewry, including Hitler's rise to power and the beginnings of persecution by the Third Reich, culminating in the horrific 'Final Solution'. You will also see exhibits devoted to the Jewish Resistance fighters, to the days in the concentration camps following liberation, and the desperate, clandestine attempts of dispossessed Jews trying to reach Palestine.

The HALL OF REMEMBRANCE next to the museum is a starkly uncompromising rectangle, with walls of huge basalt boulders topped with slabs of concrete. Inside, the floor of the chamber is inscribed with the names of the largest Nazi concentration and death camps. In front of a vault containing the ashes of many of the victims of the camps, burns an eternal flame.

Across the plaza is a complex housing a synagogue, an auditorium, an ART GALLERY and the HALL OF NAMES. The art gallery includes in its collection works produced under the terrible conditions of the ghettos and the camps. The Hall of Names houses a roll-call of the names of over three million murdered Jews – these are still being added to .

The Israelis have an inordinate fondness for modern sculpture. Here at *Yad Vashem* the medium is used with intensely powerful effect in a variety of works dotted around the gardens. Don't miss the incredibly moving statue by Lea Michelson entitled SILENT CRY or Nandor Glid's powerful evocation of the millions of Jews who perished in the death camps – THE MONUMENT TO THE VICTIMS OF THE DEATH CAMPS. Near the CHILDREN'S MEMORIAL GARDEN (over one and a half million Jewish children perished during the Holocaust) is a sculpture by Boris Saktsier entitled KORCZAK AND THE CHILDREN OF THE GHETTO. Korczak was a Polish teacher who went voluntarily with his charges to certain death in Treblinka rather than leave them to face the terror alone.

The Holyland Hotel Model

This really is worth a visit. If you put it high on your agenda it will help you a great deal when you start to explore the Old City, and try to get a picture of what Jerusalem was like around the time of Christ. In a wonderful setting in the grounds of the Holyland Hotel, a little to the south-east of the city, the model is highly detailed, and although some question its accuracy, only an expert archaeologist might be churlish enough to pick holes. Covering an area of over 1,000 square metres, the model is built on a scale of 1:50. Unless you already have extensive knowledge of the layout of Herod's city, you will get the most out of your visit if you try to join an organised tour. The guides are often very informative and interesting.

Ein Kerem

You won't be stumped for places to go and see in Jerusalem, but on a hot day, when you feel like a respite from the noise and bustle of the city, one of the most pleasant excursions is to the village of EIN KEREM.

This pastoral idyll nestles on the steep slopes of a valley just west of Mount Herzl and the *Yad Vashem* Memorial; a short bus ride west of Jerusalem. A favourite haunt of artists, the narrow streets with their picturesque old stone houses make the village pleasant enough just for a stroll, stopping at one of the restaurants for lunch or for a cool drink. But *Ein Kerem* has more to offer. Traditionally it is the birthplace of John the Baptist and the place where the Virgin Mary visited John's mother, her cousin Elizabeth, during her pregnancy.

As you come into the village from Jerusalem, look out for the police station on your left. Take the right-hand turning opposite, for ST MARY'S WELL and for the lovely Franciscan SANCTUARY AND CHURCH OF THE VISITATION – another Barluzzi gem.

You'll find St Mary's Well at the foot of the disused mosque. The well commemorates Mary's visit to Elizabeth. With graffiti scarred walls, it's barely worth a passing glance as you follow the road round and up the hill for the Sanctuary of the Visitation. Murals in the church and the small chapel below commemorate the Visit itself and the Massacre of the Innocents; Elizabeth is traditionally believed to have hidden the baby John here from the murderous intentions of Herod's soldiers. There is a particularly fine mosaic decorating the façade of the upper church. There are also multilingual inscriptions of Mary's hymn of praise – the Magnificat. It is a lovely spot, with splendid views over cypress and olive groves and ancient terraced vineyards and, unlike so many of the churches in Jerusalem, very conducive to quiet contemplation.

Return to the police station and walk up the hill for the CHURCH OF JOHN THE BAPTIST which stands over a grotto, traditionally the birthplace of John. The church is heavily decorated with blue and white tilework in a multitude of different patterns. Witness to the popularity of the site with visiting pilgrims, is the souvenir shop located in the vestry, which does a roaring trade in postcards, etc. The church, now under the care of the Franciscans, was built in the late 17th C over the ruins of a Crusader church destroyed by the Moslems.

You could combine your visit to *Ein Kerem* with a short detour to the HADASSAH HOSPITAL. (Just to complicate matters there are two hospitals with the same name; one on Mount Scopus and the other, near *Ein Kerem*, on Mount Herzl.) Here in the hospital's synagogue you can see the world famous CHAGALL WINDOWS. Twelve magnificent windows in richly coloured stained glass, and standing eleven feet high, represent the sons of Jacob from whom descended the 12 tribes of Israel. The inspiration for the intricate designs is taken from Genesis and Deuteronomy.

Tourist Offices

24 King George Street
17 Jaffa Street
Jaffa Gate (just inside on left hand side)

99 Bus (The Jerusalem Circular Line)

This is a godsend for weary tourists or those bent on seeing everything as quickly as possible. The 99 bus leaves the bus terminal near Jaffa Gate every hour Sunday through to Thursday from 9.00 am to 5.00 pm. On Fridays and eve of holidays from 9.00 to 2.00. It stops at 34 main tourist destinations and you can buy a ticket that will allow you to hop on and off at will. For further details contact Egged Central Bus Station on 02–534596 or 551868.

Walking Tours

These are usually excellent and although they are quite pricey there is simply no better way of getting a good understanding of the old city. Check with the tourist offices for up to date details.

Parking

Parking is a nightmare but don't be tempted to park illegally – the clamp has arrived in Jerusalem and tourist cars are not exempt.

C·H·A·P·T·E·R·3
West Bank

INTRODUCTION: WEST BANK

The West Bank, the kidney-shaped area of desert and hills that lies to the west of the River Jordan, is the most contentious part of Palestine today. Those Israelis who see this area as an inalienable part of the land given to them by God, or a strategically vital link for the defence of the state of Israel, prefer to call it by the Biblical names of Judea and Samaria. Many Israelis, and pretty well everybody else, know it as the 'Occupied Territories'.

In 1947 the land was designated part of the Palestinian state by the United Nations. This plan never got off the ground though, and the following year, during the Israeli War of Independence, it was annexed by Jordan. Along with Jerusalem it remained in Jordanian hands until 1967, when the Israelis took it in the Six Day War. Despite the enormous problems it poses them, the Israelis have not relinquished their hold, and seem unlikely to do so.

Many of the roots of Judaism are here, notably Hebron and Shechem, and this land was certainly part of Israel in Biblical times, but since then the population has been almost exclusively Arab. And so it remains to this day. The Israelis now find themselves saddled with a resentful and volatile population who want no part of the state that has been imposed upon them. Adding fuel to the fires, Israel is constantly engaged in stamping the West Bank with her indelible mark; everywhere are communities of settlers, hardy and often fanatical Israelis who are offered very generous incentives to colonise the area.

For the tourist or visitor though, the West Bank is not dangerous; on the contrary you will find the inhabitants friendly and welcoming. The land, in its wild and desolate way is some of the most beautiful to be seen in Israel.

Bethlehem

The birthplace of Jesus, the ancestral home-town of the poet-king David, and burial place of the Matriarch Rachel lies about 10 km from Jerusalem. BETHLEHEM, with its overwhelmingly Christian Arab population, is part of Israeli-occupied Palestine and, together with Jerusalem, a focus for millions of pilgrims. The name means 'House of Bread' in Hebrew and 'House of Meat' in Arabic.

THE BASILICA OF THE NATIVITY is why most people come to Bethlehem. Marking the spot where Jesus was born, this heavy, fortress-like building, built by Justinian and later restored and added to by the Crusaders, is one of the oldest churches in Christendom. How did it survive the Persian and Arab invasions? It is said that when the Persians arrived in 614 that they spared the church because a mosaic of the three wise men depicted them in Persian dress. The Arabs, originally led by Caliph Omar, revered Jesus as a prophet, and indeed themselves prayed in part of the church; even when other Christian sites were destroyed on the orders of later, less tolerant Caliphs, the birthplace of the 'prophet' continued to be spared.

Early Christians venerated the cave over which the later churches were built as the exact location of the birth of Christ. The Emperor Hadrian, in the 2nd C, covered the area with a woodland grove and dedicated it to the pagan cult of Adonis. It wasn't until the early 4th C that Constantine's mother, Helena, built the first church. Some 200 years later, the church was severely damaged during an uprising, and Justinian ordered St Helena's Church to be pulled down to make way for a church that was to be more splendid than any other in Jerusalem.

The Crusaders fortified the Justinian Church, and it was here on Christmas Day in the year 1100 that Baldwin I of Boulogne was crowned King of Jerusalem. When the Crusaders left, the church fell into decline with the situation made worse when squabbles broke out between the various

Christian denominations, particularly over the rights of ownership of the GROTTO OF THE NATIVITY.

The Church of the Nativity is shared by the Greek Orthodox, the Latins and the Armenians. As you cross the large courtyard note the tiny entrance doorway. You can see the outline of the original Byzantine lintel and the later Crusader arch. The Crusaders would have made the doorway smaller for defence purposes, but later work, to make the entrance smaller still, was apparently designed to stop looters driving carts inside the church or to prevent the Mamelukes from thundering into the church on horseback.

The cavernous interior is austere and sombre. Monolithic pillars of brown limestone decorated with the faded paintings of a variety of saints, an English oak wooden roof (given by Edward IV) and lack of elaborate decoration may come as something of a disappointment if you are expecting a magnificent display of church pomp. Note the trapdoors in the floor. Sometimes they are opened so you can see fragments of a lavish MOSAIC FLOOR, probably dating from as early as the 4th C.

The GROTTO OF THE NATIVITY, heavy with incense and sputtering with candles and lamps, can be reached by steps on either side of the Greek Orthodox High Altar. A silver star beneath the small, curtain-fringed Altar of the Nativity, is inscribed with the words *Hic de Virgine Maria Jesus Christus natus est*. 'Here of the Virgin Mary Jesus Christ was born.'

The grotto is not very large, and for many devout pilgrims a visit here is perhaps the most important and moving part of their visit to the Holy Land. Try to resist the temptation to take photographs, and leave as quickly and as quietly as possible to allow devout Christians to make the most of what is often the experience of a lifetime.

For many years the denominations have argued over ownership of the grotto. One incident, or series of incidents, involving the silver star, was one of the contributory factors in the build-up of tension leading to the Crimean War. It started when Roman Catholics placed the silver star in the grotto. The Orthodox Greeks, presumably seeing the move as a territorial claim, 'removed' it. Napoleon III then waded into the fray, declared himself protector of the Catholics in the Holy Land and announced, with no foundation whatsoever, that the Basilica of the Nativity was in French territory. The Greek Orthodox had their own protector in the form of the Tsar, and with his backing attempted to drive the Roman Catholics out of the church altogether. The Turks stepped in to restore some semblance of dignity and ordered the Greek Orthodox to replace the stolen star. But the various grievances still festered and even today disputes continue over who is responsible for what, and who is allowed to carry out this function or that office.

If the swarms of tourists start getting to you, head through the small door on the north side of the church. Here you will find a beautifully restored MEDIEVAL CLOISTERED GARDEN directly in front of the 19th C Roman Catholic CHURCH OF ST CATHERINE. In welcome contrast to the Church of the Nativity, St Catherine's is light and airy, and it is from here that the traditional midnight mass on 24 December is broadcast to the world. From this church a narrow stairway leads down to a maze of rock-cut grottos, some dedicated as chapels. It is in one of these that St Jerome is said to have spent much of his life translating the Bible into Latin (the Vulgate).

As with so many of the holy sites, it really does pay to try to visit as early as you can, before the swarms of tour buses descend. But what about Christmas? There are three of them. The Armenians celebrate on 19 January and the Greek Orthodox on 7 January. If you want to visit Bethlehem on either 24 or 25 December, special conditions apply. You need to obtain a permit which, at the time of writing, was only available through the Government Tourist Offices in Jerusalem, Tel Aviv and at Ben Gurion Airport. To attend midnight mass in St Catherine's, you need to make enquiries with the Christian Information Centre, which you will find near the Jaffa Gate in Jerusalem's Old City. It's difficult, but not necessarily impossible, to get a seat. If you don't succeed you can, armed with your permit, join the throngs in Manger Square, outside the church.

Take the street that runs off the south-eastern corner of Manger Square for the Franciscan SANCTUARY OF THE MILK GROTTO. Tradition has it that a drop of milk fell from the Virgin Mary's breast, whilst suckling Jesus, and turned the rock on which she sat, white. An endless succession of candles burning round the altar has long since turned the white rock sooty. But it is still a place of worship for infertile women, expectant mothers or women with babies. It was believed that pieces of rock, ground to a powder and drunk, would ensure sufficient milk for suckling. The little chapel dates from the mid 19th C, although the Franciscans have looked after the grotto itself since the 14th and there is evidence of earlier churches on the site. It is small and rather homely inside, adorned with flowers and with a basket by the altar, containing tiny scraps of folded paper – presumably petitions for fertility.

Milk Grotto, Bethlehem

Returning to Manger Square, spare some time for the Bethlehem MARKET. Although there is no shortage of souvenir shops in the town, the market itself, which you will find if you head westwards out of the square, is quite untouristy. This is a working market for the local people. It's noisy, busy, full of fruit, vegetables, spices, household items, mounds of sticky sweets and crates of chickens waiting to meet their maker.

It's a two kilometre hike, or you could take a taxi or a bus, from Manger Square to the village of *Beit Sahur* and SHEPHERDS' FIELDS. You probably won't be surprised to hear that there are two of them, one administered by the Franciscans and one by the Greek Orthodox. The Franciscan site is certainly the most attractive and if you are short of time you would be well advised to confine yourself to this site. You approach the Shepherds' Fields through ironwork gates and down a short drive. Here you can see, in a suitably pastoral setting, a natural cave, a typical shelter for shepherds, which has been turned into a small chapel. Groups of visiting pilgrims often hold short services inside, and you will have to wait for them to finish before you can enter. But it's a pleasant shady spot and while you wait, you can walk up to see the delightful, airy little church, once again designed by Barluzzi, and built in 1954.

Ten km south-east of Bethlehem you'll find the HERODION. Herod the Great, mindful of his unpopularity and very fearful of uprisings or foreign invasions, was never one to do things by half. So he found himself a mountain and cut the top off. Hollowing out the inside, he created a unique fortress. Herod was apparently buried here, but to date, no evidence has been found of his tomb. The hilltop fortress was used by rebels during both the Jewish Revolts against Rome.

The place is worth a visit for the spectacular view alone, across the Judean wilderness to the Dead Sea and towards Bethlehem and Jerusalem. The ruins have been extensively excavated and you can see the remains of the PALACE with patches of FRESCOES still visible, the BATH HOUSE and an ancient SYNAGOGUE. There are also the ruins of a BYZANTINE CHAPEL, left by monks who lived here in this strange, hollow, volcano-like mountain until after the 7th C Arab invasion.

HEBRON

Hebron is the focus of the very beginning of history for both Jews and Arabs. Abraham, the 'stranger and sojourner', who had made his way south from Ur of the Chaldees, finally settled in this hill town, surrounded as it was by fine grazing land for his flocks. He set up his tents near the OAK OF MAMRE, and on the death of his wife Sara, bought some land for use as a family burial ground. The land contained the CAVE OF MACHPELAH, where Abraham and Sara were finally laid to rest. Today the Cave of Machpelah, which also contains the tombs of Isaac and Rebecca, and Jacob and Leah, is surrounded by the magnificent walls of *Haram el Khalil*, the 'Shrine of the Friend'. (Abraham is known by the Arabs as 'The Friend of God'.)

Abraham was the father of both the Jews and the Arabs, and the place where he spent much of his life, and lies buried, is held sacred by both peoples. Before taking Jerusalem, David established his capital and the Ark of the Covenant at *Qiryat Arba*, as Hebron was then known, thus making the town doubly sacred to the Jews. Sadly but predictably, this double adoration of Hebron results not in an increase of its sanctity and peace, but rends the town with bitterness and hatred. The radical elements of both races have sought exclusive rights to the shrine and the town, and the result is constant fighting and an oppressive military presence. A very uneasy atmosphere prevails. It is understandable that Jewish feelings run high over the place where 4,000 years ago the tribes of Israel made their first recorded acquisition of land; but it is equally understandable that the Arabs should so revere the site of the Tomb of Abraham, who, apart from being the Patriarch of their race, is one of the first and most deeply loved prophets of Islam.

'Shrine of the Friend', Hebron

There is little of beauty remaining today, though the ruins suggest that the town must once have been beautiful. But dominating the town is the HARAM EL KHALIL, one of the most striking buildings in the Holy Land. Herod the Great built the original walls at the same time as he was restoring the second temple. More of his work is evident here than at Jerusalem – the huge, unmistakable blocks of stone giving a strong impression of how vast and magnificent the temple must have been. The upper courses are of Arab construction. In 1115 the Crusaders built a church on the site of the cave, much of which stands today. In the 13th C the whole building was converted to a mosque, and so it remains to this day, although Christians and Jews are permitted to pray here too. In a corner beside the catafalque of Abraham is a small window; in the window is a stone with a depression, said to be the FOOTPRINT OF ADAM.

About 2 km out of Hebron to the west is the traditional site of the OAK OF MAMRE. Here Abraham, while resting under the oak tree, received a visit from three angels on their way to the cities of the plain. He offered them hospitality, and when they told him of the imminent fate of Sodom and Gomorrah, he was able to intercede on behalf of his friend, Lot. On the hill above is a RUSSIAN ORTHODOX CHURCH built by White Russians in 1923. The Ilex oak under which Abraham was wont to rest and camp is still there on the slope of the hill; its authenticity is the subject of debate, but it is undoubtedly a very ancient oak. Enfeebled with venerable age it can no longer support its own limbs and has to rely on a contrivance of rusty iron struts.

Hebron has for long been the centre of a GLASS AND POTTERY INDUSTRY. The Arabs had developed these crafts to a highly sophisticated degree by the time the Crusaders arrived in the Holy Land. Back in Europe, pottery was still primitive and glass was virtually unknown. In Hebron today they still use the traditional methods. In the workshops dotted around the town, you will be made most welcome by the Arabs who run these businesses. The wares vary considerably in style and quality, but many of them are very attractive and extremely cheap.

If you are visiting Hebron when tensions are running high, make it quite clear that you are a tourist, and be particularly careful if you are driving a hire car that is not easily identifiable as such, and carries Israeli numberplates. Once the Arabs know you are a visitor they will be extremely friendly and helpful.

Solomon's Pools

In spring the journey from Hebron to Jerusalem, winding through the beautiful hills of the West Bank among almond trees and lush green pasture, is a delight. 4 km south of Bethlehem you come to SOLOMON'S POOLS. These are three huge reservoirs, still on the site of Herod's original work, whence they carried water by means of an aqueduct to the Temple area in Jerusalem. The pools have been restored by the Ottomans and by the British, but it's not difficult to imagine how they must have been before the time of Jesus. They are set in a beautiful forest of pines.

WILDERNESS OF JUDEA

From Jerusalem to Jericho is about 25 km, with a descent of 3,800 ft. The route has been well travelled since early history, for Jericho, the 'City of Palms', has for long been a fertile garden, as well as a popular winter retreat for the inhabitants of Jerusalem; when snow lies on the Holy City, you can gather dates and bananas in warm sunshine at Jericho. Herod, who had an eye for a good spot, built a winter palace at Jericho, and Hisham, one of the later Umayyad Caliphs, had his magnificent hunting-lodge there.

Between the two cities and stretching north and south along the Dead Sea and the Jordan, lies the WILDERNESS OF JUDEA, an ocean of dusty hills that looks like the most barren and desolate spot on earth. Yet somehow the Bedouin manage to pasture their flocks here: scattered in the desert, you will find the dark tents of these hardy people, surrounded by healthy, robust-looking sheep and goats.

The wilderness has long been a place of refuge. David, hunted 'like a partridge' by the jealous Saul, found protection here, as did the Maccabees and the Bar Kochba rebels. Of his days in the wilderness, David said 'There is but a step between me and death.' And of course this was the wilderness to which Jesus retired for 40 days. The Essenes too and, later, bands of Christian monks withdrew from the turmoil of the world to the awful barrenness of these hills. The Judean Wilderness is indeed an 'abomination of desolation', but it has also the profound and ageless beauty of the desert. Thousands of ascetics have found themselves nearer to God here in this unearthly and supernatural wasteland than anywhere else on the earth.

Today there is a busy main road between Jerusalem and Jericho. Halfway along its length it passes the INN OF THE GOOD SAMARITAN. The present building is the remains of an Ottoman police station, which now houses a cafe and a restaurant; inside is a fine mosaic from the church that stood here in Byzantine times. This of course is the site of the inn where the good Samaritan of Jesus' parable paid for the care of the traveller who had been robbed and beaten. The plight of the poor traveller was a common one until quite recently. Up until the time of the British Mandate, travellers and pilgrims would either buy protection for the journey from the local Bedouin sheikh, or hire an armed guard, for the way was infested with bandits. Today this is no longer a worry, and many people make the pilgrimage or journey from Jerusalem to Jericho on foot – although for a number of reasons it's better not to make the trip alone.

The first part of the journey from Jerusalem is very confusing, and not recommended without a guide, but the second part, from the spring of *EN QILT* to Jericho, is easy to

WEST BANK

follow, and a dramatic and beautiful walk of 10 km or so.

Take the Jericho bus and get off shortly after the Inn of the Good Samaritan, at the stop for *En Qilt*. Take the narrow rough road down the hill to your left; after fifteen minutes you find yourself in the bed of WADI QILT. There is a CAFE here, but its opening times are unpredictable. There is also one of those wonderful miracles of the desert, a clear water spring with a waterfall and deep pools surrounded by greenery. Continue about 5 km down the *wadi* – easy walking except for a little slide you have to negotiate between two rocks – until you come to ST GEORGE'S MONASTERY.

The Greeks have a genius for siting their villages and monasteries, and St George's is a fine example. The simple blue-domed monastery, with its surrounding honeycomb of hermits' cells, its airy terraces and towers, seems not the work of man, but a natural excrescence in the rock walls of the canyon, a part of the cliff itself. Beneath is a garden with vines and stately Cypress trees. A bridge and a long hill of steps lead to a gate.

The few remaining monks are hospitable but poor, so a gift of coffee, fruit, nuts or *arak* is always welcome. There are only five monks now, but they will tell you that in the glorious years of the monastery, before the Persians came in 614, there were over 5,000 monks living in the monastery and surrounding caves. The Persians massacred them as they massacred tens of thousands of Christians in Palestine at that time. The Gryphon vultures that haunt the rocks of *Wadi Qilt* picked their bones clean, and the bones now lie in the caves of the cliffs. The monastery was built in the 6th C and then extensively restored in the 19th C, but there are many fine icons in the chapel that date from before the restoration.

If you can tear yourself away from this enchanting spot, continue down to the mouth of *Wadi Qilt*, where the WADI QILT RESTAURANT provides welcome refreshment. Be careful about doing a walk like this in the heat of summer; it's easier to get sunstroke than you think. Of course there are many other places to visit in the Wilderness, but they mostly need specialised knowledge and skill. To get the most out of it try the ISRAEL SOCIETY FOR THE PROTECTION OF NATURE. They organise walks, rides and journeys thoughout Israel all year round, with guides who know and love their subject. (Tourist Office at Jaffa Gate or 13 *Heleni Hamalka* Street, Jerusalem or 4 *Hashfela* Street, Tel Aviv.)

In a similar setting, wedged into the cliffs of the Kidron Valley halfway between Jerusalem and the Dead Sea, is the MONASTERY OF MAR SABA. Again this is a beautiful monastery in incomparable if unearthly surroundings; but it is a place of fervent devotion rather than a tourist attraction; women are not admitted. This monastery played a central role in the development of the early Church, for here lived, worshipped and studied John of Damascus and Stephen the Thaumaturgist. The monastery was founded in the 5th C by Mar Saba, whose body lies today in the chapel. In the light of evening, or even early morning, the hills in this part of the West Bank, with their distant views of Jerusalem, and the stone villages of the Arabs blending into the landscape, make one of the most beautiful sights in the Holy Land.

Jericho

Jericho is believed to be the world's oldest continuously inhabited city; excavations on the *tel* to the north of the modern town have revealed traces of habitation as long ago as 8000 BC. This great age is a result of the oasis of Jericho; a continuous and reliable source of water has made of the city a green garden in the desert. Today, looking over Jericho from above, in the wilderness of Judea, the contrast between the barrenness of the surrounding desert, and the deep green of the cultivated oasis, appears miraculous.

There are three Jerichos: the ancient one at TEL ES SULTAN, encompassing the Spring of *Elisha*, now a pumping station; the New Testament one at the entrance to *Wadi Qilt*, where Herod built his winter palace with its gardens and flowing streams; and the modern town that lies between the two.

Jericho can claim the distinction of being the lowest city in the world, at 800 ft below sea level. In summer it is almost unbearably hot; but it's a fine place for a winter palace, because it's always warm in the winter. Apart from HEROD'S WINTER PALACE, of which virtually nothing now remains, there are the extensive ruins of the fabulous PALACE OF HISHAM. This palace is a couple of kilometres to the north of Jericho, an extraordinary sight and one well worth seeing.

The palace was built in the 8th C for *Hisham*, the Umayyad Caliph who ruled the Islamic Empire from Damascus. The craftsmen and architects employed on its construction were Greeks, who were able to give much freer rein to their ideas when working for the Umayyads than they had been able to do working for the more straight-laced Byzantines. The result is an exuberance of style and decoration. Note, too, how the Islamic injunction against the depiction of humans or animals in art has been flouted.

The mosaic floor in the bath-house is one of the finest and

most unusual examples of this sort of decoration you're likely to see. There's an exquisitely executed tree of life with birds and three deer browsing beneath; a lion is springing for the kill. The plan of the palace, and those stones and gates and arches that remain, give one the impression that this was a really magnificent and beautiful work.

Just to the west of Hisham's Palace is the TEL OF ANCIENT JERICHO, where you can walk on the dust and rubble of the world's oldest city, and imagine Joshua and the warriors and priests of Israel marching seven times round the walls, blowing their ram's horn trumpets.

The walled city that was so spectacularly conquered by Joshua was never rebuilt, and although Jericho was given as a gift by Mark Antony to Cleopatra, it has never been more than a pale shadow of that early city.

Above and to the west of Tel Jericho you can just make out the MONASTERY OF ST JOHN THE BAPTIST – *Deir el Qarantal* in Arabic. This is said to be the spot where Jesus spent 40 days in the wilderness. Here, on this very hill perhaps, He was tempted by the Devil to turn stones to bread to assuage his terrible hunger, and in return for worshipping the Devil, He would be given all the kingdoms of the world. This monastery on the Mount of Temptation is now reduced to a solitary monk. He will patiently show you round the deserted courts and chapels that once heard the chanting of thousands of monks.

The modern city of Jericho is something of a ramshackle affair. There is a HOTEL in the centre – the Hisham Palace – and a number of very good RESTAURANTS AND CAFÉS, in particular the Mount of Temptation, at the northern entrance to the town, and the Wadi Qilt, just outside the southern exit. It is a pleasant and friendly Arab town, blessed with the most spectacular vegetation.

The original site of Jesus' baptism in the JORDAN lies just east of Jericho. Thousands of pilgrims used to come here to immerse themselves in the sacred waters; but since the First World War, the site has been closed to pilgrims, and the place of baptism moved upstream to the Sea of Galilee, for convenience. Still, it's the same river.

Nablus – Shechem

From Jericho you can take the spectacular road that leads through the wilderness to RAMALLAH: at 3,000 ft above sea level, Ramallah should be cool and breezy after the stifling heat of Jericho. For this reason it's a popular holiday area among the Arabs, and is adorned with fine parks and gardens. For the tourist it's a pleasant town to stop for a stroll and a meal, but there is nothing of specific interest to merit a stay.

Heading north on Highway 60, after 40 km of winding through spectacular rocky countryside, you reach NABLUS, a busy Arab town which occupies the site of biblical Shechem. When Abraham arrived in the land of Canaan from Ur of the Chaldees, he set up an altar where his followers could worship; the altar stood on MOUNT GERIZIM, up whose northern slope the modern town of Nablus straggles. Thus Mt Gerizim can be seen as the first holy place in Palestine. Many years later, after the death of Solomon, when the Kingdom of Israel split in to two, the southern half became the Kingdom of Judah with Jerusalem as its capital, while Rehoboam, king of the northern Kingdom of Israel, set up his capital and holy altar at Shechem. But when the 'Ten Lost Tribes' of northern Israel were taken into captivity and dispersed by the Assyrians, Shechem declined in importance.

In 72 AD the Roman Emperor Vespasian founded a new city between the mountains of Gerizim and Ebal, and called it Neapolis (New City). The city grew to be a stronghold of the Samaritans, those early Jews of the Ten Lost Tribes. Through the centuries the city flourished under different rulers, the Byzantines, the Arabs, the Crusaders who took it in 1100, and back to the Moslems again. Today it is a thriving Arab town, and one of the most exciting and architecturally interesting towns in the Holy Land.

Today's town still lies between the slopes of the two mountains. The most interesting part is just south of the centre, the old Arab quarter and *Souk*. Here is a warren of tiny alleys and passages, lined with innumerable stalls and shops, selling herbs and spices, ironmongery and saddlery, materials and clothes, etc.; everywhere are coffee-shops and cafes, selling delicious snacks, roast chickens, *falafel* and sweets. But the finest thing here is the architecture. There have been many influences on Nablus. The Romans, the Armenians and Byzantines, the Arabs, Crusaders, Mamelukes and finally the Ottomans all added their particular styles to the architecture of the city. Sadly Nablus, like almost everywhere else, hasn't escaped the undistinguished and ugly mess that characterises so much of the architecture of the 20th C.

As you stroll through the old quarters of the town, all built of grey and gold stone, you will see traces of all these periods in the graceful curve of an arch, the stone corbelling of a tower, and the vaults and domes of all ages and faiths. The GREAT MOSQUE – *Jamia el Kebir* – is the largest of the city's eight mosques; it is built on Crusader foundations and retains many interesting Crusader features, i.e. the Gothic portal, similar to that of the Holy Sepulchre. Another of the mosques was once a Byzantine church.

The WELL OF JACOB on the lower slopes of Mt Gerizim, is about 6 ft in diameter and 100 ft deep; it is still full of good clear water. Jacob bought land here and gave it to Joseph, whose body was interred on this mountain after he returned from Egypt. The first church was built on the spot at the end of the 4th C; the present structure, on Crusader foundations, dates from 1903. Today the site of Jacob's Well is quiet and unspoiled, one of those rare peaceful spots in Palestine.

One of the interesting aspects of Nablus is that it is the main seat of the modern community of Samaritans. When the Assyrians overran northern Israel in the 8th C BC, they dispersed the 'Ten Lost Tribes', who had split from the tribes of Judah in the south. Most were carried into captivity or sold as slaves, and the vacuum was filled by relocating alien populations from elsewhere in the Assyrian Empire – this disorientation of populations was the Assyrians' standard procedure for running their Empire. But many Jews of the northern kingdom remained and, over the years, they inter-bred with the new races. This is generally believed to be the origin of the Samaritans.

Today they live on a hill in the western part of the city, called the Street of the Samaritans. On the summit of Gerizim they observe the Feast of the Passover by the sacrifice of lambs. Near the summit is the remains of their temple, which was destroyed by the Maccabees. In the town they have a synagogue where the scroll of the Samaritan Pentateuch, the only part of the Old Testament which they regard as sacred, is kept. The community is reduced now to 300 or so; another 300 Samaritans live in Holon, near Tel Aviv. This antique offshoot of Jewry once numbered several millions, scattered about the ancient lands of Samaria and Syria, But over the ages, the tribes were decimated by frequent massacres, conducted by John Hyracanus, Pontius Pilate and the Christian emperors of Byzantium among others. The race nearly became extinct when, at the end of the last century, their numbers dropped to 120. Today, with some 600 members their strength is reviving, though perhaps at the expense of doctrinal purity; the reason behind their steady increase is that they now permit marriage with non-Samaritans, which was previously forbidden.

Three miles to the west of Nablus in the ROMAN CITY OF SEBASTIA, built by Herod the Great in 27 BC. Little remains to be seen today.

C·H·A·P·T·E·R·4
The Coast

Rosh Haniqra – The White Cliffs – Ladder of Tyre

At the northernmost tip of the coast of Israel are the stark limestone cliffs of ROSH HANIQRA. Stand on the windy hill and look over the fields of bananas down the rocky sweep of the coast to Akko; the view to the south is impressive. The sea is clear and blue and there are woods along the dusty foreshore, with rocks and the occasional beach to swim from; rock-pooling and the study of inshore marine life are popular activities here.

This is as far north as you can go on the coast of Israel, and a dismal reminder the place is of the bitterness of the conflicts of the Middle East and the intransigence of the protagonists. The twisted and torn tracks of the railway, built to link Syria, Palestine and Egypt, remind one of how closed this route is today. The tunnel is bricked up and the rails ripped away.

You can take a cable-car down over the cliffs to get to the LIMESTONE CAVES below. Over the ages the sea has worn deep holes into the soft white rock. Now there is a walkway through a gallery in the caves. Compared to the wealth of startling natural phenomena to be seen elsewhere in the Holy Land, the caves of *Rosh Haniqra* are not wildly exciting. By the fortified customs post at the top of the hill is a CAFE and RESTAURANT.

If you're heading south from here towards Akko, with its incomparable Crusader halls, take some time to visit the

Crusader Castle of MONTFORT; it's not far off the route and is well worth the trouble.

Montfort

Turn inland along the first road south of *Rosh Haniqra*, signposted *Shomera*, and continue about 10 km. On the right of the road you will see some brown and white signs of the Nature Conservancy Authority. Follow the signs and you will soon find yourself in a car park among the pines. This is a lovely peaceful spot which so far has escaped the worst attentions of the National Parks Authority – there is no toll-booth and no barbed wire fencing; the place is all yours for nothing, and you're more than likely to have it all to yourself as well.

If you look across the deep valley from the picnic site, you will see, on a promontory, the remains of the CASTLE OF MONTFORT. There is a path that winds down the side of the valley, across the river and up to the castle.

The castle was built by the Teutonic Knights in 1226, as an important link in the chain of fortresses guarding Acre. Some 45 years later it was surrendered to the Mameluke, Baybars, who destroyed much of it. Regrettably, time has ravaged the rest of it and today it is in a sorry state. But it is still well worth the effort of the 40-minute walk to get there. Perhaps the finest remaining part of the castle is the fortified hostelry beside the river. Although the ruins are full of earth and rubble, you can still see the magnificent arched transept supported by great stone pillars. The castle above, on its steep thickly wooded bluff, must have been a particularly beautiful and spectacular stronghold, tiny compared to the vastness of Belvoir or Crac des Chevaliers in Syria, but dramatic in its setting and design. Picnic here in the cool of the evening.

Nahariyya

Nahariyya is a seaside resort, set on some of the best BEACHES in Israel. It's a modern town, for there was nothing here until Jewish settlers arrived in 1934, intent on farming the land. The main street, *Sederot Ga'aton*, lined with tall eucalyptus trees and with a dribble of a river running down the centre, is where the life of Nahariyya takes place. Here there are scores of pavement cafes, hamburger joints, strudel shops, ice-cream parlours, restaurants and night-clubs. Gay little carriages with the thinnest horses I've ever seen wait to take you round the town.

At the end of the street is the sea, with a park of pines behind the beach. As always there are pay-beaches where you enjoy the benefit of piped music, crowds and hamburger stalls, and free-beaches where there is a little more tar and rubbish. There are plenty of HOTELS and GUEST-HOUSES so there's no shortage of anywhere to stay or eat, should you decide to stay here. But apart from the sea and the main street, the town has little charm and not much to offer.

Akko – Acre

Keep going south from Nahariyya through the flat coastal plain of maize and bananas; after about 10 km you reach the suburbs of Akko. The suburbs are much like any other suburbs, but once you've negotiated them and got through to the kernel of the Old City, you have a real treat in store.

Acre was for centuries known as 'The wickedest city in the world'. Since the days of the Phoenicians it had been a town of some importance, for it possessed one of the few harbours anywhere along this coast. But it was not until the age of the Crusades that the city reached its full flowering. By the 12th C St Jean d'Acre had become one of the busiest and most important ports in the Mediterranean, rivalling even Constantinople. It was also the second city of the Latin Kingdom of Palestine.

By all accounts it must have been a lively place; among other things it had become a sort of penal colony, where criminals from Europe could escape long sentences in return for a lifetime of penitential service in the Holy Land. The city contained autonomous quarters of French, Genoese, Venetians, Pisans and many others – a thriving merchant trading centre. Here the great mercantile empires of the medieval world were happy to do business with anyone, Christian or Moslem. The high and holy ideals of crusading were a far cry from the cynical opportunism of these Christian westerners.

There was little harmony among the different factions of Christians within the city; at best they tolerated one another with guarded hostility. During the 1250s there were pitched battles in the streets, the 'War at St Sabas', when the Venetians and Genoese even used siege machines against one another's quarters, in a lengthy quarrel over the rights to trade concessions.

In July 1187, after the defeat at the Horns of Hattin, Acre fell to Saladin. Four years later, in 1191, a new force of Crusaders laid siege to the city – a disunited army of quarrelling French under Philip, and British under Richard the Lionheart. The

THE COAST

besiegers were themselves besieged by Saladin's forces in a ring behind them. Eventually the Crusaders' superior might prevailed and, with the help of a blockade of Crusader ships, the town was forced to surrender in July 1191. Some 200,000 gold pieces were paid to the Crusaders, 1,500 prisoners set free, and the piece of the True Cross taken at the Horns of Hattin – where it had been carried into battle by a bishop at the head of the army – returned. Richard took 3,000 hostages. A certain amount of prevarication was shown by Saladin when it came to handing over the ransom, whereupon Richard promptly butchered every one of the 3,000 in full view of Saladin's army.

It was perhaps the arrival of the 5th Crusade at Acre in 1290 that finally put paid to the Crusaders' activities in the Holy Land. A somewhat disorganised and brutish rabble – not drawn exclusively from the ranks of the nobility – they were peasants and townspeople from Lombardy and Tuscany. The new Crusaders got drunk and went on the rampage, beating up and murdering any Moslems they could lay their hands on. As there was a truce at the time between the Templars and the Mameluke Sultan Qalawun, there was no shortage of Moslems in the city, going about their legitimate business, and the drunken brawl turned into a full-scale massacre. Qalawun took a dim view of this, and turning his full attention upon Acre, he besieged the city with a vengeance; after a long siege, he drove the Christians out for good.

Untold numbers lost their lives or were carried off to slavery in the aftermath of the siege. The last bastion in Acre to fall was the great Templar fortress on the shore at the south-western end of the city. The Knights agreed to surrender, then changed their minds because of the behaviour of the Moslem soldiers and fought on until Qalawuns's mines toppled the huge edifice, crushing hundreds of Templars and Moslem soldiers fighting among the ruins.

Today a tumbled wall washed by the sea marks the site of the last heroic hours of the defence of Acre, and of Christian power in Palestine. As a poignant postscript to Acre's violent end, a traveller is reputed to have come across some once-proud Templar Knights, 30 years after the fall of Acre, serving their Moslem masters as woodcutters by the Dead Sea – although what wood they found to cut by the Dead Sea I cannot fathom.

The TOWER OF THE FLIES, the ruined pile of masonry at the south-east end of the harbour, is all that is left of the traditional medieval harbour fortification – a chain that could be raised or lowered to admit or bar shipping.

THE COAST

The present FORTIFICATIONS are the remains of 19th C Ottoman work, but the walls and the streets of the city follow almost exactly the medieval plan. The magnificent CUSTOMS HOUSE on the port is also a 19th C reconstruction of the original. Very much of the medieval city remains though, and with a careful eye and a little imagination, it is almost possible to imagine that one is indeed walking along the streets of the Middle Ages. In the 13th C there were some 38 churches in the city, the greatest of which was the great Gothic Church of St Andrew, used as a navigation mark by mariners. It's on the tourist map, but there's barely a trace of it today.

AL JAZZAR MOSQUE, built for the Mameluke governor of Acre, *Al Jazzar*, the Butcher – for his disagreeable habits – is a typical Mameluke mosque. It is painfully disappointing, with dull raw-boned geometric decoration in black, white and red marble. Beneath the courtyard, down some steps on the south side, is an underground cistern; again this is not as imposing as one would hope.

But the wonder of Acre is the beautiful CRUSADER CITY opposite the *Al Jazzar* mosque. Here is one of the finest remaining examples of Crusader architecture in the world. Massive, rude elegance, Romanesque and early Gothic – built in the late 12th C. This is believed to be one of the first examples of the flowering of Gothic architecture – imposing stone-flagged refectories and chapels with lovely cross-vaulted ceilings. It gladdens your heart and makes you ponder on how far behind was the cultural development of medieval Europe when compared with the delicate and refined sophistication of Islamic architecture.

The underground Crusader city is certainly the finest sight in Acre, if not the finest Crusader remains in the Holy Land. Its remarkable state of preservation is due to the fact that it was filled with rubble to act as foundations for later building above. But there are also many other fine buildings in the city. Tiny architectural details, the curve of an arch, here, the line of a street, the mullion of a window, and throughout, the golden glow of the old limestone, offer rare glimpses of the beauty of a medieval city.

The LAND AND SEA WALLS of Akko are in a good state of preservation and well worth a look even if you are not interested in 19th C Ottoman military architecture. At the north end of the land walls is a citadel; most of it is modern, used as a prison by the British during the Mandate period. This has now been turned into a MUSEUM OF THE HAGANAH, many of whom were imprisoned and executed here. It is an interesting and moving subject, but the museum is wretched; either through lack of money or lack of will, the display is poor and unimaginative.

The best way to enjoy Akko is just to stroll through the streets and transport yourself back to the 12th C. The LIGHTHOUSE end of the sea wall has been restored and there are some pleasant RESTAURANTS AND CAFES here, but I recommend the FISH RESTAURANTS on the harbour front; this is the finest place in old Acre to sit on a summer night and eat fresh fish. A boat takes regular tours around the harbour from here.

You can get all the information you need about the town from the TOURIST INFORMATION CENTRE opposite the *Al Jazzar* Mosque; they are friendly, helpful and efficient. There is a large YOUTH HOSTEL and a number of small hotels in the Old City, but the main hotels are outside in the suburbs or along the beach to the south. There is a small pay bathing beach just outside the south gate of the city, but the water here is filthy – there is a sewage outlet just beside the beach. If you want to swim you would do better to head south towards the big BEACH HOTELS, where there are some fair beaches.

Haifa and Mount Carmel

Fifteen km south of Akko is the industrial sprawl of the port of HAIFA. This is the second industrial centre of Israel, after Tel Aviv. Israelis wax lyrical over the charms of Haifa, and the inhabitants won't hear a word said against it. Its setting on this horn of the Israeli coast, the only irregularity on an otherwise flat and featureless coastline, is certainly magnificent, and the surrounding countryside on MOUNT CARMEL is one of the greenest and most attractive parts of Israel.

Haifa is a modern town, though; little survives from before the beginning of this century. The town was mostly built by German settlers, spreading up the steep northwestern bluff of Mount Carmel, and their love of neatness, precision and order strikes you immediately. At the foot is the port and industrial area, grey, smoky and dull, though this is where most of the MUSEUMS are to be found. Halfway up the hill is HADAR, the commercial and business quarter. If you wish to eat or go shopping in Haifa, this is the place to do it. There are also a number of hotels in this area. Finally, at the very top, is Carmel itself. Here are the big international hotels, in the very best part of Haifa, for in the hot summer it is delightfully cool and breezy. The view, too is striking; on a clear day you can see all the way up to the white cliffs of *Rosh Haniqra,* and at night the web of lights spreading far below into the darkness is impressive.

The *Carmelit* rack and pinion railway is the best means of getting about vertically, for it runs in an almost vertical track between the top and bottom of the city. (In 1987 it was closed for repairs.) Otherwise there is an excellent bus service which somehow manages to haul the inhabitants up and down the hills.

Plumb in the centre of the town is the beautiful garden surrounding the SHRINE OF THE BAB, the world centre of the Baha'i faith. The garden itself is the most beautiful in Israel. The shrine is as graceful and fine a modern monument as you will find anywhere. You are welcome to visit, but only in the mornings, although the garden is open all day. This you should certainly not miss.

Baha'i Shrine and Gardens, Haifa

THE COAST

Today there are more than two million followers of the Baha'i faith, throughout SW Asia, Africa, Europe and the Americas. Their religion has developed from the teachings of two 19th C Persian mystics, Mirza Ali Mohammed – the *Bab* or 'Gate' – and Mirza Husain Ali – *Baha'u'llah* or 'Glory of God'.

The Baha'i see *Baha'u'llah* as the Messiah, following a long line of prophets including Moses, Buddha, Christ and Mohammed. They believe that salvation will come through racial and social equality and world peace, brought about by an inner change in man and society. This salvation will be attainable by all mankind, not just the faithful. The Baha'i have been persecuted since the beginning of their religion, and are cruelly oppressed to this day in Iran. Although derived from Islam, Baha'i claims to be one of the great world universal religions.

To the west of the town, over the busy main road to Tel Aviv, are some fine BATHING BEACHES. At the north-west extremity of the town is the CAVE OF ELIJAH, just below the CARMELITE MONASTERY. Here Elijah is said to have found refuge from the wrath of King Ahab. This is a very holy place indeed, for Christians, Jews and Moslems – Elijah, as *El Khader,* is sacred to the Moslems as well as to the Jews. There are always people inside the dank grotto, engaged in fervent prayer, and the little garden outside is a favourite spot for a picnic.

A little to the east of Elijah's Cave are the CLANDESTINE IMMIGRATION AND NAVAL MUSEUM. These are both worth a visit; the maritime museum has some impressive models and artefacts from all over the world. The Immigration Museum brings to life the history of these remarkable events with some of the ships that took part. I recommend both museums. If you're really stuck for something to do, there are other museums in town – the DAGON GRAIN SILO MUSEUM, the EDIBLE OILS MUSEUM, and the RAILWAY MUSEUM – although these are unlikely to be anybody's idea of a wild afternoon out.

The thing to do in Haifa is to leave the city by the top, out past the UNIVERSITY into the NATIONAL PARK of Mount Carmel. Carmel means 'vineyard' in Hebrew. The mountain range extends about 25 km south-east of Haifa, at an average height of 1,600 ft. Since ancient times, Carmel has been a place of sanctuary and holiness. It is referred to in the Bible less as a specific place than as a symbol of beauty and fertility. It is indeed greener and lusher than the rest of Israel, for it is blessed with heavy year-round dewfall, which makes it a delightful place to go wandering.

Here was the stamping ground of the Prophet Elijah. The

cave where he sought refuge is at the western end, while 15 km to the east, at one of the highest parts of the Carmel range, is the site of his dramatic confrontation with the prophets of Baal. On the summit is a MONASTERY – *Muhraqa* – on the site of the sacrifice; tourists and visitors are not encouraged.

From the early years of Byzantium, Mount Carmel was a favourite abode of hermits, who built chapels and refuges on the thickly wooded slopes. The Carmelite order was founded by St Brochard in 1212, but although they grew powerful in Europe, their hold on Mount Carmel was shaky, as they were under constant threat from militant Moslems to whom monasticism was something of an aberration. Several times the order was all but exterminated, and it was not until 1827 that they succeeded in establishing themselves finally in the monastery that stands to this day.

As you head south-east along the spine of Mount Carmel, you pass the DRUZE VILLAGES of *Isfiya* and *Daliyat el Karmil*. The Druze seem to favour this sort of situation; the other Druze villages in Israel are to be found in the high valleys on the slopes of Mount Hermon. Here they sell handicrafts – rugs, pottery and the like – and run TEA-SHOPS and RESTAURANTS, welcome spots to break the journey.

The Druze are a heretical sect of the Moslem faith who do not follow the Koran, nor have any outward religious ceremonies or chapels. Their origin dates from Caliph Hakim of Egypt. The Druze did not join the Arabs in their struggle against the Zionists in 1948. The details of their religion are secret even from most of its adherents.

The most infamous leader of the Fatimid dynasty was the Caliph Hakim who ruled from 996 to 1021. He became insane and declared himself to be the Messiah. The Druze still revere him as an incarnate deity. In 1009 Hakim ordered the destruction of all the churches of Palestine, apart from the Nativity at Bethlehem. This senseless act was one of the major factors contributing to the launching of the Crusades.

The Druze movement dates from a palace coup during Hakim's reign when, proclaiming that he was the divine incarnation, he disappeared (he is believed to be in occlusion – that is, hidden with promise of return). However the mastermind behind the Druze organisation was *Hamza ben 'Ali*, a Persian whose teachings are incorporated into several letters that, along with other writings, represent the Druze scriptures.

The Druze now occupy mountainous regions of Lebanon, Syria and the Holy Land, with an estimated population of 200,000. Intermarriage with outsiders is strictly prohibited and new adherents are not actively encouraged, so the sect has remained for centuries a close-knit community and has developed a distinct racial identity.

Two main classes may be distinguished amongst the Druze; the learned and the ignorant. High moral character, daily religious exercises and distinctive clothing featuring white turbans distinguish the former group. The most learned and pious among them are considered spiritual chiefs, or *shaykhs*, from whom each village or district appoints its head. The latter are subordinate to the learned group.

The further southeast you go, the lovelier the mountain becomes. As it reaches its highest point, just after *Daliyat el Karmil*, and starts to drop down towards the pass of *Yoqne'am*, you enter the area known as 'LITTLE SWITZERLAND' – a bit fanciful perhaps, but this is the loveliest part of Carmel, lush green with valleys of pine and small flowing rivers. It is no surprise that such a miraculously temperate spot in the midst of the harsh climate of the Holy Land should have been considered so blest. Beneath the mountain here is the unexcavated *tel* of *Yoqne'am*, an ancient fortress-city, now a tall, steep overgrown mound.

From *Daliyat el Karmil*, a path leads down the more gentle eastern slope of Carmel, about 5 km to EN HOD – or you can reach the village from the main Haifa–Tel Aviv road.

En Hod

EN HOD is another one of these odd villages that one comes across now and then in Israel, where artists, with their superior eye for a delightful place to live, have grasped the opportunity and moved in. It's a little Arab village nestling among trees on the foothills of Mount Carmel, with a fine view over the sea below. It's a curious sort of a place, part forest, part wilderness of scrub and thistles with paths winding to and fro through it, leading you to pottery workshops or to the imaginatively adapted shacks of textile designers, weavers, painters and sculptors. There's a BAR/RESTAURANT at the entrance to the village – nice for an afternoon stroll and a brief sortie into the airy realms of art.

A couple of kilometres up the road is the KIBBUTZ GUEST-HOUSE *Nir Etzion*, set in a spectacular garden. This is a lovely place; the people are friendly, the garden is pretty, there's a swimming-pool (no mixed bathing, *Nir Etzion* tends towards the religious) and it's a good spot for wandering about on the slopes of Mount Carmel, on foot or on horseback, for the Kibbutz organises pony-trekking.

Plain of Sharon

Before the plain of Sharon became one of the finest citrus-growing areas in the world, as it is today, the whole area was a virtually impassable swamp. The coast here is uniform from top to bottom, with no natural harbours except for Haifa, Acre and Jaffa; the rest consists of a thin strip of sand bordering the sea, with a belt of dunes behind. The streams, rivers and *wadis* that drain the hills in the hinterland, cannot easily flow into the sea, and thus disperse their waters in the surrounding flatlands.

Until the Romans came, the area was virtually uninhabitable and completely impassable; the ancient *Via Maris,* Way of the Sea, turned inland long before it reached the Plain of Sharon. The Romans bridged the streams, making the whole area accessible. In the Middle Ages, though, the bridges and development instigated by the Romans wasted away and the area reverted to a hot desert swamp under the careless Ottomans, who cared not a fig for the backwoods province of Palestine, except for what it could yield in the short term in the way of revenues. General Allenby too had trouble passing this way in 1917. But the British Mandate and the Zionists bridged the rivers, drained the swamps and transformed the whole area into what it is today. The crocodiles who had previously made life so disagreeable for the inhabitants of the area and such travellers as passed this way, found the new environment uncongenial and departed for new swamps.

Caesarea

Although there had been a Phoenician settlement here, known as STRATO'S TOWER, since early in the 4th C BC, it was Herod the Great who really put this place on the map. The Emperor Augustus gave him the small fortified town, and Herod set about creating, in a mere 12 years, a city to glorify the Emperor. According to the historian Josephus, the building feats were phenomenal even by Herod's standards.

He constructed a theatre, a temple (dedicated to Augustus), a sophisticated sewage system, a market, a palace and an amphitheatre. For his deep-harbour, he sank huge blocks of stone measuring 50 ft long, 10 ft wide and 9 ft deep in 20 fathoms of water, to serve as the foundation for a massive breakwater.

Roman Amphitheatre, Caesarea

After Herod's death in 4 BC the job of governing Caesarea fell to one of his sons. He survived as king a scant ten years before the Romans decided he wasn't man enough for the task, and replaced him with their own choice of governor (procurator), who now governed Judea with an army of occupation based in the city.

From now onwards the city's population, a mixture of Jew and Hellenised gentile, lived uneasily with each other and with their Roman overlords. The Hellenised Greek-speaking gentiles were the élite, taking plum civil service and tax-collecting jobs, and even augmenting the Roman army. A succession of procurators were appointed from Greek Asia Minor; all anti-semitic and mostly incompetent. To complicate matters further, Christianity was beginning to take root – the Acts of the Apostles report a number of Christian activities here, including Peter's conversion of the Roman centurion, Cornelius, and Paul's two-year imprisonment in the city. The Romans often saw Christianity as just another Jewish sect and so the tensions increased.

In 66 AD a major clash between gentiles and Jews, which the Romans, in spite of pleas from the Jewish community, did nothing to prevent, resulted in the massacre of thousands of the Jewish population. (Josephus, who was prone to exaggeration, claims 20,000 were killed in an hour.) This was one of the sparks that set off the first Jewish Revolt against Rome.

The Romans suppressed the Jewish revolt, returning from Jerusalem to Caesarea to celebrate their victory by throwing 2,500 hapless Jews to their menagerie of wild animals in a single day. Following the second Jewish Revolt, the Romans were more restrained and contented themselves with the torture and execution in public of the spiritual leader of the revolt – one of the greatest Jewish scholars, Rabbi Akiva.

Now Caesarea settled down to two centuries or so of relative peace and considerable prosperity. The Jewish community was left virtually alone and Caesarea flourished as a seat of great Jewish learning. With the coming of the Byzantines and the adoption of Christianity as the empire's official religion, Caesarea became an important Christian centre; the great church-historian Eusebius studied here and became bishop in the early 4th C AD.

Caesarea capitulated along with everywhere else to the Arabs in 640 AD. The harbour was neglected but the city continued to prosper and the inhabitants were left much to their own devices. But peace was not to last. The beginning of the 11th C saw the first of the Crusades, and Caesarea seemed to bear the brunt of all the toing and froing. First it was King Baldwin I who in true Christian Crusader fashion destroyed the town, slaughtered the inhabitants and carted off the Holy Grail, a goblet reputedly used by Christ at the Last Supper. In 1187, Saladin defeated the Crusaders and destroyed the city. Along came Richard the Lionheart who occupied the ruins for a while in 1191, but it wasn't until 1251 that any major work was carried out, when Louis IX of France rebuilt and fortified the town; though not sufficiently to keep the Mamelukes, led by Sultan Baybars, at bay. Some 26 years later the Mamelukes totally destroyed the city to prevent any further Crusader invasions from the sea.

As a city, Caesarea never regained its importance, and even today there is no town as such, apart from a collection of fancy 'villas', a deluxe hotel and golf course. The main attraction is, of course, the ruins – predominantly Crusader but with vestiges of Byzantine and Roman remains. Considering how much of Caesarea was plundered for building projects elsewhere, there's still a great deal to see. The main site is now under the dubious auspices of the Caesarea Development Authority, which appears to be doing its best to trivialise the ruins with a development of cafés, shops, restaurants and a disco, all virtually in the ruins themselves.

One ticket will admit you to the two main sites; the Roman theatre facing the Mediterranean, and the Crusader city. The theatre was extensively restored in 1970 and is used today in the summer months for drama, classical music and rock concerts.

The entrance to the Crusader city, through an excellently restored Crusader gate, is just down the road. Louis IX is mainly responsible for the walls and the extant Crusader remains you see today, having apparently helped to build the city with his own hands. The site has been very well marked, so you can guide yourself round.

Just over the road by the car park and the snack bar, you can take a look at the remnants of a section of a Byzantine street, paved in part with marble slabs, some in excellent condition, and in part with rather faded mosaics. The two huge headless statues, one fashioned from porphyry and believed to be the Emperor Hadrian, were imported here from Roman temples and date from around the 2nd or 3rd C AD.

East of the Byzantine Street you will find the Hippodrome. This was another of Herod's large-scale building projects and could seat up to 20,000 spectators. The site appears rather uncared for now, but use your imagination and think of the fantastic races for which Caesarea was famous, held on this very spot over 1,500 years ago.

The Roman Aqueduct is some way from the main site, but it's worth a look. You could walk or drive to it along a bumpy road that skirts the ruins and then runs over the sand dunes, or drive northwards, turning left for the Aqueduct and passing through Caesarea's cluster of expensive villas. The Aqueduct is a spectacular sight and in excellent condition. It was originally built by the tireless Herod to bring fresh water to the city from Mount Carmel some 16 km away.

Netanya

Netanya was founded on the sandy Sharon Plain in 1928, as a centre for the area's citrus fruit production, and named after the American philanthropist Nathan Strauss. Immigrants from South Africa and Belgium established a diamond-cutting industry here which still flourishes today, although Netanya's main *raison d'être* is tourism.

If you're looking for a beach holiday with occasional excursions to soak up a bit of history then this might be the place for you.

The town is built on a clifftop at the foot of which are 10 km of excellent sandy beaches. There is an attractive park-like promenade which runs along the clifftop whilst the town behind is a network of streets offering hotels, hotels and more hotels as well as plenty of shops, restaurants and sidewalk cafés.

Make a visit to the Tourist Office, which you will find in *Ha'Atzma'ut* Square. In season, Netanya offers all kinds of free entertainment in the evenings, and the tourist office will be able to tell you what's on offer. You can also amuse yourself by taking one of the guided tours to the diamond-cutting and polishing centres – the odds are you'll come away with a dent in your holiday budget.

Herzliya

HERZLIYA is 15 km north of Tel Aviv and is in effect a ritzy suburb of the city. If you are staying in Tel Aviv, for good beaches head for Herzliya on Sea, not the town of Herzliya itself. The sea front is commandeered by the big luxury hotels and you have to pay to use the beaches.

Tel Aviv

Your first impressions of TEL AVIV are likely to be of a concrete jungle; gleaming and modern in parts, shabby and run down in others. You're likely to find it brash, noisy and frenetic. But pause a moment before you take the first bus out of town. Only 80 years ago this was desert and swamp land. Israel was, and still is to a large degree, a country in a hurry, with territory to stake a claim to and defend, an economy to build and millions of immigrants to house; no time then for the luxuries of aesthetic planning, grandiose architecture and organic growth. But here, if you are in any way interested in the birth of the Israeli nation (and whatever your views, it is a fascinating story) you'll find the landmarks of a nation's birth – not lofty and exalted but the workday monuments of a state very recently and painfully born. And Tel Aviv is nothing if not vigorous. It just takes a while to feel its pulse.

Late in the 19th C, when the early Jewish pioneers started to trickle into Palestine, most of them arrived via the nearby Port of Jaffa. Some headed out for the swamplands of Galilee to establish agricultural settlements, but many remained in the Arab port and lived in a considerable degree of harmony with the Arab population.

In 1908 a small band of Jews led by Dizengoff (later to become the first Mayor of Tel Aviv) left the crowded and narrow confines of Jaffa and, with help from the Jewish

THE COAST

National Fund, purchased a small stretch of land a little to the north of the port. What was, in 1908, little more than a string of barren sand dunes became the foundation for the first all-Jewish city to be established in Israel for over 2,000 years. Some 80 years later this place was to become the economic, social and cultural heart of the state of Israel.

The pioneers changed the name of their little settlement from *Ahuzit Bayit* to Tel Aviv – Hill of Spring. In 1917 at the outbreak of the First World War, the Turks expelled the Jewish settlers from their rapidly expanding town, but they returned under the British, and the building of the city continued apace. In the face of increasing hostility and rioting from the Arab population of Jaffa, more Jews packed up and moved to swell the population of Tel Aviv to around 15,000.

After the Second World War, Tel Aviv, now a sizeable town, became the centre of resistance to British immigration policies, and the base of operations for Israel's Underground Defence Forces – the *Haganah*. When the British withdrew from Palestine, the Jews launched an immediate, and successful, attack on nearby Jaffa – a hotbed of Arab resistance to the emerging Jewish state. From Tel Aviv's Independence Hall, the new state of Israel was proclaimed on 14 May 1948.

The city is a bit daunting when you first arrive; a huge urban sprawl merging with Jaffa in the south and Herzliya in the north. But it's easier than you might think to orient yourself; just take your bearings from the sea to the west.

All the monolithic hotels line up along Tel Aviv's long seaside promenade. The BEACHES are good, especially at the southern end, but don't be fooled by the inviting Mediterranean water. There's a very nasty undertow that claims the lives of many swimmers every year. Take your cue from the flags planted intermittently along the beach; white means it's safe, red means be wary and black means you're an idiot if you attempt to swim. On some of the beaches there are lifeguards – you'll see their viewing platforms – and if you're not a strong swimmer or you're with children, you'd be advised to stick to them.

All along the beach promenade, in between the big hotels, are cafés, restaurants and ice cream parlours. The prices are high but you can nurse one drink here for hours and watch the endless stream of people go by. It'll cost you nothing to sit on one of the many benches all along the promenade and watch the beach life or the sun go down in the evening. Avoid the northern end of the beach parade, the area known as KIKAR NAMIR, at night. This hideous modern shopping and restaurant complex is fairly nasty during the day and even seedier after dark.

The tourist office is on Mendele Street, so before you start a detailed exploration of the city, get yourself equipped with a good map; they'll provide one free of charge. All the major tour companies are based near the tourist office, so you can book yourself excursions to such places as Jerusalem, the Dead Sea, Masada and Caesarea at the same time.

The hub of Tel Aviv's café life is in and around DIZENGOFF CIRCLE and the northern part of Dizengoff street. Busy during the day, it has a positively carnival atmosphere at night. You can find almost every type of take-away and junk food here, together with restaurants and cafés whose diversity of offerings is evidence of the broad ethnic mix of Jewish immigrants. In between all these eateries and drinkeries are expensive fashion shops. By the way, you'll find plenty of places open here on the Sabbath. Compared to other parts of Israel Tel Aviv is 'sin city' and this area is where most of the sinning goes on.

Dizengoff Circle itself is raised above the hustle and bustle of the street, and crowned with an extraordinary FOUNTAIN 'SCULPTURE'. The Israelis are fond of large-scale, modern, arty edifices. This one whirls at regular intervals to the accompaniment of unlikely music, such as Ravel's 'Bolero' and Lloyd Webber's 'Don't cry for me, Argentina'. But that's not all. After a while a flame appears at the top and, in spite of a regular spraying with the water that squirts all over it while the contraption whirls, refuses to be doused. Tourists and locals alike sit around the circle on benches munching their take-away snacks and staring bemused at this inexplicable spectacle. Sit downwind and you're likely to get sprayed.

When you've had enough of the beach and the bright lights of Dizengoff, start your exploration of Tel Aviv at the southern edge, where the city begins to merge with Jaffa.

The neighbourhood known as NEVE TZEDEK started life as a suburb of Jaffa and is the oldest quarter in Tel Aviv. The old stone houses are now being refurbished and this shabby area is gradually becoming a fashionable address, especially for Tel Aviv's artists and avant garde. You can find some interesting little galleries and boutiques around here. A tour of this quarter starts from the Dan Panorama Hotel immediately west of the area on the sea-front. If there aren't too many guests wanting to go, they might let you tag along.

A little east of *Neve Tzedek* on Herzl Street is the SHALOM MAYER TOWER. Constructed in 1957, it occupies the site of the Hebrew School built by the early settlers. It's a shabby affair

THE COAST

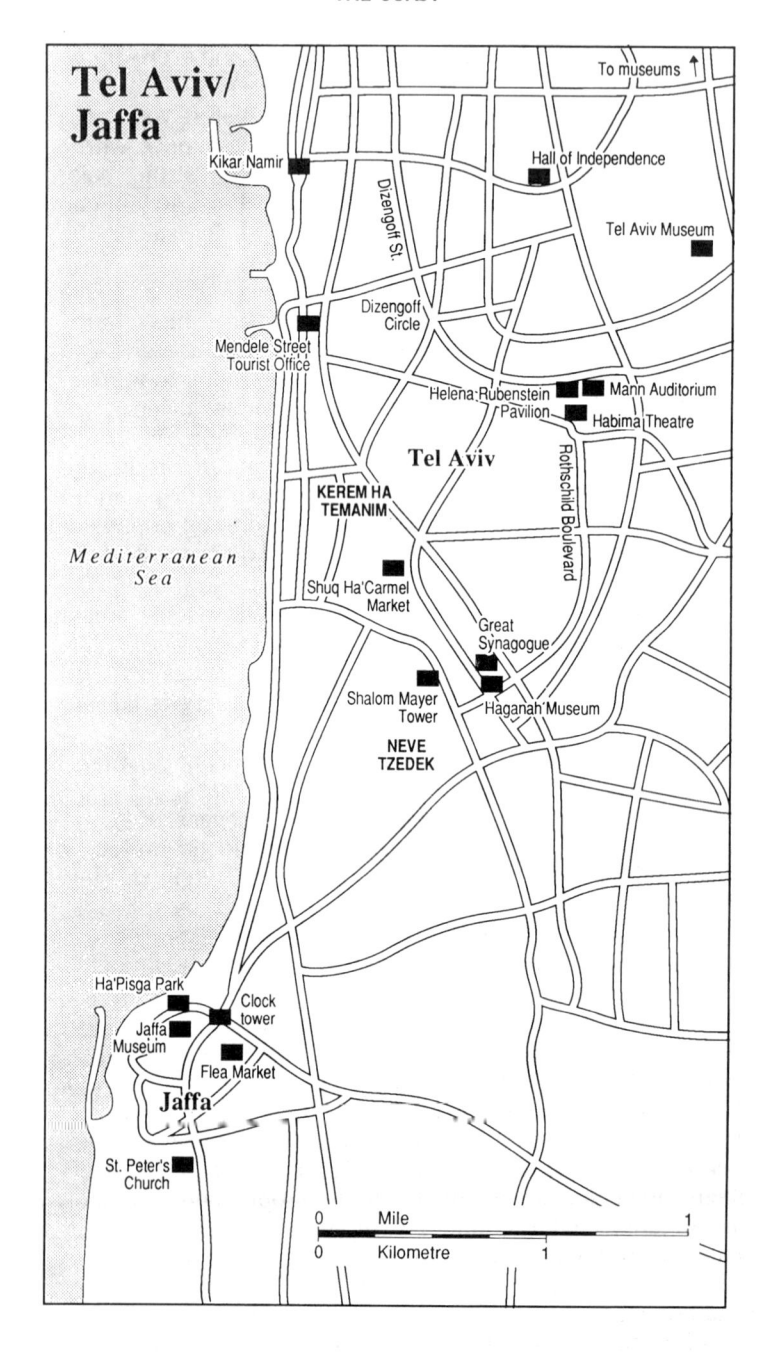

both inside and out. It houses shops and offices as well as a WAXWORKS MUSEUM, an AMUSEMENT ARCADE and an OBSERVATORY with a panoramic view of Tel Aviv. The admission price for the waxworks and the observatory is steep and quite frankly not worth it. Give this one a miss.

Before you leave the area, take a look at the GREAT SYNAGOGUE on *Ashad Ha'am* Street. It was renovated in the 1970s and with its stained-glass windows and dome is really quite handsome.

A little to the north-west is the SHUQ HA' CARMEL – a good place to give your eyes a feast and your ears a bashing. It doesn't quite know whether it's an eastern bazaar or a Levantine version of Petticoat Lane, but it certainly must be one of the noisiest markets in the world. At the northern end you'll find clothing, mundane household goods and bric-à-brac, whilst at the southern end there's a wonderfully colourful display of fruit and vegetables, cured meats, olives and pickled vegetables.

Nearby to the north, is the *Keren HaTemanim,* or YEMENITE QUARTER. A maze of narrow streets, this is where to find some of the best and most atmospheric restaurants in Tel Aviv. Yemeni food is spicy but it won't blow your socks off.

ROTHSCHILD BOULEVARD is one of the most elegant streets in Tel Aviv, with a lovely tree-lined central promenade interspersed with little refreshment kiosks selling cold drinks and freshly squeezed juices. It's one of the most fruitful areas if you are interested in the history of the birth of Israel. Starting at the southern end of the street, at number 23 is the HAGANAH MUSEUM. The museum is next door to one of the first houses to be built in Tel Aviv, and the home of Eliyahu Golomb, one of the founders of the *Haganah*. His house was for years the illegal HQ of the defence movement.

The British disbanded the Jewish Legion after the First World War; it had served its purpose but was now considered to have no rôle to play in the British Mandate rule of Palestine. But from the early 1920s as Arab opposition to Zionism, the Balfour Agreement and increasing Jewish immigration translated into violence, a covert self-defence organisation was formed with a brief to guard the settlements in Galilee, Samaria and Judea. This organisation eventually evolved into the *Haganah*. The British, unwilling to alienate the Arabs, did little to protect Jewish settlements from attack and so the *Haganah* did what they could with a limited supply of arms and relatively few men.

Following the Second World War the *Haganah* played a major rôle in frustrating British attempts to stop the immigra-

THE COAST

tion of thousands of Jews fleeing post-Holocaust Europe. When the British left and the State of Israel was declared in 1948, the new country was plunged immediately into a war against the Arab Nationalists. The *Haganah* now emerged as Israel's regular army. Although they were massively outnumbered, there is little doubt that Israel would never have survived without them. They had, since their illegal formation, painstakingly recruited and trained their forces, built up a supply of arms, some homemade, some smuggled in under the noses of the British, and cut their teeth on years of sporadic undercover activities.

Not many of the exhibits are marked in English and unless you have a knowledge of weaponry most of it will be lost on you. But the photographs are interesting, as are such exhibits as the propaganda leaflets aimed at demoralising the British troops. One such leaflet issued illegally during the harsh days of restricted immigration reads: 'Belsen was liberated on April 14th 1945 – 31,000 Jews have died since then.' On the third floor you can see some of the ways the *Haganah* managed to build up its supplies of arms right under the suspicious noses of the British.

Just over the road from the *Haganah* Museum at number 16 is INDEPENDENCE HALL. Only open in the mornings this place is the favourite haunt of hordes of incredibly noisy Jewish schoolchildren engaged in absorbing the recent history of their little country. When you think of the ramifications of the event that took place in here on 14 May 1948 you might expect a grand edifice marking the spot. Instead you will find a simple stone house, the former home of Dizengoff, the first Mayor of Tel Aviv, which was later converted into a museum.

Displays in the ground-floor rooms tell the story of the years leading up to the proclamation of the State of Israel. They start with Theodor Herzl's pronouncement at the first Zionist Congress in Basel, that 'if you will it, it is no idle dream', through the years of struggle under the British Mandate, to the United Nations Partition vote, and David Ben Gurion's announcement: 'By virtue of our national and intrinsic right and on the strength of the resolution of the United Nations General Assembly, we hereby declare the establishment of a Jewish state in Palestine, which shall be known as the State of Israel.' The whole proclamation ceremony took barely half an hour.

Next door to the hall itself is a small room where documents relating to the foundation of the state, many of them in English and including the Declaration of Independence itself, are displayed. In the upstairs rooms you'll find a rather scruffy BIBLE MUSEUM and MODERN ART GALLERY.

Tel Aviv, not Jerusalem, is the cultural heartland of Israel and its major 'monuments' are to be found at the extreme northern end of the Rothschild Boulevard, clustered around *Habima* Square; the HABIMA THEATRE was founded by a Russian theatre group and is now the National Theatre of Israel, with a worldwide reputation for excellence. Next door is the huge 3,000-seater MANN AUDITORIUM, home of the world-famous Israel Philharmonic Orchestra. In between the two complexes you'll find a shady respite known as *Gan Ya'akov*, meaning JACOB'S GARDENS.

Just round the corner on *Tarsat* Boulevard is the HELENA RUBENSTEIN PAVILION displaying a constantly changing selection of Israeli modern art from the 1960s onwards. You can buy a combined ticket for this and the TEL AVIV MUSEUM which can be found to the north-east on *Shaul Hamalek* street. You need to check with the Tourist Office or the press to find out if there are any special exhibitions. Permanent exhibits include a selection of 17th C Dutch and Flemish paintings, 18th C Italian painting, impressionist and post-impressionist and 20th C art. The museum is usually open on the Sabbath but it is very popular with the Israelis so expect to queue, especially if there's a new temporary exhibition. There's also a cinema here which regularly shows foreign films – often in English; check the press for details.

Further north and over the Yarkon River are two more museums worth a visit. The first is the HA'ARETZ MUSEUM COMPLEX, a series of 'pavilions' laid out in pleasant gardens and encompassing the TEL QASILE excavations. These excavations, Israel's first archaelogical dig, have partially uncovered a PHILISTINE CITY dating from around 1200 BC. There are layers testifying to the possibility of an Israelite settlement during King David and King Solomon's reigns, and much later remains from medieval and Crusader periods. The site is interesting, especially the temple area, which can be examined from a viewing platform and is numbered and colour coded to make it easier to 'read'. You can pick up a free walking tour leaflet from the little *Tel Qasile*, MUSEUM which will help you identify the different levels.

Within the grounds you will find a small PLANETARIUM with a display of some interesting early concepts of the universe. The Planetarium programmes are in Hebrew only, except by special arrangement for tour groups. Near the Planetarium is SUNDIAL SQUARE, a display of nine different kinds of sundial. As you walk further through the grounds you'll come across the old diesel engine TRAIN with carriages and cargo trucks dating from the British Mandate period. Climb inside and look at the 1934 Palestine train timetable. The FOLKLORE PAVILION is worth a stop, particularly for its wonderful display of elaborate Jewish marriage contracts, dating from 1700 onwards and collected from such places as India, Africa, Holland and Italy. You could give the OIL EXTRACTING PLANT a miss; a reconstruction of a traditional mill and press for production of olive oil, explanatory signs in English are conspicuous by their absence. The MAN AND HIS WORK MUSEUM exhibits the very first tools and processes used by man. Detailed explanations are in Hebrew, but many of the displays are self-explanatory. Outside the pavilion is a series of RECONSTRUCTED WORKSHOPS – a working glass-blowing workshop, a blacksmith, woodturner, carpenter, silver and goldsmith, shoemaker and a weaver. Have a look at the GLASS MUSEUM for an explanation of the production process of glass and a fascinating collection of wine jugs, jewellery, ointment bottles, glass lamps, etc. Don't miss the beautiful 14th C mosque lamp donated to the museum by the Rothschilds.

Still left to see are the CERAMICS PAVILION, THE ALPHABET MUSEUM, NUMISMATIC MUSEUM, SCIENCE AND TECHNOLOGY MUSEUM and the COPPER MUSEUM – a small but well laid out exhibition of the story of man's progress from stone age to present times. Admission to the complex is free except on the Sabbath and holidays (you have to pay for the Planetarium).

If you don't do anything else in Tel Aviv you really should stir yourself to see the MUSEUM OF THE JEWISH DIASPORA (BETH HATEFUTSOTH) in the grounds of the university campus. Even if museums leave you cold this one is likely to fascinate you. Theoretically, this isn't really a museum at all – not in the sense that displays of ancient objects and works of art constitute a museum. It tells the story, with the clever and imaginative use of video, slides, sound and wonderfully intricate models, of 'a people scattered over the world, who yet remained a single family, a nation which time and time again was doomed to destruction and yet, out of the ruins, rose to new life'.

It is in fact a reconstruction of Jewish history and culture from the exile right up to the present day. You can't possibly do it justice in a few hours and I guarantee you'll be hooked after your first visit, so be prepared to return to complete your tour. By the way, you can feed your name into a computer here to see if it is a Jewish name, and what its origins are. You can

JAFFA

JAFFA is the oldest port city in the world and its history is rich with biblical associations, myths and legends. According to Jewish tradition Noah's youngest son, Japheth, settled here after the flood, and Mark Twain relates in his *Innocents Abroad* that 'it was from Jaffa that Jonah sailed when he was told to go and prophecy against Nineveh, and, no doubt it was not far from the town that the whale threw him up when he discovered he had no ticket'.

The Egyptians invaded in 1486 BC and a story relates that the reigning Pharaoh, one Thutmose III, captured the city by concealing his troops, Ali Baba style, in vast storage jars. Jaffa crops up in Chronicles; Solomon having decided to rebuild the Temple in Jerusalem asked King Hiram of Tyre to send the cedarwood. Hiram replied, 'we will cut you all the logs from Lebanon you need and will float them in rafts by sea down to Joppa. You can then take them up to Jerusalem.' The Greeks were here too, leaving behind a myth whose landmark is still being shown to tourists today. Apparently the reigning king's wife got a bit above herself and declared herself more beautiful than Poseidon's nereids. Much affronted, the sea-god sent a flood upon the land and a particularly voracious sea-monster to terrify the populace. Appeasement was only to be gained by the sacrifice of the couple's hapless daughter Andromeda, who was to be offered as a snack to the monster and was accordingly chained to a rock in the harbour. As with all good fairy tales the unfortunate princess was both rescued and married at the eleventh hour by one Perseus astride his winged horse.

Passing under the yoke of Romans, Moslems, Crusaders and Mamelukes the city fell into decline in the 14th C, and didn't revive until the late 18th C, when it served as a port for pilgrims on their way to Jerusalem and subsequently as a gateway for Jewish immigration. Jaffa had been predominantly Arab from the 13th C onwards and became a centre of resistance to the formation of the new Jewish state. In 1948, just before the Declaration of Independence, the *Irgun* and *Haganah* captured the city and thousands of the Arab population fled. Today, there is still a sizeable Arab population and in spite of being cheek by jowl with modern Tel Aviv, a real atmosphere of the old Middle East prevails, although officially it has been incorporated into Tel Aviv since 1950.

THE COAST

If you prefer crumbling historic towns, the extensive redevelopment of the old city above the harbour of Jaffa may not be to your taste. But the Israelis seem to have an exceptional ability to blend the old with the new. The work here is as good as, if not better than, the restoration and modernisation of the Jewish Quarter in Jerusalem. You can reach this area by turning right on *Mifraz Shlomo* Street, just past the CLOCK TOWER which you will see as soon as you come into Jaffa from Tel Aviv.

As you walk up the hill, to your left is the JAFFA MUSEUM (the adjoining Turkish *hamam* is now a nightclub) and behind it the small HA' PISGA PARK. Here you can see EXCAVATIONS of a town dating from the 13th C BC. The ruins are quite well marked but not extensive enough to warrant a special visit. The park is attractive, though, but I'll leave you to decide about the arched MEMORIAL SCULPTURE atop the hill.

Returning to *Mifraz Shlomo*, continue up the hill towards *Kikar Kedumin,* an open square with the attractive 17th C CHURCH OF ST PETER as its focal point. This is the renovated area, full of cafés, fancy restaurants and even fancier boutiques, galleries and artists' studios with prices to match. But the view from here, especially at night with the lights twinkling across the water, makes even Tel Aviv look attractive.

Just south of the square is *Shimon Ha-Burski*, a narrow street leading down towards the harbour. Here you will find the HOUSE OF SIMON THE TANNER. Christian tradition holds that St Peter stayed here after miraculously restoring Tabitha to life (Acts 9). Casual visitors are discouraged and you might give this one a miss unless you are a serious pilgrim.

Right at the top of the hill is a modern complex which houses the 'ISRAEL EXPERIENCE'. This is what is known as a multi-media show with 51 projectors, a giant screen and 'breathtaking special effects' (this includes a 'burning bush' that glows rather unconvincingly at the appropriate biblical moment, just below the screen). It aims to tell you the story of 'Israel Past and Present'. It's all rather over the top and will either amaze you or make you want to giggle.

JAFFA HARBOUR, below the restored old city, is earmarked for development as a marina. But at the moment it's scruffy, lively and a great place to go for fish restaurants. They don't have the gloss of the restaurants on the hill above, but the prices are lower and the atmosphere is just as good.

Everyone who visits Tel Aviv or Jaffa makes a beeline for the JAFFA FLEA MARKET. Head southwards on *Yefet* Street from the Clock Tower and you'll see it on your left in *Aleytsion*

Street. Go early if you want to see it at its liveliest, but don't expect an oriental bazaar glowing with rich antique copper and brass, bolts of silk and brocade, jewellery, etc. The 'finds' here are few and far between and have to be rooted out between the bric-à-brac, tatty household items and second-hand carpets.

All around the Clock Tower and in the streets off *Yefet* Street there are Arab shops selling incredibly sweet middle-eastern sweetmeats and pastries – you'll be hard pressed to manage one, two will probably make you sick and three will rot your teeth! There are scruffy restaurants here that will charge you a fraction of the price that you will pay for a meal up on the hill.

Ashkelon

Ten km of beautiful beaches, a fascinating history and an attractive National Park encompassing the archaeological remains of ancient ASHKELON, make this town, Israel's southernmost coastal resort, popular with the Israelis.

Ancient Ashkelon has an interesting history. One of the oldest cities in the world, Ashkelon first came to prominence as a port on the great sea trading route from Mesopotamia to Egypt. A Canaanite town, under Egyptian protection, it fell to the predatory Philistines in the 12th C BC round about the same time as the Israelites occupied the rest of the land. The Bible is rich in its descriptions of the bitter struggles between the militarily superior Philistines and the Israelites. One of the best known is the account in Judges of Samson ultimately avenging himself on the Philistines for putting out his eyes, by pulling down the temple dedicated to their god, Dagon. But the Israelites never succeeded in conquering Ashkelon, or any of the other four Philistine cities.

The city changed hands numerous times, becoming Hellenised in the process, until around 200 BC when it decided to throw itself on the mercy of Rome and asked for protection. The city flourished from then on.

It is thought that Herod the Great was born here. Whether he was or wasn't, he was certainly moved to endow the city with some fine buildings – 'he furnished the city with magnificent bath-houses and fountains as well as with an arcaded chamber of astonishing size and craftsmanship' (Josephus). For many years the city prospered, becoming a noted seat of learning. But, along with pretty well everywhere else, Ashkelon fell to the Arabs in the 7th C AD, was taken in turn by the Crusaders five centuries later and then utterly destroyed by the Mamelukes in 1270.

It has taken seven centuries for Ashkelon to be rebuilt. Now it is a modern town and a major centre for 'acclimatising' newly arrived immigrants. You'll see signs which rather ominously read 'absorption centre' all around the town. Here the *olim* are housed in apartments and attend orientation classes for their first three months in Israel. For the tourist there is a near perfect climate, miles of magnificent, clean and generally uncrowded beaches and the AQUELUNA. But Ashkelon's tourist potential has hardly been tapped at all as yet. You won't find miles of promenade hotels, cafés and shops. The promenade is there alright. Squeaky clean and shiny new and at an estimated cost in excess of £2 million. But so far either a lack of resources or the town's innate conservatism has prevented any major development. It can only be a matter of time; this is a potential gold-mine for tourist development.

Don't expect to find evidence of Ashkelon's multi-layered past in the town itself, which is uncompromisingly modern. Except for two remarkably preserved and beautifully detailed ROMAN SARCOPHAGI displayed in a courtyard in Afridar, the 'tourist' area of town, the ruins of Herod's vast buildings, columns and statuary from Greek and Roman periods and Crusader fortification walls, are instead enclosed in a beautiful seaside NATIONAL PARK a little to the north of the town, you can go down to the beach from the park itself where you will see the remains of Roman columns jutting out of the Byzantine sea-walls like so many cannon.

Further north, just above the DELILAH BEACH is a ROMAN TOMB dating from the 3rd C AD. The frescoes are in a remarkably good state of preservation; the colours still vivid and the detail still clear. Further south, the ruins of a BYZANTINE CHURCH and a faded MOSAIC FLOOR are sited prosaically, in the middle of Barnea, a suburb of the town. Neither the mosaic nor the church is particularly spectacular.

C·H·A·P·T·E·R·5
Galilee

Galilee: Introduction

For anybody who ever went to Sunday School or listened to the Bible story, the name of Galilee, a name that sounds so sweet in English, evokes the profoundest memories and associations; for this is where the brief candle of Jesus Christ's ministry flamed for three years, before it kindled the empire that ruled the world.

If you come in March, April or May, Galilee won't disappoint you, for this northern part of Israel has the highest rainfall in the country, and in those spring months the hills are cloaked in deep green grass and starred with flowers. After the scorching desolation of the deserts to the south, or after the tumult and pollution of the cities, Galilee offers a gentle respite. In the summer months Galilee is still strikingly beautiful, but much of the green on the hills turns to a parched, thorny scrub. The region used to be known as *Galil Ha-Goim*, Region of the Gentiles, now shortened to *Ha-Galil*, or Galilee.

Sea of Galilee

The focal point of the region is Lake Tiberias, known as *Kinneret* – the Harp – because of its shape. Approach this, the Sea of Galilee, with caution, for whether or not you are familiar with the New Testament story, you cannot fail to feel some echo of a response at the very sound of the name. With care you should be able to mitigate what can be disappointment. The obvious place to make for would seem to be Tiberias, often mentioned in the Bible and one of the old Holy cities of the Jews. Tiberias should in fact be avoided by anyone not in search of constant loud disco-music, parades of ice-cream parlours, noisy bathing beaches with piped music, and the all-night thump and clatter of disco-boats on the lake.

Driving up the Jordan valley is again the obvious way to get to *Kinneret*, but from here the first view is disappointing. The best way is to arrive from the hills on the western side, ideally from Safed, from whose high road there are wonderful views of the lake and its surrounding mountains. The roads from Nazareth and Afula also give you a fine first view. Try to make it early evening, just before sunset, when the mountains recede in misty ranks of blue and purple.

The Sea of Galilee is a freshwater lake 25 km long by 12 km wide. It is fed by the Jordan River, which rises at the springs of Banyas and Dan to the north. At the southern end the Jordan flows out, limpid and green between banks of eucalyptus. The lake is teeming with fish of many different kinds, notably St Peter's Fish (White Mullet), the local speciality – a bit bony, a bit bland and a bit expensive, but not bad for all that. The water of the lake is cool and clear, lovely for swimming.

Galilee also acts as a reservoir for much of the country to the south; a conduit takes water from the northern end of the lake all the way down to the Negev, for desert irrigation schemes. And of course the lake supplies irrigation during the dry months for the intensively cultivated Jordan Valley. But the water-level is alarmingly low at the moment. Many years of below average rainfall and excessive drawing on water resources, wells, springs and rivers have lowered the water-table so that the lake lies about ten feet below its normal level. There is very real cause for concern over this.

According to Josephus, the Jewish-Roman historian who wrote the *Jewish Wars*, there were in his time no fewer than nine cities surrounding the lake, each with a population of over 15,000: Tiberias, Magdala, Khorazim, Capernaum, Gadara, Susita, Gamla and others. Thus in the time of Jesus this was a populous area. Today, as a result of wars, earthquakes and the general decline that settled on the land under the later Ottomans, that population has dwindled considerably; Tiberias is the only town of any size, and the others have died and worn to barely discernible heaps of dust and stones.

GALILEE

Tiberias

George Adam Smith – author of *Historical Geography of the Holy Land* – described Tiberias as 'repellent', and there is no shortage of travellers and chroniclers to support him, but you will almost inevitably find yourself here, for Tiberias has all the hotels and facilities. It is also the place from which to take tours of Galilee. 'Egged' at the bus station operate a number of tours to various sites in northern Israel, but these have a tendency to be propaganda exercises; much better are the smaller private operators who take you in fleets of taxis.

There has been a city on this spot since ancient times; the Romans made it an important administrative centre. The young Herod the Great cut his teeth here as governor, and had a great deal to do with the planning and building of the Roman city; one of his opulent palaces formerly stood here. But perhaps by design, perhaps not, he had desecrated a Jewish cemetery in the building of the town, and thus the place became accursed to the Jews, who refused to come and live in Tiberias when Herod sought to re-populate it.

Within 100 years though, Tiberias had been ritually purified and the Jews began to move in. A number of notable rabbis, *Yohanan ben Zakkai, Maimonides* and Rabbi *Akiva*, made Tiberias the centre of Jewish scholarship through the later Roman years and into the Byzantine period. It was also the seat of the Sanhedrin during the long years when Jerusalem was denied to the Jews. Tiberias became one of the four Jewish Holy Cities, the others being Safed, Jerusalem and Hebron.

Today the town has moved north from its original position near the thermal springs which made it one of the major spa towns of the Roman empire; now it spreads round a cape and from the waterside up to the residential quarters high on the hill. This must be a welcome relief to the residents for, lying at about 210 metres below sea-level, Tiberias can be very hot indeed in the summer.

As you enter the town from the south, you pass the modern CLINIC which has grown around the HOT SPRINGS; the hot sulphurous water is said to be effective in the treatment of many ailments of the skin and other disorders. Beside the clinic are the ruins of the ROMAN BATH. A small MUSEUM, which helps to make sense of the foundations and stones of the ancient baths, is housed in the beautiful Ottoman *Hamam*, or Turkish Bath.

Then you pass the dark walls of the Crusaders, now ruined

but with enough of the towers and stones still standing to give an impression of what the town would have looked like at that time. Leaving behind the great masses of the luxury hotels – the Plaza and the Jordan River – you find yourself in the centre of Tiberias.

There are two spots of note in the town; the TOMB OF THE RABBI MAIMONIDES lies in a little park to the north-west of the town centre. Maimonides, or Rambam as he is known, is held in great reverence by the Jews, and his tomb is a very holy spot, as evidenced by the number of worshippers in devout prayer. The tomb has recently been extensively refurbished with new paths and walls. Right in the centre of town is the sorry GREAT MOSQUE, a small classical mosque from the late Ottoman period, once the centre of devotion for the Moslems of the area, now surrounded by a shabby shopping development and used as a rubbish-dump and latrine.

The town has luxury HOTELS, HOSTELS and HOSPICES in plenty, so although it is a very popular resort in summer and winter alike, there is usually somewhere to stay. Highly recommended, beautiful and reasonable, is the Scottish Hospice, set in its own gardens near the lake just north of the town centre.

Along the water-front is a PROMENADE, shaded by ilexes and lined with RESTAURANTS; here the speciality is St Peter's Fish, but it's also the nicest place in the town to sit with a beer and watch the sun set over the Sea of Galilee. As soon as the sun sets, if you don't want your reverie disturbed, I recommend that you move elsewhere; for when darkness falls, the disco boats berth along here, and shatter the stillness of the lake. It looks like fun, but somehow it seems a little incongruous, so you may want to seek spots for quieter reflection.

At the south end of the promenade is a street leading up to the town centre. The prices at the restaurants that line this street are more reasonable than those on the front, and there's an alluring variety of coffees, cakes and ice-creams on offer; but again the cacophony of a dozen different sound systems turned up to compete with one another, detracts somewhat from the ambience.

But you can't go wrong in Tiberias with a *falafel;* they're the best in the country. Up in the centre of town, where the buses stop, is the finest selection of falafel-stalls you'll see in Israel. So grab a falafel and head north out of the town for more appealing spots. Immediately to the north and south of the town are bathing 'Lidos', landscaped waterside gardens with loungers, lawns, water-sports facilities, water-slides, cafés, fish-restaurants, crowds, piped music and hefty entrance fee. Bathing near the town from anywhere but these lidos means forcing through barbed-wire to bathe from a rubbish-dump scattered with broken glass and rusty tin cans. About 2 km away from the town the pay beaches give way to public beaches, dusty and rocky and beside the main road, but the water's still clear and cool.

Leaving Tiberias

Heading north from Tiberias along the lakeside road, the first place you come to is the site of the ancient city of MAGDALA; the site is marked by a tiny blue-domed Moslem tomb under some eucalyptus trees between the road and the lake. Josephus records it as a town of 40,000 inhabitants, but he was given to exaggeration. This is the reputed home of Mary Magdalen.

Rearing up to the west is the dramatic red stone cliff of WADI HAMAM, the 'Valley of the Pigeons'. When Herod was made governor of Galilee, he distinguished his early career by flushing out the bandits who lived in the caves on this cliff. It is said that he lowered his soldiers in baskets and smoked the unfortunate bandits out. At the head of the valley here is the TOMB OF JETHRO, *Nebi Shuweib*. Jethro was the father-in-law of Moses, and is held in high esteem by the Druze of Israel.

After Magdala the road leaves the shore, and the flat plain between the two towns starts to fill with the lush green of banana plantations, citrus trees, avocados and even a domesticated version of the *Sabra*, or prickly pear – without prickles. In the midst of this startling greenery is KIBBUTZ GINNOSAR. This is one of the many Kibbutzim which, taking advantage of the demand for tourist accommodation, have diversified into the hotel industry. Ginnosar is a fairly luxurious establishment with swimming pool, well landscaped gardens and a high standard of facilities and service. Ginnosar is a pleasant alternative to staying in Tiberias; the tour-buses stop here to pick up customers on the way out from town, it's on the shore of the lake and it's peaceful.

Tabgha

A couple of kilometres north of Ginnosar, turn right off the main road to TABGHA. Here there is a YOUTH HOSTEL and a CAMPSITE on the banks of the lake; it's cheap and basic but idyllic, set in a grove of trees right on the edge of the water. A

Mosaic of the Loaves and Fishes, Tabgha

little further on is Tabgha itself (Tabgha is an arabisation of the Greek *Heptapegon* – seven springs). This is the site of the miracle of the loaves and fishes. A modern BENEDICTINE CHURCH, simple and pleasing, marks the spot. Inside the church is the stone where Jesus broke the bread and fishes; set within the stone is a 5th C mosaic depicting two Galilee mullet, while the floor is a wonderful mosaic representation of the flora and fauna of Galilee. Nearby is a much older GREEK ORTHODOX CHURCH set in a beautiful little garden, peaceful and lovely on the shore of Galilee.

It is in these tiny unassuming churches in the rural areas of the Holy Land that one feels closest to the events that marked this part of the world as the spring of Christianity.

CAPERNAUM

Continuing along the shore of the lake, you soon reach *Kfar Nahum*, CAPERNAUM, the town where Jesus lived and preached and cursed the inhabitants. Jesus' ministry in His home town of Nazareth got off to a poor start when the townsfolk tried to throw Him over a cliff; accordingly He decided to try at Capernaum, probably teaching in the synagogue that antedates the present one. His teachings created a profound impression; even more so did His casting out of an unclean spirit and the later healing of the man with the crippled hand. It was here that He healed the centurion's servant and raised a dead girl to life (Mark 5: 41). Here Peter's mother-in-law was healed, along with many others. Later at the synagogue He explained to His disciples and others that unless they drank His blood and ate His flesh, they would have no life in them. After this 'hard saying', many forsook him (John 6: 1–66).

This was a major town in the time of Jesus, and is today one of the most important archaeological sites in the area. As a lakeside port it was probably the site of the customs house where Jesus found Matthew. The most striking part of the ruins is the beautiful 3rd C synagogue. This is to be seen in the centre of the town, a partly reconstructed building of white limestone with much of the fine decorative detail still intact.

The synagogue is a noble and beautifully proportioned building, but the carved decorations, are particularly striking. Notable among these is the insignia of the Roman Tenth Legion, two eagles holding a wreath of laurel in their beaks – a curious mingling of Roman military with Jewish religious motifs. It is believed that the actual stones of the decoration came from an earlier synagogue which would have stood on the site in the time of Jesus.

Capernaum is a holy site, and whether you get there by car, coach or by one of the ferries from Tiberias, you will be expected to 'dress modestly'. Interesting though Capernaum is, it would be a great deal more interesting with the provision of some sort of museum or display to inform the visitor.

CHURCH OF THE BEATITUDES

Back to the main road and up the hill to the MOUNT OF THE BEATITUDES. There used to be a Franciscan convent hospice here, but it's no longer open – a pity, because it must have been one of the loveliest places in the Holy Land to stay. In the 1930s the Italians built a church on the long hill sloping down to the lake, where the multitudes gathered to hear Jesus preach the Sermon on the Mount. The church is unashamedly modern, octagonal and surrounded by an arcaded gallery, with the Stations of the Cross depicted round the walls, and the Virtues in marble on the floor. It's a lovely church, in a beautiful evocative spot. If you can get here by about 8:00, before the tour buses arrive, you can have the garden all to yourself.

Mount of Beatitudes

Khorazin

Back on the main road, continuing uphill past the Mount of Beatitudes, a red sign after 5 km points right to KHORAZIN. It seems impossible that Khorazin could once have been a town of over 15,000 inhabitants. What remains today looks as if it had been a small village, crudely hacked from the black basalt. Some arches and walls still stand, and there's a graceful black synagogue and an olive-press.

But to be truthful, Khorazin is poor fare for the tourist in search of tangible and inspiring remains from the past. Many sites are similarly disappointing in the Holy Land; the great temples and statues are fallen to the ground, and the wind and weather of the ages, and the folly of man, have made of them shapeless mounds of stones and dust. What they do have though, is evocative atmosphere; they awaken a sense of history and time and if you have the time and inclination to sit for an hour as the sun rises or sets, or in the heat of the day as the sun bakes the ancient stones and cracks the seed-pods of the brittle scrub all around, you can feel the ghosts of these old villages and cities swarming around you.

As you turn right off the main road to go down to Khorazin, you will see on the left a neat-looking ranch with horses running around in a corral, and beautiful landscaped gardens. This is *Vered Ha Galil*, the Rose of Galilee, a centre for riding and trekking in the hills of Galilee. Accommodation is in chalets dotted around the grounds or more cheaply in the bunk-house. They offer guided riding and hiking by the hour or by the day, even riding trips all round Israel. This is certainly one of the best ways of seeing and enjoying the country, with guides who have been travelling around like this for years and really know where to go. Ring 06–935785, or write Vered Hagalil, M.P. Korazim 12385, Galilee Israel.

As you continue along the road past Capernaum and round the northern shore of the Sea of Galilee, you come to the delta of the Jordan River where it flows into Kinneret. You cross the river by a Bailey-bridge just north of where it spreads out into a broad delta of marshy vegetation. This is a fine spot for watching water-birds and waders, but mind the mosquitoes.

EN GEV

From the front at Tiberias, boats leave several times a day for *En Gev*, on the eastern shore of Galilee. This is the better shore for bathing or strolling by the water's edge. There are FREE PUBLIC BEACHES, backed by shady woods all the way, without the barbed wire and rubbish that characterises the western shore. It's quieter too. Midway along the eastern side is the Kibbutz *En Gev*, at the foot of the steep scarp of the Golan Heights. Here is a bathing beach and a fine FISH RESTAURANT as well as comfortable Kibbutz accommodation. In spring the Kibbutz hosts a celebrated Israeli FESTIVAL OF MUSIC AND DANCE. On the hill above the Kibbutz lie the ruins of Susita, one of the ancient cities of Galilee, although little remains to see today.

GOLAN HEIGHTS

The Golan Heights have only been part of Israel since 1967, when they were taken from Syria during the Six Day War.

On a clear day from the Golan Heights you can see right across Northern Israel to the sea. In the days when the heights were Syrian territory, the Syrians were not averse to using this strategic advantage to shell settlements in the Hula Valley and Northern Israel. Understandably the Israelis resented this, so they took the Heights, and are now engaged in stamping it with their indelible mark. There are Kibbutzim, Moshavim and new settlements dotted all over the place. Generous tax incentives are given to settlers in order to encourage them to live in this potentially volatile and somewhat godforsaken place; army camps abound, along with barbed wire, minefields and bunkers – the handiwork of both sides. Despite all this, for the traveller or tourist, the place is quite safe.

Once you have climbed up the steep western flank of the Heights, you are faced with a great expanse of steeply rolling hill-country with hardly a tree to be seen. In summer the vegetation is limited to tall dense scrub of vicious thorns and thistles, baked brittle and hard by the intense sunshine. The colours are amber, ochre and yellow, broken by piles of dark basalt stones. Overhead wheel eagles, vultures and a rich variety of other wild birds. In autumn and spring this forbidding and inhospitable vegetation becomes a carpet of green, shot with hundreds of different species of wild flowers, for this area has the highest rainfall of anywhere in the country.

Qazrin

There are no big towns up here; the biggest is QAZRIN, a little one-horse new town, rising starkly out of the bare plain. It's a curious phenomenon, for the road to Qazrin is little more than a rough and rutted back-road, and all of a sudden you find yourself sweeping along a brand new dual carriageway built for huge volumes of city traffic; pedestrian bridges arch overhead to carry the ceaseless throng safely across the endless flow of traffic – but there is nobody about; the place is like a ghost town during working hours. The thorny scrub has been banished from the the new town, and gardens of oleanders, bougainvillaea and plumbago sprout from carefully tended lawns. A leisure complex with a swimming-pool and tennis courts keeps the inhabitants happy and healthy.

If you have taken an Egged tour to Qazrin, you may be deposited for half an hour to ruminate among the wares of the town's jewellery and gew-gaw workshop. Here the discerning can buy a number of interesting gold and silver artefacts, including diamond-encrusted playboy bunnies. This is an arrangement worked between the tour guides and the proprietors of the jewellery company, and is not really in the best interests of the tourist.

When you have had your fill of the cave of wonders aforementioned, you can visit Qazrin's ARCHAEOLOGY MUSEUM. Here are displayed many of the finds from the area. In the garden are the pillars and lintels, capitals and carvings of the various synagogues that have been found up here, all hacked from the dull black basalt that furnished the only building material in the region. The rest of the museum is devoted to a good display of the early civilisation that bloomed in this area, well explained and illustrated by means of display cases full of artefacts, drawings and charts. Just outside the town are the impressive remains of one of the synagogues, stark and black on the hillside. You are not encouraged to go wandering about up here though, as there are said to be minefields everywhere!

Gamla

About 15 km south of Qazrin is GAMLA. Gamla is sometimes described as the 'Masada of the North', because of the historical and geographical similarities. Gamla again is built of the black basalt stones, an extensive walled city set on a mighty promontory among the scrub. The best way to approach Gamla is to take the road running east from the shore of Galilee, climbing up the spur of a long hill. The valley below you to your left contains a ribbon of greenery where the river runs among the rocks.

The setting of the city is magnificent – on a high rocky promontory between two deep gorges. On the east side would have been a fortified wall to complete the defence provided by nature. Opposite the city, on the rocks of the northern gorge, is a colony of eagles, their eyries perched among tall pinnacles of rock. Swifts and eagles swirl to and fro on the thermals below the city walls. This position made the city virtually impregnable, and it took the resourceful Romans, to whom Gamla was a constant thorn, much time and effort to take it. When they finally did take it, the story goes that the inhabitants hurled themselves from the cliffs rather than suffer dishonour at the hands of the Romans – hence the Masada parallel.

The city is more than 2,000 years old, but it seems that the area was not colonised after its destruction; until recently the only inhabitants were semi-nomadic shepherds and their flocks. So the original city plan remains almost intact. Of course the buildings are in a sorry state, but one can still easily make out the synagogues, oil-presses, granaries and private houses of the people who lived here long ago. As yet the site had only newly been adopted by the Parks and Monuments Commission; as always they've got the toll-booth up, but there's no display, museum, or anything else to help you orient yourself. A few signs and a leaflet in Hebrew do little to dispel the gloom. Hopefully something will be done about this, because Gamla is an important and fascinating historical link.

From the car-park a marked path leads north and south. At both ends are WATERFALLS at the head of the two flanking valleys. The north path takes you after half an hour to a small waterfall, just dribbling in summer, not far from the eagle colony. The south path takes you to a full-blown cascade spraying down to a deep rock-pool and a stream shaded by oleanders and willow. This seems like a miracle in these shadeless hills. The water is clear, fresh, cold and good to drink; the pool is perfect for bathing. The walk takes you along the edge of the steep valley, where you may be lucky and see rock-badgers scuttling and chucking in the crags below. Eagles and lizards and the strange harsh flora of this country you will see in profusion. Much recommended – nobody goes to Gamla, which makes it all the better.

Dotted on the side of the road leading to the town are many DOLMENS, the curious evidence of even older civilisations.

Hammat Gader

From the southern tip of the Sea of Galilee, take the yellow road – 98 – east up through the hills to HAMMAT GADER. For 6 or 7 km the road follows a dramatic valley up through the mountains. On the south side is a river, and a wrecked railway with broken bridges. A business-like barbed wire fence follows the road; on the other side is a minefield, then Jordan. The valley and the hills are dry and barren – a place of stones and scorpions – until suddenly a rich green oasis appears spread out below; huge pools of a fish-farm, forests of bananas and a park. Here is Hammat Gader, one of the great spa-towns of the Roman Empire. Today it's enjoying a revival with its alligator park, fish restaurant, trampolines, children's park – wonderful remains of the Roman baths – for me one of the finest Roman remains in Israel, though very poorly displayed – and its own new sulphurous hot pool in which to bathe. This really is a great treat, though signs tell you that bathing in the smelly water for more than 15 minutes can be 'hazardous to your life'.

Once you've been through the toll-booth, the first thing you come to is the ALLIGATOR PARK. This may seem a curious phenomenon, for one does not generally associate the land of Palestine with alligators; but as late as the turn of the century the rivers and swamps that then made up the coastal plain were infested with crocodiles. These may have been the 'Behemoths' or 'Leviathans' referred to in the book of Job – 40 41. Alligators are said to live to as much as a hundred years in captivity. They are certainly economical with their energy; it's not easy to tell whether they are dead or alive as they float phlegmatically with just the tips of their nostrils and their beady eyes above the water. This is a sort of alligator farm as well as being edifying for the visitor. The alligators live in a well landscaped park with ponds, trees and islands; they seem well contented with this environment, though the inscrutable alligator gives little away about his feelings. The visitor surveys the scene from a wooden walkway of bridges and paths, just above snapping height.

The display takes you right through from the hatching eggs and the endearing little ones in the terrarium, through frisky youth – a phenomenon which is distinguishable from the torpor of age by an occasional raffish flick of the tail and a wink. Then comes venerable age, and finally a dignified metamorphosis into a handbag, shoe or belt – available in the souvenir shop. Even for those who are unenthusiastic about alligators, this park is a very worthwhile visit.

From the alligators, follow the perimeter of the park round to the ROMAN BATHS. Much still remains here and from what you can still see this must have been a magnificent spa. Round the back is a pool and a stream of blue-green sulphurous water – at boiling point. The water was channelled by a sophisticated system of pipes through the various steam, hot, warm and cool rooms. The site was excavated in 1979; a museum and a coherent display is planned and will be very welcome. These baths are really worth seeing.

On the lawns under the tall date-palms are the CHILDREN'S PLAYGROUND, WATER-SLIDES and much vaunted FISH-RESTAURANT. There are also the remains of a 5th C SYNAGOGUE on a hill at the western end of the park, looking down the Yarmuk River valley.

Ancient synagogue of Bar'am

More in keeping with modern trends and styles is the great blue steaming pool, fed by the hot waters of the sulphur springs. The water is *very* hot near the source, and is about as difficult to get into as a very hot bath, but the temperature becomes more bearable once you get out into the open pool. It's rather pleasant, swimming in a huge hot bath beneath a blazing sun. Extravagant claims about the youth-restoring properties of the water are not to be taken too seriously! There are showers to stop you smelling like a rotten egg as the mineral-rich water dries on you.

Rosh Pinna

If you're leaving Galilee for the west, the most spectacular route to take is the road 89, from Rosh Pinna up to Safed. From the high forests in the hills that the road passes through, you have a startling view of the mountains of Galilee with the lake glittering far below. Up in the forest are miles of trails, a lovely spot to do some walking.

At the junction of the Safed road with the main Tiberias – *Qiryat Shemona* road, lies the village of ROSH PINNA.

In the 1880s a group of Romanian Jews came to Palestine to buy land and set up a farming community, far from the harsh oppression of Jews in their native land of Romania. This was to be one of the very first communities of settlers to return to Israel from the Diaspora. The land they bought was good and although they were not farmers – as was often the case with these earlier settlers; rather they were merchants, lawyers, doctors, etc. – for the Jews were generally forbidden to engage in soldiering or agriculture – their idealising of the dignity and glory of physical labour paid off and the enterprise became very successful. The village grew and today it is a large and prosperous community with smart modern houses lining neatly landscaped roads.

The old part of the village, built to echo the style familiar to the Romanians, still survives. It is up the hill to the north-west of the main road junction. At the foot of the old town is the YOUTH HOSTEL, whence a cobbled stone road leads up to a couple of streets of old Rosh Pinna. There is a BAR/CAFE on a terrace with fine views of the valley below. The old stone houses of the village are being restored; soon it may look something less of a ghost town. The Youth Hostel here is good to stay in, and the bar is good for a beer and a snack, but Rosh Pinna itself is not really worth a long journey unless you have a speciality interest here. After a stroll and some refreshment in the bar, continue up the road towards Safed.

GALILEE

HAZOR

Leaving the Sea of Galilee by the main *Qiryat Shemona* road to the north, you climb a long hill with beautiful views over the lake. After the pass you drop steadily down towards the Hula Valley. Before entering the plain, the road sinks into a deep cleft, dominated by an imposing hill on the west side. This hill is the *tel* of the city of HAZOR.

Hazor was one of the three great ancient cities of the land of Canaan, prominent as long ago as 2,000 BC; the other two being Megiddo and Gezer. It was in the 13th C BC that Joshua, at the head of the tribes of Israel, routed the Canaanites in confederation under the king of Hazor. 'Joshua smote its king with the sword . . . and burned Hazor with fire' (Josh 11.) Under the reigns of David, Solomon and Ahab, the city maintained its importance. Its final destruction came with the Assyrians under Tigrath-Pileser in 732 BC; in roughly 2,000 years the city was destroyed and rebuilt 21 times – once in 100 years. Such a well-fortified and strategic city must have been a desperate place to live!

There were two main factors determining the site of major cities in the ancient world: strategic situation, and access to water during peace and war. The site upon which Hazor is built is a perfect illustration of a fortress city guarding an important highway and trade-route. Even today the main road from the great centres and fertile valleys of the south, which would have led in less troubled times to the cities and trading centres of lands to the north, passes through a narrow defile to the east of the city. Hemmed between the impassable marshes in the Hula Valley to the east, and the mountains of *Naftalya* to the west.

As for water, a well with an abundant supply of water has been unearthed by the archaeologists. This well and the tunnel bringing the water into the heart of the city is twice as big as that of Megiddo, as indeed is the city.

Hazor was the greatest among the cities, 'head of all those kingdoms', according to a contemporary document. Archaeological research was carried out in the 1950s and 1960s. Many of the finds have been placed in the museum over the road, though the major ones are in the Israel Museum in Jerusalem. The museum, with its model of the old city, is worth visiting, for the *tel*, much like other *tels*, doesn't reveal much by itself. In fact a *tel* is indistinguishable from a slag-heap to the uninitiated. What you do get from a *tel* is a wonderful sense of place; a place to ponder the immensity of history, the cursory nature of civilisations. Here there are no less than 21 different periods of them.

These *tels* are the 'Cities fortified up to Heaven' that we hear of in the Bible – against which the Israelites were sent. After each successive destruction of the city, the ruins would be flattened and used as a foundation for the next city to be built on the site. They grew considerably in height and defensive advantage each time. This practice, although obviously sensible, did not take into consideration the work of archaeologists in years to come, for the problems of excavating a *tel* are mind-boggling. The archaeologists had little trouble identifying the layer of the Canaanite city – that laid low by Joshua – for, as was the case with all of Joshua's handiwork, this was the charred and blackened layer.

HULA VALLEY AND NATURE RESERVE

Drop down off the hill from the heights above Hazor, and you will see to the east a great green plain, lush and fertile. This is the HULA VALLEY, one of Israel's major agricultural successes. Older maps of Palestine show three great inland seas, like beads threaded upon the Jordan River: the largest, in the south, is the Dead Sea, the next, the Sea of Galilee; and the small one to the north, the Lake of Hula, which no longer exists. Today the lake has become the Hula Valley, a fertile agricultural area. Lake Hula and its surrounding marshes used to be a paradise for wildlife, flora and fauna. It was home to an astonishing variety of creatures – water-buffalo, storks, cranes, kingfishers, dragonflies. etc.

In 1950 the Israelis started an ambitious drainage scheme to convert the beautiful but pestilential marshes into farmland. The young country, with so many geographical and political factors arrayed against it, could not afford to waste a single acre of the potentially fertile land, so, despite protests from international conservation societies, they went ahead. It worked; and today the area is one of the richest and best watered farmlands in the whole of Israel. But having destroyed the natural habitat of so many species, and effectively banished them from the country for ever, something had to be done to redress the balance.

The result was the Hula Nature Reserve, a small concession to the departed creatures who had either died out or were now living in exile. Today you can see again the buffalo, wild boar, herons, storks, ducks, etc. that used to live here. One of the guided tours round the reserve is well worth the small investment. The best time to visit, as with everywhere else, is in April when thousands of migrating birds break their journey here in the marshes.

Hurshat Tal

Continue along the main road north along the western edge of the Hula Valley, until you reach QIRYAT SHEMONA; there are some good HOTELS here for those spending a few days visiting the area, but the town has little to recommend it. Turn east along the 99, and after about 3 km on the right you will see the sign for HURSHAT TAL.

'Forest of Dew' is the name of this nature reserve, a lovely park full of ancient Ilexes shading the banks of the Dan river. It is curious that these trees should have survived in a land where every scrap of wood has traditionally been grabbed and used for firewood or building materials, and, until now, not replanted. Some of the trees are said to be 2,000 years old.

The survival of the younger ones may be attributed to a legend that has made the trees sacred to the Moslems. Ten Messengers of Mohammed halted one day in the barren wilderness that was then *Hurshat Tal*. There was not a stitch of wood for shade or for tethering their horses. Disgusted with the spot, they drove their sticks into the ground to tether their horses and lay down to sleep with no fire for comfort, pleasure and safety. In the morning, when they awoke, they found themselves shaded by a forest of immense leafy oaks which had grown overnight from the planted sticks. It's a lovely legend, another one of the tests of the faith in which the Holy Land abounds.

As a result of this, this spot has long been holy to the Moslems – several tombs are nearby – and they have been able to protect the trees from desecration. Lovely spot for a cool swim and a picnic in the shade on a hot day.

Dan

'From Dan to Beersheba' is how the Bible delineates the extent of the Land of the Israelites. Dan is almost as far north as you can go in today's Israel. The *tel* of Dan, although the site of the important Canaanite city of Laish, some 5,000 years ago, is only of interest to the most specialised visitor; indeed it's a job to recognise it as a *tel* at all.

The attraction of Dan today is as one of the principal sources of the Jordan, and as a NATURE RESERVE. The source of the Jordan here is already a furiously rushing river. No tinkling mountain stream this, but a roaring torrent raging straight out of the ground. It winds its way in several streams intertwining and parting only to unite again, through a curious and unique forest. This has been tended and landscaped by the local Kibbutz and, with the addition of the ubiquitous toll-booth, car-park and cafe, turned into a regular tourist site. If you happen to be passing, it's a pleasant, cool shady wood, with big streams rushing through. It also has a certain number of interesting botanical specimens, such as pistachio trees – but the flora, and the elusive and invisible fauna, are not striking enough to make it a place for a long detour.

This was where Jeroboam I set up the golden calves when Israel and Judah split after the reign of Solomon. The prophets ranted, for this was one of the most heinous crimes against the Covenant, and a failing to which the Israelites were particularly given. But in mitigation it must be remembered that the northern tribes of Israel no longer had access to the Temple in Jerusalem for worship, and thus were unable to fulfil their duty of worshipping there three times a year. They needed something through which to direct their prayers and sacrifices to God.

The graven images were probably set up here just because of the general delightfulness of the place, and the fact that it marked the northern boundary of Jeroboam's kingdom rather than for any orthodox pious reason. The ancients rightly believed that the beauty spots of nature were the abodes of the gods.

Banyas

At the foot of the slopes of Mt Hermon lie the spectacular SPRINGS AND FALLS of Banyas. The River Jordan has a number of different sources up here, but none quite so startling as the springs of Banyas; the water pours out from beneath a wall of rock, already a full-blown rushing river. Running crystal clear over a bed of shingle, it runs beneath the SELF-SERVICE RESTAURANT, under the road, and away down to the magnificent falls. Unfortunately the great cave from which it used to emerge has fallen in, probably as the result of one of the many earthquakes that have troubled this area.

The springs and the falls are considered as two separate sites, so you have to pay for entry to both; what you're paying for is a toll-booth, car-park, a souvenir shop and someone to pick up some of the rubbish. The springs are a very popular picnic and tourist spot in the summer. Swimming is forbidden here but at least you can go for a dip in the pool below the waterfall. These falls are one of those miraculous green spots in the parched desert, but less agreeable than Gamla because of all the people.

Dusty paths and steps lead up the hill from the main spring.

There are some nondescript and unimpressive caves, little more than indentations in the rock; a rock-cut shrine to the god Pan, he with the pipes and the legs of a faun. This takes the form of a small niche, about a yard across, with a vault in the shape of a shell. Farther up the hill is the tiny Moslem shrine of *El Khader*, the ubiquitous St George.

NIMROD CASTLE

From Banyas, look upward to the east and you may catch a glimpse of the spectacular Castle of NIMROD, or *Surbaiya*. It's just a few kilometres away, along the main road on the way to Mount Hermon.

The northernmost of Palestine's Crusader castles, Nimrod stands on a dizzy perch, a southern spur of Mount Hermon, dominating the important trade routes from Acre and Tyre to Damascus. The site is stupendous and you find yourself wondering at the skill and hardiness of the Crusaders in building their magnificent fortifications in such lofty and inaccessible spots. Of course it was all done by slave labour, the Crusaders themselves being so few in number. Nevertheless the achievements are spectacular, and few places demonstrate this better than Nimrod.

The fortress guards one of the main northern passes into Palestine. It was built by the Crusaders in the 12th C, though the Moslems have held it at various time since then and added their own additions. The castle is in a sad state of decay, but there is enough left standing to give you an idea of the magnificence of the original building.

What will always remain though is the beauty of the site; it's a place to come in the evening, when the castle is shut, sneak up over the walls and enjoy the view as the sun sets over the receding ridges of mountains to the west. Shadows and ghosts are your only companions, save flocks of mosquitoes as big as sparrows – if you plan to do some ruminating up here, which I strongly recommend, bring some insect repellent.

THE DRUZE VILLAGES OF UPPER GALILEE

High on the lower slopes of Mt Hermon are the two Druze villages of MAJDAL SHAMS and MASADA, set beside the curious crater-lake of *Berekhat Ram*. There are outposts of Druze dotted all over Israel, as well as major communities in Syria, Lebanon and elsewhere. The setting of the villages is spectacular and high for Israel, though it's not particularly beautiful. There are few trees up here; the land is sparse-looking pasture for the flocks of the villagers. They also grow fruit; a great apple orchard spreads a patch of green against the dry hills beneath Majdal Shams. The villages have an air of developing prosperity; large villas are starting to spring up on the outskirts, but all in all they are not attractive, and have nothing to offer the tourist, apart from a café and souvenir-shop above the lake.

The lake has been credited as the source of the Jordan at odd times, but subsequent investigations have not borne this out. Philip, the son of Herod threw chaff into the lake in the hope of seeing it come out in the river below; but a zealous and loyal attendant, not wanting his master to be disappointed, and careless of the dissemination of truth, cast chaff into the river where it emerges from the rocks at Banyas. The plot was discovered though; Birket Ram is not the source of the Jordan.

Mount Hermon

The Druze villages are on the lower slopes of Mount Hermon, the highest mountain in Israel at 9,000 ft. With one foot in Israel, one in Syria and one in Lebanon, you would expect it to be as volatile as an active volcano; it is quiet though, at the moment. Perhaps the enduring nature of this contentiously sited mountain could be seen as a sign of hope for an eventual agreement and understanding between the warring countries of the Middle East; for what are 50 years to a mountain?

Anyway, it's so peaceful now that beneath the international surveillance posts on the summit, there is a SKI CENTRE and a NATURE RESERVE. The skiing may not be the best in the world, but it's very popular with the Israelis. If you visit in the winter, try and make it a weekday as the lifts and slopes are packed on *Shabat*.

You can stay at *Moshav Neve Ativ* for visiting the area in summer or winter, the most convenient spot for exploring the high part of northern Israel.

Szfat

Ringing a high hilltop in the mountains to the northwest of Galilee is SAFED. At over 2,800 ft, it is the highest town in Israel. In summer this makes the air a little cooler than the rest of the country, and in July and August the little town becomes a very popular holiday spot for the Israelis. It's only about 25 km from the Sea of Galilee, and makes a good centre for exploring all parts of Northern Israel. It has HOTELS to suit every pocket; there's the expensive and beautifully appointed Rimon, cleverly converted from the old Ottoman Post Office. With it gardens, swimming pool and fine situation right in the middle of the artists' quarter, it's probably about the most agreeable hotel in the north of the country. More reasonable, and still in a nice part of town, just off Jerusalem Road, are a number of other hotels: the Carmel, the Tel Aviv, the Hadar and the Galil.

Zefat is a very ancient city, one of four holy cities of the Jews, and for hundreds of years one of the most important centres of Jewish scholarship; but it has so often been destroyed that virtually nothing of the old city remains today. Today the oldest and most attractive part of the town, the Arab Quarter, has been preserved as an 'Artists' Quarter'. Apart from this, the only other buildings of any note in the town are the four SYNAGOGUES and the OTTOMAN MOSQUE which is now shamefully and shortsightedly used as a municipal rubbish dump and urinal. The massive arches and vaults of this mosque are strikingly beautiful; but they are in desperate need of restoration. The existence of this mosque seems to be denied; it doesn't appear on any maps or in any books, though it is certainly the most distinctive building in Safed.

Just off *Kikar ha Meginim*, below the Carmel Hotel, is the synagogue quarter, one of the prettiest parts of the city. There are a number of notable and very old synagogues here, though all much restored due to the ravages of earthquakes. The ABUHAV Synagogue, named after Rabbi Isaac Abuhav, the 15th C cabalist and scholar, was destroyed in the earthquake of 1837 – all, that is, except the south wall that faced Jerusalem. This singular fact was attributed to the holiness of Abuhav's Torah scroll.

The CARO Synagogue, from the 16th C, is notable for its beauty and simplicity. The *Ashkenazi* HA'ARI Synagogue, destroyed by an earthquake in 1852, has a beautiful ark with 19th C carving.

The Artists' Quarter is Safed's reason for being, for a town cannot survive by its views alone. The artists of Israel know when they're on to a good thing. At Safed they have taken the old Arab village, picturesquely straggling down the hillside, adorned it with flowers and gardens and wooden balconies and sculptures, and converted all the houses to studios. It's undeniably attractive, and one finds oneself wishing that the inhabitants of more Israeli towns and villages were blessed with this aesthetic sensibility. Over 200 artists and their studios live in the quarter. All the galleries are open to the street and you are more than welcome to wander in, peruse the wares and chat to the incumbent. Unless you are going to spend a week or more here though, you will need to choose which galleries to visit. At the north-west end of the quarter is a general gallery containing samples of all the artists' work; have a look in here until you find something which interests you, find the name on the map, and go and visit the artist of your choice. It's a most agreeable way to spend a day.

The other sights of Safed are pretty thin on the ground. The TOURIST OFFICE is on *Rehov Yerushelayim*. The METZUDE GARDENS, on the hill leading up to the old CRUSADER CITADEL, are shady and peaceful. At the top is a modern AMPHITHEATRE. At the other end of the top are the remains of the Crusader Citadel, built in 1140 by Foulques of Anjou, and subsequently destroyed by the Mameluke Baybars – whom we have to thank for a good part of the destruction of Crusader remains in the Holy Land. The combination of frequent earthquakes and the expansion of the Jewish and Arab quarters in the town below have ensured that scarcely a stone of the old castle remains in place. The excavators have left nothing here to inform the casual visitor, and the whole thing is fenced off anyway – a big disappointment for Crusader enthusiasts. At the top of the steps leading down to Jerusalem street is a BIBLE MUSEUM.

In the hills around Safed are HIKING TRAILS AND PICNIC SPOTS.

Seven km to the west, at MERON, are the tombs of Rabbi Shimon and his son Rabbi Eleazar. These tombs are perhaps the most important Jewish place of pilgrimage in the Holy Land today. The Rabbis lived in the 2nd C AD and were leading exponents of Talmudic literature. Fleeing from the Romans, Shimon took refuge in a cave where he devoted himself to the composition of his cabalistic treatise, *Zohar*, the Brightness. His cave was blessed with a carob tree and a spring, and off these he lived for thirteen years. The great pilgrimage takes place on the feast of *Lag Beomer*, on the 33rd day after the Feast of Passover. The Rabbis Hillel and Shammai also have their tombs on Mount Meron.

BAR'AM

Heading west out of Zefat on the main road to Akko, you're in rough hilly country dotted with Mediterranean pine. A few miles winding long the back road towards Sasa, takes you to BAR'AM. It's a fair way out, along narrow hill-roads, which means it is not so peopled with sightseers as are more accessible sites. A lone Arab boy dozes in the shade by his toll-booth, waiting for the rare visitor.

Once you get there, you know it's worth it, for Bar'am has one of the best preserved early SYNAGOGUES in the country (see p. 141): sophisticated, beautiful work, carefully sculpted and carved from the limestone. The pillars and friezes still standing testify to the existence of an artistically advanced culture in Byzantine times. The synagogue is rich and lavish and worth the trouble of a visit. Scattered around are the ruins of an Arab village and the wrecked remains of a Christian Arab church.

'Let my people return' is the slogan daubed on the wall of the building on the edge of the site – therein lies a story. In 1948 *Kafr Bir'im,* as it was then known, had a population of 950 Marronite Christian Arabs. These people had for many years lived in harmony and co-operation with the Jews of Palestine. In 1945 they were known to have given assistance to the Zionists in bringing in Jewish immigrants from Lebanon, at considerable risk to themselves. In 1948, when fighting broke out between the Arabs and Jews, the people of *Kafr Bir'im* refused to join the Arabs or give them support.

When the Israeli forces arrived in the village in October 1948, they were welcomed by the villagers. Two weeks later the villagers were ordered to move out temporarily because of the strategic location of their village in the light of an expected Arab offensive. They complied and moved to temporary shelter in nearby caves. Shortly afterwards they were moved to the nearby village of Jish, where they were promised that they would soon be able to return to their homes. That was 40 years ago, and despite constant requests to the authorities, these trusting and peaceful people have been ignored, the promises forgotten.

Lower Galilee

Nazareth

The town of Nazareth is a great test of faith. Of course there is no doubt that Jesus spent the formative years of his life here, but one always has a faint hope that Nazareth will still be a quiet little hilltown with a street of carpenters' shops. But you know it won't be – and it isn't. It's an ugly seething modern town; along with Tiberias perhaps the greatest disappointment in Israel.

From the south, you arrive in the town on Paulus VI street at the bottom of the hill. You can't help noticing the BASILICA OF

THE ANNUNCIATION; it's the grandest church in the town, towering, octagonal with a hideous dome, but wealthy, sophisticated and modern – completed in 1966. The church, which is much more agreeable inside than out, is built upon the preserved remains of a Byzantine and a Crusader church, on the supposed site of Mary's home; here, it is said, the Angel Gabriel appeared to Mary and told her of the birth of her son.

The Greek Orthodox Church would have it otherwise. They take the site of the Annunciation to be Mary's Well – the Angel appeared to her while she was drawing water. In fact the Bible says that Gabriel appeared to Mary twice, once at the well and once in her home. The Greek Church of St Gabriel is half a km up the main road to the northeast; on the corner is a curious modern brick contrivance built round the well; turn left and continue up the hill to the castellated gate in the walls of St Gabriel's. The Greeks have built their church over the spot where the spring still gushes to this day. This, to me, is the finest church in the town; the interior is Byzantine, richly decorated with frescoes. At the back, behind the altar, is a clear rushing spring which used to feed the well down the road. Tall domes and vaults rear into the gloom swirling with vibrant paintings from the life of Christ – a cool, quiet and holy place. The Crusaders built the first church here, and their arches still survive in the Crypt.

There are RESTAURANTS and CAFÉS outside this church, should you require sustenance; if not, back to the Church of the Annunciation. To reach it you must walk up the hill on Casa Nova St, past the TOURIST OFFICE on the left; after a few bauble and gewgaw emporia, the entrance will be seen on the right. Enter through the great west door.

Church of the Annunciation

Recent archaeological evidence has uncovered a church dating from before the time of Constantine, although this was destroyed long before the building of the second church in the 4th and 5th Centuries, under the aegis of Helena. The Cave of the Annunciation lay below the level of the church. By the end of the 11th C, when the crusaders arrived, the church was ruined. Tancred built a new one and very magnificent, too – see the astonishing capitals of this church with their beautiful carving in the Monastery Museum – but it was destroyed along with the Christian population of Nazareth in 1263 by the Mameluke Baybars.

Under the first years of Turkish rule, Nazareth was destroyed, as was the church, the only surviving part being the

Church of the Annunciation, Nazareth

actual Cave of the Annunciation. In 1620 the Franciscans succeeded in establishing a monastery; in 1730 they set about building a new church on the sacred spot. It was a very modest church, cobbled together in a mere six months, but it was all they had. In 1877 they were able to add a rather grander façade. The new church lay across the foundations and ruins of the early Basilica and the Crusader church. It was tolerable as a functional church, but didn't really fit the bill for such an important holy site, and certainly could not accommodate the increasing throngs of pilgrims who came at the festivals.

In 1907 excavations were carried out to discover the churches that had previously occupied the site. It was only during these excavations that the earliest church was discovered. In 1955 it was decided to pull down the 1730 church and have a really good look at the site; much of interest to archaeologists was discovered. When the site was properly cleared, Signor Muzio, the Italian architect, set about erecting the enormous church that occupies the spot today.

He had to build something grand enough for the dignity of the place, big enough to accommodate the thousands of pilgrims who visit Nazareth, incorporate and preserve the Cave and the remains of the three earlier churches, and cram the whole in between the building of the existing convent and the streets of Nazareth.

He decided to build not one but two churches, an upper and a lower. The outer walls more or less follow the lines of the Crusader Basilica. The surviving relics of the Crusader church, including its mosaics, are preserved in the lower church. The supports of the great tower are of reinforced

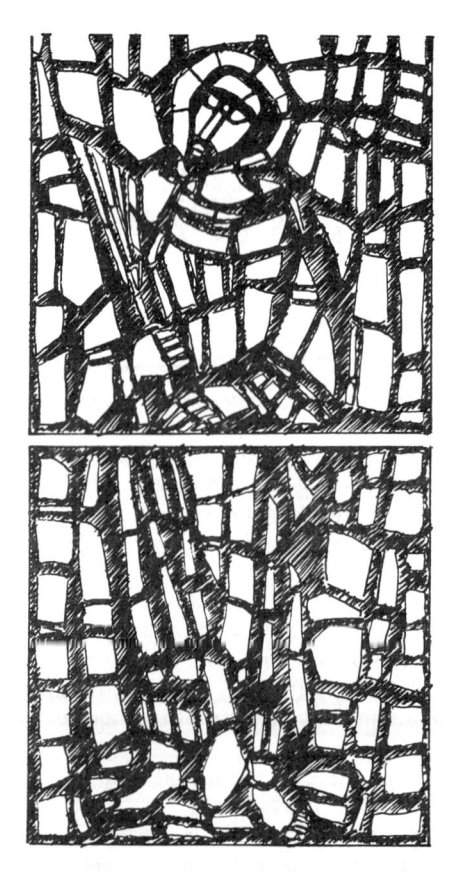

Church of the Annunciation, Nazareth

Church of the Annunciation, Nazareth

concrete, hopefully strong enough to withstand the earthquakes to which the region is subject.

The west front of the church is decorated with statues illustrating the story of the Incarnation and, on the south side, the Annunciation. The upper church is used for more populous gatherings, while the lower is designed rather for quieter devotion and private meditation.

The great church strikes one first of all as being brash and grandiose, overbearing and downright ugly; but on reflection and acquaintance, one realises that it is a remarkable achievement, and as one learns to find one's way about its complexities, its corners become fascinating and beautiful; it lends a pride and dignity to the former churches preserved in its heart.

Beneath the arcade to the north of the church is an ARCHAEOLOGICAL MUSEUM with artefacts discovered over the years on the site. The big building on the right is the Terra Sancta FRANCISCAN MONASTERY. North of the Annunciation church is the CHURCH OF ST JOSEPH, built on the ruins of a 13th C Crusader church, over the probable site of the carpentry shop where Jesus spent the first years of his life. Beneath the church in the crypt is a fine Byzantine Mosaic, as well as a cave and an olive-press. The church itself is simple and beautiful with fine stained-glass windows.

To the west of Casa Nova St is the Arab *souk*, the narrow winding lanes of the domestic shopping area. Just inside this area you come across the two white towers of the Greek Catholic 'SYNAGOGUE CHURCH'. This is the Synagogue where Jesus and his family would have worshipped, and where Jesus himself would have spoken. A simple stone undergound vault is the site. Although the actual vaulted building is reckoned to date from about 300 years after Christ, the floor is probably the original. If the door is locked the key is kept in the flat above the steps.

All over the town are hospitals run by Christian orders. This is a legacy from the days when the town would be thronged with thousands of pilgrims, most of whom would be wretched with poverty, hunger, disease or fatigue after the long

Synagogue Church, Nazareth

unimaginably arduous journey they would have made to get here. Charitable orders were established for the succour and relief of these pilgrims. They remain to this day, although with the journey being rather less arduous for the thousands of Christian pilgrims, people from the town and the surrounding country make up the majority of inmates.

Also there are many hospices where modern pilgrims can stay; they are generally happy to accept ordinary travellers as well.

There are two major churches in the town, both on top of the hill – the SALESIAN CHURCH OF JESUS THE ADOLESCENT, and the CONVENT OF THE FRANCISCAN SISTERS OF MARY. It is important to check what time these churches are open, because it's a long hot haul up here.

Big HOTELS are here too – the Grand New Hotel, the Nazareth and the Hagalil, all with three stars and prices to match.

The town has a population of about 40,000 Arabs, half Moslem and half Christian. A new Jewish quarter is in *Nazerat Illit*.

Nazareth is, along with Jerusalem and Bethlehem, one of the three main Christian Holy Cities of Palestine; but its standing is not quite so exalted as the other two, for although Jesus spent 30 years of his life here, his ministry was away in Galilee, his birth in Bethlehem and his trial and Crucifixion and Resurrection in Jerusalem. The only supernatural event to have happened here was the Annunciation by the Angel Gabriel to the Virgin Mary.

After the death of Christ, Nazareth became a predominantly Jewish town. When the Jews joined the Persians in attacking the Christians in 614, Nazareth supplied a large contingent, undoubtedly on account of the intolerable oppression to which they had been subjected by the Christians.

Zippori – Sepphoris

Just 6 km northwest along the country path from Nazareth is the ruined town of Zippori. Mary's parents, Anne and Joachim lived here; and when Nazareth was just a little village, Sepphoris, as Zippori was then known, was a major town with between 20,000 and 40,000 inhabitants, the largest and most important city in Galilee.

Today there is an ITALIAN CONVENT at the bottom of the hill, and a little CHURCH (key at the convent). On top of the hill the first thing you see is the remains of the CRUSADER TOWER: this in turn was built over what looks like a Herodian foundation – note the immense blocks, as in the Wall at Jerusalem. Recently the tower has been used as a school for the Arab village that used to be here, but which was flattened when the population was re-located after the Six Day War. Many of the Arabs who used to live here now live in a suburb of Nazareth; this suburb has a green-topped minaret and looks over the plain towards the old village of Zippori.

Surrounding the tower are the excavations currently being carried out by American and Israeli archaeologists. Work started five years ago; to date they have discovered a large ROMAN AND JEWISH TOWN with substantial public buildings, a theatre, some extremely well-preserved mosaics and a number of fine private houses, some with the Jewish ritual baths with their seven steps.

It was here that the armies of the Crusaders gathered before their march to the Horns of Hattin on 4 July 1187; it's about 15 km as the crow flies.

Cana

Jesus performed his first miracle at Cana. He was invited to a wedding with his mother, Mary; long before the proceedings were over, the wine ran out. Mary, knowing that her son was capable of working miracles, persuaded Him to change the pitchers of spring water into wine. This He did, and the feast continued. This was the first time Jesus performed a miracle in public.

To mark the auspicious event, there has long been a church on the spot; the FRANCISCAN CATHOLIC CHURCH was built in 1879 on the ruins of a mosque, beneath which were found the remains of a synagogue dated 500. It's a pretty church, with lovely frescoes of the events at the wedding – all from the 19th C; the Greek Orthodox Church on the west side of the street, a beautiful simple little Byzantinesque church, was built in 1566. Both churches, with their simple altars and collections of ancient water-pitchers, are a breath of fresh air after the immense and pompous edifices that dominate Nazareth. 'It is a simple matter of the "Primacy of Engineers"', explains the Italian Priest at Cana.

Cana is perhaps not the most beautiful spot on earth, but the simple charm and devotion of these little churches make this one of the most moving holy sites of the Holy Land.

The Arab name for the village is *Kafr Kanna,* and you can find it 6 km north of Nazareth on the road to Tiberias, set on a hillock in a plain of olive groves and barley fields.

GALILEE

Mount Tabor

For your first glimpse of Mount Tabor, try to see it in the evening mists from Belvoir Castle to the southeast. Seen from here it seems impossible for there NOT to have been some miracle there. Rising up sheer out of the plain of the *Yizre'el* valley, it looks like an ant-hill, a sugar-loaf, a perfect picture-book mountain. As you approach its distant perfection fades, but it's still an impressive hill, 1900 ft high, thickly forested with pines and topped with a MONASTERY and a CONVENT. From the north side a road leads by narrow hairpin bends to the top. Buses from Nazareth and elsewhere drop groups of tourists at the bottom whence they are ferried up by a small fleet of taxis. The enterprising traveller with some time and energy to spare for a rewarding experience, will take one of the many paths up the south side, and experience the joy of the measureless view unfolding with dignity and composure before him. It's a steep path, and a fair old haul, but the feeling of arriving at the top on foot and beholding the monasteries and churches for the first time, is wonderful.

Although many will argue the case of Mount Hermon for the site of the Transfiguration, Mount Tabor is a strong contender, and once you've seen it and felt the atmosphere of the place, you will be convinced that this was the very spot where Jesus appeared to Peter, James and John shining with the glorious light of God; this was one of the first intimations of Christ's divinity. Again there is a very old church here, in ruins, and replaced by the modern Franciscan and Greek Orthodox churches, monasteries and hospices. The views over the Valley of Yizre'el, stretching away into the haze like a patchwork quilt, are beyond description.

The FRANCISCAN HOSPICE here welcomes pilgrims and travellers, and is surely one of the best places to stay in the Holy Land.

Horns of Hattin

Leaving Tiberias on the main road to Nazareth or Haifa, as you climb back up to sea-level, cast an eye back for the wonderful views of the lake with Tiberias obscured behind its hill. On the north side of the road, on the heights above the Sea of Galilee, you will see two curious hillocks, like rocky breasts. These are the Horns of Hattin, or Horns of Hittin as they are known in Hebrew. Here, on 5 July 1187, was the final battle between Saladin and the Crusaders; the crushing defeat inflicted on the Christians brought about the end of the Latin Empire of

Jerusalem. Stroll around the battlefield – there is no monument, no nothing, it's just another evocative spot. On a summer day, with the heat of the sun baking the rocks, you can imagine the terrible scene as the heavily armed Crusaders, maddened by heat and thirst, were cut down in their thousands by the darting attacks of Saladin's lightly encumbered horsemen.

MEGIDDO

In the fertile plain of MEGIDDO, the scene of some of the world's bloodiest battles but now the peaceful bread-basket of Palestine, it is prophesied that the final conflict between the forces of Theism and those who defy the rule of God, will take place (Rev 16:16 20:8 Ezek 39:4).

Megiddo was one of the few Canaanite fortress cities that survived the onslaught of the Israelites. Along with *Yoqne'am* to the north-west, the city of Megiddo dominates the main passes through the Carmel range; according to military strategists who understand this sort of thing, the *Yizre'el* Valley before the ancient fortresses of Yoqne'am, Megiddo and Jenin, is the most strategically important part of Palestine; whoever holds power here holds the key to the whole land. This has been ominously demonstrated in the great battles that have already been enacted on the plain below *Har Megiddo* – or Armageddon. Here Barak battered the Canaanites, Gideon the Midianites, Josiah the forces of Pharaoh Necho; Holofernes (Judith 12) and later the Persians (Macc I 9:4) met their makers here. More recently Allenby ousted the Turks in the First World War – for which he earned the title Viscount Megiddo. In 1967 Israeli tanks drove back the Arab Legion.

Before the 20th C, the routes at the foot of Carmel range, from the Jordan Valley to Acre, and the route from the pass at Megiddo north-east to Afula and Mt Tabor, were almost impassable; a survey team in 1880 reported that the ways were so deep in dust that even their horses found it impossible to continue, while in the winter the whole area became a treacherous marsh. The one exception to this, and it was this that contributed to Megiddo's strategic importance as a great crossroad on the highways of the ancient world, was a basaltic highway which led north-east to Mt Tabor, creating an excellent all-weather route. Looking at the well-tamed fertility of the great valley of *Yizre'el* today, this is hard to imagine.

Tel Megiddo is perhaps the most interesting excavated *tel* in Israel. Twenty layers have been exposed, starting 6,000 years ago in the Chalcolithic period. There is evidence of early Canaanites, Egyptians, Persians and Assyrians, but the most interesting period was under Solomon and Ahab, when Megiddo reached its zenith as a 'Chariot city'. From this time dates the magnificent gate, whose lower blockwork is still visible.

There's a good MUSEUM on the site, with displays of pottery, ornaments, jewellery and statues, and a fine model of the city as it was in the time of King Solomon.

Bet She'arim

In the north-west corner of the *Yizre'el* Valley is a range of chalk hills. Here lies the ancient town of *Bet She'arim* and its catacombs. In the 2nd C AD, the leader of the Jewish people under Roman domination was Rabbi *Yehuda Ha Nasi*, 'the Prince'. He established the Sanhedrin at *Bet She'arim* and made the town his teaching centre. He was held in great reverence by the Jews, and as people flocked to hear his teaching, the town expanded. He was buried at *Bet She'arim* when he died in 217 AD.

Under Hadrian Jerusalem was forbidden to the Jews, and the most favoured burial ground, on the Kidron Valley side of the Mount of Olives, was no longer open to them. To be buried in the same ground as the revered Rabbi was a good alternative. In the 2nd and 3rd C, *Bet She'arim* became the most popular burial ground for the Jews throughout Palestine and in the Diaspora. The town thrived on the business.

All you can see of the actual town today is the foundations of some public buildings, a ruined synagogue and an olive-press, set on a hill overlooking the Plain of *Yizre'el.* Below the town are the CATACOMBS, an extensive system of tunnels and caves dug into the rock. Here rested hundreds of coffins, some beautifully carved and decorated, but regrettably damaged and despoiled by grave-robbers. You can visit the catacombs, and there is a small MUSEUM on the site.

The Jordan Valley – El Ghor – Rift Valley

The Jordan Valley is part of the great geological fault in the earth's crust, known as the Syrian-African Rift, or the Great Rift Valley. It starts well north of the Sea of Galilee, in Syria and, deepening all the way, follows the course of the Jordan down to the Dead Sea, thence through the Red Sea to Africa.

North of Galilee it manifests itself gently and reasonably in the flat fertile valley of Hula. The river flows swiftly down through the valley until it debouches into the Sea of Galilee, a freshwater lake surrounded on all sides by steep hills, and already 700 ft below sea level. At the southern end of the lake the River Jordan curls green and slow on the start of its 200-mile journey down the valley to the Dead Sea (as the crow flies the distance is only 60 miles, but the Jordan winds and meanders so convolutedly that the total river distance is 200 miles).

The irrigated river plain is rich in green plantations of fruit, vegetables and cotton, a striking contrast to the parched look of the hills that border the valley. The further south you go, the wilder this barren landscape becomes; the hills of barley-stubble give way to the astonishingly meagre grazing lands of the Bedouin, and finally to the cracked dry hills of dust and stones around Jericho. A few km south of Jericho the river ends its journey in the Dead Sea, at 1,400 ft below sea level. The Jordan and several other lesser rivers flow into the Dead Sea, but there is no outlet; the rate of evaporation is so high that the sea maintains a constant level. This seems quite beyond belief until you go there, when it seems hardly surprising, on account of the searing heat and the dryness.

Belvoir Crusader Castle

Another magnificent example of a Crusader castle, Belvoir commands the upper Jordan Valley. If, as I was, you are foolhardy enough to attempt an assault upon this castle on a summer day, you are unlikely to be successful in the enterprise. From Kibbutz GESHER a path leads across the scrub up the hill to the castle. Alternatively you can keep going south down the road and then turn right up the secondary road to the top, about 5 km and a stiff climb.

When you get to the top, you find yourself standing on the impressive remains of a dark stone Crusader castle. The massive lower walls and moats, tapering obliquely like a Tibetan palace, are still intact. The castle was built at the end of the 12th C. It was the last bastion of the Crusaders to fall, and suffered a long siege. But eventually it was forced to surrender; the enthusiasm of the knights waned when they realised that they were the last ones, and at the end of the century, they laid down their arms. Saladin, in recognition of their bravery, allowed them safe passage to Tyre.

Shortly afterwards the castle was pulled down, to prevent it falling into Crusader hands again. Everybody knew by now that once the Crusaders were allowed to take advantage of the fortifications at which they so excelled, you could never get them out. Their superb techniques of construction and design are well in evidence here. The view down the valley of the Jordan River is vast and impressive.

BET SHE'AN

Bet She'an is known for its ROMAN THEATRE. Down through the park to the north of the town, basking in the dust beneath a wooded hill is the well-preserved AMPHITHEATRE; dark grey basalt and pale limestone create a pleasing contrast. The theatre is in a fair state of preservation, particularly the fine stage-building, and is worth coming to see; but the real prize of *Bet She'an* is the great BYZANTINE CITY that was only discovered in the spring of 1987. Feverish excavations are now taking place and the city promises to be one of the most important and well-preserved archaeological finds in the Middle East.

A huge public bath and a broad main street, or 'Cardo' as at Jerusalem, have been discovered to date. Many fine marble columns and a host of fine carvings are coming to light.

To the north of the site towers the *tel*, another huge city mound that makes the newly revealed Byzantine city at its foot look like a modern urban development. A dusty hill with trees, this is a *tel* for wandering and musing on. The latest stratum contains remains from the Crusader period, much later than the city below.

Bet She'an is in fact an ancient Canaanite city, its dark walls made gruesome in history by the mutilated bodies of Saul and his sons, which were hung there after the Philistine victory at nearby Mt Gilboa. The city lies 320 ft below sea-level, dominating the confluence of the two great valleys of *Yizre'el* and Jordan. For thousands of years skilful political manoeuvring maintained as near a precarious neutrality as was possible to achieve in this tormented land. *Bet She'an*'s method was placation of conquerors, but in the 12th C they failed to placate the Crusaders, whereupon the whole city was destroyed.

Follow the signs out of the town to the west for GAN HASHELOSHA: 6 km from the town an avenue of poplar trees leads to a lush forest beneath the mountain of Gilboa. Here, where the waters from the Gilboa mountains gush out from the spring of *Ein Harod*, and irrigate the fertile Harod Valley, is a cool wooded park with fresh pools of clear green water for swimming. A summer afternoon spent lazing on the well manicured lawns beneath shady trees, and dipping in the lovely water is an afternoon well spent. There's a CAFE and RESTAURANT, as well as lifeguards to save you. Finest spot for swimming in Israel.

C·H·A·P·T·E·R·6
The Dead Sea, Northern and Central Negev

Dead Sea

So hot and dry is this region in summer, that it's surprising it can support any life at all. But amidst the harsh, desert landscape are oases of lush vegetation teeming with animal and birdlife, fertile Kibbutzim, waterfalls, clear pools, sulphur springs, ancient ruins and the extraordinary DEAD SEA itself.

At 1,320 ft below sea level, the Dead Sea, part of the Great Rift Valley that extends all the way to East Africa, is the lowest point on earth. Towards the south, it is fringed with rims of whitish salt crystals; in places the salt content is so dense that solid flats float like pack-ice on the surface of the water.

The cliché snapshot, floating unsupported on your back whilst nonchalantly reading a newspaper, will probably prove irresistible. You really do float, even if you don't know how to. Indeed, so great is the buoyancy, that it's quite impossible to swim in the normal way at all.

The water feels strangely thick and oily. You should be careful not to get it in your eyes, and don't be tempted to take a dip if you have any cuts or bruises or are sunburnt. It really will sting you very badly – hardly surprising when you think there's about 2½ lbs of salt to every litre of water!

There are all sorts of claims about the health-giving and curative powers of both the water and the atmosphere here. Certainly, the air is rich in oxygen, and there is a very high concentration of magnesium, bromine and iodine in the

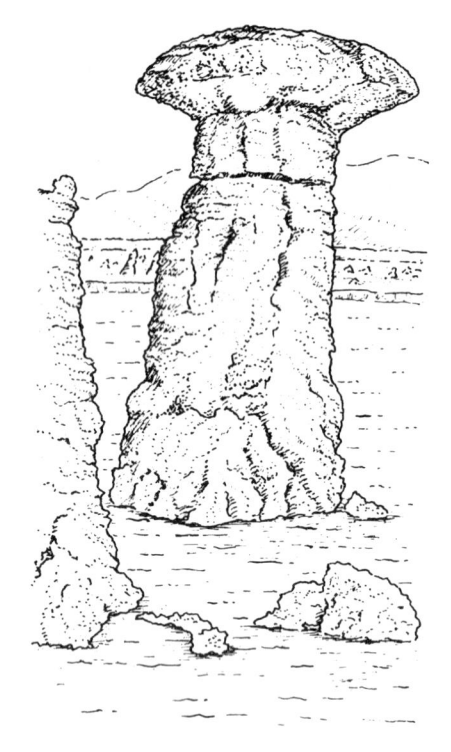

Salt formations in the Dead Sea

water. And everyone is crazy about the black mud. You'll find it available everywhere. The idea is to coat yourself with the thick, slimey muck, and sit back while the sun bakes it dry. Whatever it does or doesn't do for you, it's amusing to listen to the chorus of 'you're not going to put that on your *face* too!?' When the beaches are busy the spectacle is something akin to an offbeat black and white minstrel show.

Qumran

In 1947, in a barren spot on the western shore of the Dead Sea, just south of Jericho, a Bedouin shepherd boy stumbled on a cave containing shards of ancient pottery and a number of earthenware jugs. Inside some of the jugs he found dusty bundles wrapped in linen cloth. The place was QUMRAN and the dusty bundles were the DEAD SEA SCROLLS; their discovery changed the face of biblical scholarship and have been described as the 'greatest find of manuscripts in modern times'.

You can see some of the Dead Sea Scrolls in the SHRINE OF THE BOOK in Jerusalem and learn more about their contents. But Qumran is certainly worth a visit in itself.

Aside from the scrolls, the excavations are important because they throw light on the way of life of an extreme ascetic religious sect – the Essenes. In the three hundred years before Christ, Greek colonists poured into Palestine bringing with them a new, hedonistic way of life, a new way of thought, and considerable wealth. Many Jews welcomed this cultural invasion, becoming semi-Hellenised themselves. But some, seeing Greek influence as a threat to their spirituality, retreated into the desert to 'prepare the path of the Lord'. One such group, the Essenes, founded a community, run on strict religious lines, at Qumran around 150 BC. They flourished here until the Romans flushed them out during the Great Jewish Revolt.

Excavations commenced in 1951 have uncovered and identified a number of buildings; amongst them the SCRIPTORIUM, where it is more than likely that the Dead Sea Scrolls were written; the WATCHTOWER – walk up to this for a good overview of the site and the Dead Sea – and a number of CISTERNS. You have to be sure-footed to get to the caves where the Scrolls were found; you'd be well advised to view them from afar.

The site is well marked with signs and there are numerous guided tours. You could tag on the back of one of these for an in-depth understanding of the site. There's a good modern restaurant/snack shop run by the local Kibbutz here, as well as a souvenir shop.

Some two miles south of Qumran itself, is your first opportunity to experience the Dead Sea. *EIN FESHKHA* is where the Essenes farmed, and where they buried their dead, in strict accordance with the Jewish law that all cemeteries should be kept well apart from living quarters. There are FRESH WATER SPRINGS here, so you can take a refreshing dip and wash off the salt from the Dead Sea.

Ein Gedi

There are two beaches here. Both consist mainly of small sharp stones, so you should bring a pair of shoes you can wear on the beach and in the water. You'll find the public beach first, but it's not up to much. There's no shade on the beach itself (essential in the oven-like heat) and the whole area is scruffy. You'll be better off travelling a little further south for the EIN GEDI SPA. Here sunchairs and sunshades are provided, the black mud is freely available from a 'box' on the beach, and ramps have been built out over the sea making it easier to get in and out of the water. There is also a good snack bar and restaurant, and if the fancy takes you, you can languish in one of the spa's hot and smelly sulphur baths.

But the main attraction of *Ein Gedi* is the NATURE RESERVE of Kibbutz *Ein Gedi* and *Nahal Arugot*. You enter the Kibbutz of *Ein Gedi* by a great plantation of bananas before arriving at the entrance to the trail. A marked path takes you up through a deep cleft in the mountains of the desert. Beside the path runs a cool river, with the occasional pool for bathing. Above tower some of the most startling mountains I've ever seen. The desert light plays curious tricks, turning every rock into a castle or a palace soaring high among the eagles.

As for the wildlife, the canyon is rich in startling vegetation and alive with butterflies. Rock badgers regard you phlegmatically from the rocks – quite without fear – small herds of Ibex trip down almost vertical mountain slopes to drink in the pools; eagles and vultures whirl overhead. These are all commonplace. Occasionally though, you are obliged to walk in the reserve with an armed guide, for there are leopards about, and these can be dangerous. *Ein Gedi* Nature Reserve is for me one of the most spectacular sights in Israel.

Masada

Herod the Great spent the early part of his reign in constant fear of being deposed or attacked from Egypt by Cleopatra. To protect his family and to provide him with an impregnable fortress should civil war break out, he embarked on one of his most ambitious building projects – choosing a 1,500 ft high plateau-topped mountain on the western shore of the Dead Sea and in the midst of the Judean Wilderness for the site of his great fortress and sanctuary – MASADA.

Seventy years after Herod's death Masada was a Roman outpost protected only by a small garrison. In 66 AD at the beginning of the Great Jewish Revolt against Rome, a party of zealots overpowered the garrison and, as the revolt progressed, Masada became a haven for supporters of the revolt escaping from the Romans. Although the revolt ended in 70 AD with the capture of Jerusalem and the destruction of the Temple, in Masada resistance continued for three more years.

Eventually the Romans despatched the might of the 10th Legion to flush out this last vestige of resistance to their authority. And so began one of the most heroic and tragic chapters in Jewish history. Atop the barren cliff, 960 men, women and children watched as the vast army, serviced by hundreds of Jewish slave labourers, encircled the base of their eyrie. The Romans had no intention of sitting out a long siege, but the storehouses and water-cisterns originally constructed by Herod to service the fortress might well have held out longer than their patience. An early victory obviously called for ingenious tactics and, above all, skilful military engineering; the Romans excelled in this division.

On the west side of the mountain, a natural spur provided the foundation for an immense ramp; Jewish slaves provided the necessary labour. As the ramp gradually crept up the mountainside, the dismayed rebels took a decision which has become a great symbol for Jewish bravery. In the reported words of their leader, 'we shall die before we become slaves to the enemy and remain free as we leave the lands of the living – we, our wives and our children.' Ten men were chosen by lots to slaughter every man, woman and child and then each other. The last man plunged his own sword into his exhausted body. Before they died all their possessions were burnt to frustrate the Romans of any loot, with the exception of the contents of the storerooms. These were deliberately left intact so that the advancing Romans would know 'that they perished not through want, but because, as we resolved at the beginning, we chose death rather than slavery'.

According to Josephus, whose writings provide the back-up for this tragic story, just two women and five children who had apparently hidden themselves in a cistern, escaped the mass suicide.

Some 300 years later Christian monks during the Byzantine period came here to dwell among the ruins. When they left, Masada eventually settled undiscovered under the desert dust for some 1,400 years.

To get to the summit today you won't need to build a ramp but if you choose to ascend by the 'snake path' you might think the former course would have been an easier option. Depending on how fit you are, the climb to the top by this route can take upwards of an hour; don't even think of attempting it unless you start early in the morning before the desert sun does its worst. Take water with you and wear a hat. You'll need to, anyway, for exploring the summit; there are no cafes or snack stands and precious little in the way of shade up at the top. Coming down is nearly as difficult. Don't do it unless you are fairly sure-footed.

You'll be glad to hear there are two alternative routes. The laziest way is to take the cable car. As it ascends you can look down on your fellow tourists struggling up the path and feel either smug or guilty depending on your disposition. Mind you, when you get to the cable car terminus, you still have to climb the steps to the summit itself. On the west side of the mountain, only advisable if you are coming to Masada from Arad, you can walk up via the Roman Ramp. This will take about 20 minutes.

At the summit you can wander at will or follow one of the three suggested tours outlined on a board display. The 'short tour' takes one and a half hours, the 'intermediate' about two hours and the 'extensive' tour as much as four hours. Once again, don't forget to take water and head coverings.

Some 1,900 years after Masada fell to the 10th Legion, another army attacked. In 1963 and 1964, thousands of volunteers came from all over the world to work under the blistering sun and in incredibly harsh conditions to help excavate the most important archaeological find in Israel. They completed in two years what might have taken up to 26 years under normal circumstances!

Highlights of the site include the impressive remains of Herod's NORTHERN PALACE which hangs over the cliff in a series of three terraces. It was designed not for official functions but as a place of sanctuary and solitude for Herod alone. He couldn't have picked a better spot. The view over the desert to the Dead Sea is truly spectacular.

Herod was fond of his creature comforts; the Palace BATH HOUSE can be seen just behind the Northern Palace. Behind the Bath House are the ruins of the STORE ROOMS – big enough to hold provisions to withstand long sieges.

To the east of the Northern Palace complex, you'll find the ruins of what is probably one of the oldest SYNAGOGUES in the world. If you share your journey up the mountain with an exuberant party of Jews the odds are they are on their way to celebrate a *Bar Mitzva* here; uppermost in their minds too will be the incredible fact that 1,800 years ago the rebel Zealot community would have performed similar rituals on this very spot.

Immediately south of the synagogue are the ruins of a small BYZANTINE CHAPEL, and a little further on Herod's WESTERN PALACE, built for court functions and to house his nine wives. There is a wonderful MOSAIC still in a good state of preservation at the southern end of the complex.

Heading south again you'll find the SWIMMING POOL. You may wonder how they managed to get enough water to drink, let alone swim and bathe in. Huge water cisterns were carved out of solid rock on the summit and the winter floodwaters that filled the surrounding *wadis* were diverted by damming

Mosaic from the Herodian Period – Masada

into twelve huge cisterns gouged out of the face of the mountainside.

Elsewhere on the site are the less grandiose, but still fascinating testaments to the presence here of the Zealots. In the face even of the Roman siege, the Zealots still managed to adhere to all the stringent requirements of their religion. Note the MIKVE (immersion baths) which orthodox Jews must use regularly for ritual purification.

Ein Bokek, Neve Zohar and Sodom

Heading south on the coast road from Masada you'll come to EIN BOKEK. The place is little more than a collection of big, ugly and expensive hotels set around the shore of the Dead Sea. A little further on at NEVE ZOHAR is another fancy spa where you can, for a price, take all sorts of curative treatments and immerse yourself in more mineral-rich waters. At both places you can take a swim in the Dead Sea.

You can turn off for ARAD, just a little south of here. If you do, be sure to watch out for the OBSERVATION POINTS as you climb in to the hills. They afford wonderful views of the Dead Sea and great opportunities for photographs.

If you continue south the road drops down towards Sodom; the heat intensifies, the air is heavy with the smell of sulphur, the landscape becomes even more twisted and tortured. Here the sea is clogged with great flats of salt and it isn't hard to believe that the Lord is still raining down burning sulphur on the wicked city.

There's no city here today not even a small town, and it is unlikely that anyone would come here at all if it wasn't for the sprawling hulk of the Dead Sea Works, and the strange salt formations. One, to be seen above SODOM CAVE, is claimed to be the unfortunate wife of Lot, who looked back at Sodom whilst God was doing his worst, and was promptly turned into a pillar of salt for her temerity.

Arad

In the midst of the Negev Desert, perched on a high plateau, the modern town of ARAD appears almost like a mirage out of the parched landscape. Ancient Arad was established some 5,000 years ago. Its modern counterpart, 8 km away, was built in the early 1960s. It's a little town with big ideas; wide boulevards and shady squares designed on a grand scale ideal for coping with the fierce desert heat.

The climate and altitude here are perfect for people with respiratory problems and as a consequence many of the hotels are equipped with a clinic for treatment of asthma. Arad has little else to offer other than a good base for exploring the Negev and the Dead Sea area. Masada can be reached by the ROMAN RAMP on the west side most easily from here. Check with the Tourist Office to find out if you can join a tour for a *son et lumière* at Masada; it really is a wonderful experience. At the eastern edge of the town just past the main hotel area, a promontory juts out into the desert. Pass the dramatic white modern sculpture to the very tip, and if you are lucky enough to find yourself alone, you'll be awestruck by the intense quiet and the beauty of the desert hills rolling endlessly before you.

TEL ARAD is an interesting site with reconstructed remains from the Canaanite and Israelite periods. The excavations are marked and a leaflet is available which will help you understand what you are seeing.

Beersheba

BEERSHEBA is home to thousands of immigrants from all over Europe and the Middle East, who settled in this dusty desert town after 1948. The area is also home to the increasing number of Bedouins persuaded to give up their traditional nomadic way of life. There has been no time here for the niceties of modern planning. What was little more than a watering hole for Bedouin flocks, at the turn of the century, became a town and an administrative centre for the Ottoman Turks. Flushed out by the British, the town remained a backwater and a settlement only for the toughest immigrants. The Egyptians occupied Beersheba when the British left, but it was won by the Israelis during the War of Independence and has since exploded into the 'capital' of the Negev. Now it boasts a large and impressive university and, appropriately enough, an important Research and Development Institute engaged in the study of the special conditions that pertain to this desert area, finding ways to harness and exploit its natural resources.

When you arrive in the ugly, modern town it's hard to believe that this is the Beersheba of the Patriarchs. The town takes its name from either 'Well of the Oath', referring to a covenant made between Abraham and Abimelech, when the latter agreed to accept that Abraham had rights to the well, or 'Well of the Seven', referring to the seven lambs Abraham gave Abimelech to seal the treaty. Isaac's servants redug the same well here, after the Philistines had filled it in, and Jacob 'went out from Beersheba' with his family to Egypt. According to Judges, Beersheba was the southernmost border of the Israelite territory.

You can see what is claimed as ABRAHAM'S WELL in Beersheba today; in spite of what you are told, nothing here dates from earlier than the Byzantine period. In fact, besides the well and the small, but well laid out MUNICIPAL MUSEUM, housed in a former mosque, there's little reason to tarry in Beersheba. Unless, that is, you happen to be here on a Thursday for the BEDOUIN MARKET. If you can wade through the mundane household goods and the touristy rubbish, there are still some examples of fine Bedouin handicrafts to haggle over. Keep your wits about you. The Bedouins are well used to tourists, and will switch from currency to currency at the drop of a hat; if you're not careful you'll end up paying much more than you bargained for!

Six km east of the city you'll find the excavations of an early Israelite town at TEL BEERSHEBA. If you are going to spend some time here, you would be well advised to visit the Museum in Beersheba first. Many of the finds from *Tel* Beersheba are displayed here and the accompanying explanations and site plan will make your exploration much more rewarding. Next to the site is a small BEDOUIN MUSEUM and a restaurant inside a large Bedouin tent. Both are worth stopping for. While you are here you will notice a settlement near the site. This is TEL SHEVA. The Israeli government is constantly attempting to persuade the Bedouin to give up their nomadic way of life and *Tel* Sheva is a permanent Bedouin settlement. You'll probably notice plenty of characteristic

A Bedouin tent

black Bedouin tents pitched in the area. Obviously, many of the nomads are keeping their options open.

Returning to the city, take a right turn off the main road to see the MEMORIAL OF THE NEGEV PALMAH BRIGADE, a series of vast concrete sculptures atop a hill overlooking the desert, commemorating the brigade who captured the Negev from the Egyptians in the War of Independence.

SDE BOKER

David Ben Gurion, one of the founding fathers of modern Israel, knew that if the new state was to become a viable home for millions of Jewish immigrants, its resources would have to be harnessed and its barren wastes made to bloom. About 45 km south of Beersheba, as living proof that his dream was and still is being fulfilled, the Kibbutz of SDE BOKER appears, green and lush, out of the harsh terrain of the Negev Desert.

Sde Boker was established by hardy pioneers in 1952. A year later, Ben Gurion elected to join the Kibbutz, and, interspersed with his political life, he lived and worked here with his wife until his death at the age of 86. The great man's humble home here has been maintained as he left it and can be visited. Combine this with a stroll around the Kibbutz grounds.

A little further south is the NEGEV INSTITUTE which was founded by Ben Gurion to study the best methods of reclaiming desert land. He is buried nearby with his wife. Two simple tombs mark the spot, looking out over the desert he loved so much.

Ein Avdat

Not to be confused with the Nabataean city of AVDAT, further south, EIN AVDAT is just beyond *Sde Boker*. Here in the midst of the desert the 'Spring of Avdat' is an icy cold pool set deep in a steep-sided canyon, fed by flash flood waters that over the millennia have furrowed out channels in the rock. This dramatically beautiful area is now a National Park, and if you are lucky and it's fairly deserted you might catch a glimpse of desert creatures such as the wild ibex coming here to slake their thirst. If you decided to climb down to the pool for a swim be warned that the water is very deep, and it can be almost impossible to climb out without a helping hand; don't attempt it if you are alone.

Avdat

AVDAT is one of the most beautiful, the most interesting and the most easy to 'read' archaeological sites in all Israel. Here some 4,000 years ago the inhabitants showed the same aptitude for 'making the desert bloom' as the Israelis do today. Indeed below the ruins is an original Nabataean farm, reconstructed to study the ancient irrigation methods of the Nabataeans for academic interest, but now flourishing and accepted as a practical means to farm today without a secondary water supply in this bone dry area.

The Nabataeans were a canny Arab tribe who, aside from their remarkable ability to sustain themselves in desert settlements, also took advantage of their position on the most important and profitable trade routes of the day. With their capital city at Petra (today in the Kingdom of Jordan) they developed a string of settlements westwards all the way to Gaza – their gateway to the Mediterranean – and prospered mightily by offering 'protection' to the rich caravans that passed under their noses, levying stiff taxes.

But even this remarkable people fell prey to the Romans in AD 106 when the whole of the Negev was annexed. As the Roman Empire crumbled and the Byzantines took control of the area, Avdat enjoyed a revival. Most of the well-preserved ruins you will see here date from the Byzantine era. The

Moslem invasion followed hard on the heels of the Persians and Avdat fell into decline, to be eventually deserted.

As with so many of the sites in Israel, it will pay you to get here early in the morning. Aside from the fact that the heat will be less intense, it's well worth trying to beat the coach tours and have the place to yourself.

The majority of ruins are perched high on a hill and it's a very stiff climb. You can leave your car at the top and walk down and then try to cadge a lift up again to collect it. Otherwise, come what may, you are going to have to walk.

On your way up don't overlook the Byzantine bath house, just in front of the lower car park. It is one of the best preserved in Israel. Much further up towards the summit, a right-hand fork takes you down a track to a Nabataean burial cave. Cut deep in to the rock, the cave has 22 'shelves' on which corpses would have been laid.

At the summit itself, you can explore the Roman and Byzantine ruins. To do them the justice they deserve, arm yourself with a leaflet from the gatekeeper. As you leave the car park and head towards the FORTRESS WALLS, climb to the top of a RECONSTRUCTED 3RD C TOWER and survey the ROMAN QUARTER and the BYZANTINE WINE PRESS, before you move on. Once inside the walls, to your right is the Byzantine fortress, with its huge CISTERN sunk in the centre of the courtyard. In the far corner are the ruins of a BYZANTINE CHAPEL. Adjoining the fortress is an area devoted to churches and a monastery. Built by the Byzantines over the sites of Roman and Nabataean temples, to the left as you enter the area you will find the ruins of the CHURCH OF ST THEODORUS, a 4th C Greek martyr, and the remains of a BYZANTINE MONASTERY. On the other side of the courtyard are the ruins of the NORTH CHURCH and wonderful views over the desert.

You can climb down steps at this point and explore the CAVE OF THE CROSSES, THE SAINT'S CAVE and a cluster of ruined BYZANTINE HOUSES on your way back to the lower car park.

MITZPE RAMON

A little further south from Avdat is the modern town of MITZPE RAMON. There would seem to be nothing to recommend stopping here until you step into the OBSERVATORY of the proud new VISITORS' CENTRE and peer 3,180 ft dizzily downwards into the vast RAMON CRATER. As you look at the dramatic landscape, it's not too difficult to believe that fossilised finds dating back 200 million years have been found here.

The visitors' centre has an excellent geological exhibition and an audio visual show – although you might have to hang around for a while for the English version.

There are ambitious plans afoot to develop this whole area further as a major tourist attraction, but for now it's only worth a detour on your way to or from Eliat.

C·H·A·P·T·E·R·7
Eilat, Southern Negev and Sinai

Eilat

In 1917, at the beginning of the British Mandate in Palestine, Eilat was little more than a few ramshackle huts at the southernmost point of Israel.

Today Eilat is a rapidly expanding city of fancy, high-rise hotels set round the beaches at the northern tip of the Red Sea. This Israeli outpost lies quite literally cheek by jowl with Jordan to the east and the Egyptian Sinai Desert to the south-west.

The first mention of Eilat, under the name of *Ezion Geber* is in Deuteronomy, in connection with the route taken by the Children of Israel on their return from Egypt. Under Solomon, Eilat flourished as a ship-building centre and port, giving the Israelites access to the lucrative trade with Arabia.

About 100 years later, in the reign of Jehoshaphat, King of Judah, Eilat was again in the news when the royal fleet was destroyed by a storm in the Gulf. From now onwards, Eilat fell prey to the vicissitudes that beset the rest of Palestine, as successive conquerors marched through. They were all here; Edomites, Nabataeans, Greeks, Romans, Byzantines, Mamelukes, Crusaders and Turks. Under Ottoman rule, Eilat was never much more that a forgotten outpost, and it stayed that way throughout the British Mandate.

When Eilat was included in the Israeli portion of the United Nations Partition Plan, the Israeli army fell over themselves to

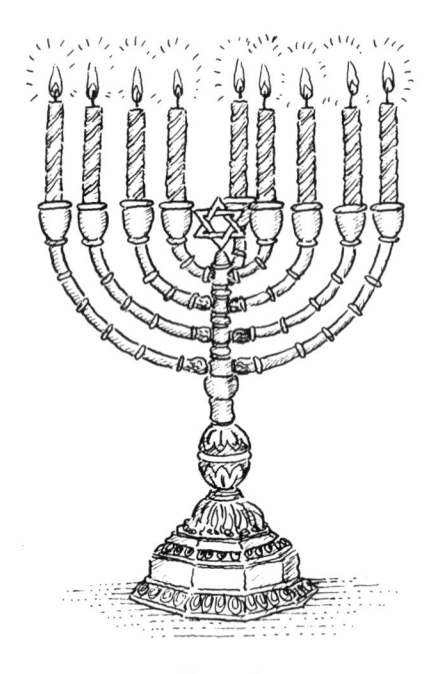

Menorah

get to the outpost and stake their claim, forgetting in their haste to take their new state flag. A sheet and some blue ink were hastily requisitioned and the makeshift standard was raised over Israel's only access to oil supplies from pre-revolutionary Iran, and to trade with Africa and the Far East.

This was no tourist paradise during the period between the late 1940s and the 1967 war with Egypt. It was a hastily constructed town, designed to absorb the hardier immigrants fleeing from post-Holocaust Europe. With temperatures in the 120s, little water and no decent road connections with the north, Eilat was a rough and ready place. Nor was its harbour of any real practical use. The Egyptians, not satisfied with denying the Suez Canal to Israeli shipping, blockaded the Gulf of Eilat too. The blockade didn't ease until after the UN took control of the Sinai and the Egyptian border with Eilat, following the Suez crisis in 1956.

In the lull in hostilities that followed, the town began to develop and the population to swell with new waves of immigrants. But the peace lasted for only eleven years. In 1967 Egypt, in alliance with Jordan, slapped another blockade on the Gulf and took control from the UN forces in the Sinai. The Six Day War that followed amazed the world nearly as much as it must have staggered the Arabs. The Israeli troops took the whole of the Sinai as far as the Suez Canal.

Now Eilat was no longer a small town sandwiched between two hostile borders. It had the whole of the magnificent Sinai Desert, with its beaches and coral reefs, extending to the south-west. Eilat started to develop its own tourist industry and that of the coastal Sinai strip. With typical Israeli determination and industry, money and sweat were poured into turning Eilat and the Sinai into an area fit for international tourism.

Whatever the wrongs and rights of the situation, when the 1978 Camp David Agreement eventually resulted in the return of the Sinai to Egypt, and the reinstatement of the border at Taba, only 10 km from the town, the Eilatis, whose vistas were now severely curtailed, were bitter and disillusioned. Then, as today, many Eilatis, who can still visit the Sinai but only with visas and frontier documentation, cannot come to terms with the miles of undeveloped potential on the Sinai coast.

None the less, Eilat itself began to develop its tourist industry within the new confines. After all, the town itself was quite small but they still had the magnificent Negev Desert stretching for miles behind. That development continues today.

If the idea of block after block of modern, high-rise hotels, and beaches packed with Israeli holidaymakers and tourists leaves you cold, you would still be advised not to dismiss Eilat. The town itself is surrounded by magnificent mountains, whose colours change dramatically from dawn to dusk; with the sea and the sky they create an unforgettable backdrop.

To the north is the Negev Desert. Not acres of sandscape but a spectacular rocky expanse where the effect of erosion over the millennia has twisted and tortured the rocks into a beautiful, unearthly landscape. To the south is the Red Sea. And it's what lies beneath the clear blue waters that makes any shortcomings Eilat may have pale into insignificance. It is one of the most popular diving centres in the world; there are no rivers running into the gulf and therefore no silt to muddy the crystal clear waters. Visibility is superb and the vibrant colours of the underwater scenery have an almost fairytale quality.

You won't have to spend long getting your bearings in the town itself. There are two main beaches. NORTH BEACH is on the eastern side and stretches either side of the marina and the ambitious man-made 'lagoon'. This is the area where all the big fancy hotels are situated and it's the most popular and noisy spot. You can hire windsurfers, pedaloes and canoes here. The eastern extreme of North Beach is currently a haven for budget tourists. There's cheaper accommodation or camping on the beach itself.

To find more beaches you have to head southwards past the port and towards the Egyptian border. The first stop is CORAL BEACH. Officially a nature reserve, you have to pay for this one, but it's worth every shekel. If you can't pluck up the courage for a spot of scuba diving (more about this later) you can get a good idea of the coral reef and its multi-coloured marine life by hiring snorkel, masks and flippers. The reserve has even provided underwater signs and pointers to help you. Don't be tempted to take bits of coral. The area is rightly protected by law and tourists are not spared from swift legal action if they're caught.

What of scuba-diving? If you are an experienced diver you must bring your licence and log book. Without these the diving clubs won't supply you with equipment. If you arrive with all the relevant documentation they will often be able to match you up with a diving partner.

If you want to learn, you can book a five-day diving course, during which you will go down for three full dives, and after a final exam, will get an internationally recognised certificate. Most of the clubs will require you to present a medical certificate, so check it out before you go, to avoid disappointment.

If you don't want to spend all your holiday in fishy pursuits you can take an introductory dive. This is very reasonably priced as clubs know that a high proportion of the beginners will get completely hooked! If you're in reasonable health and can swim, anyone from 9 to 90 can dive. You'll spend about half and hour being kitted out and shown the equipment and how it works. Then you'll be taken in a party by boat or mini-bus to Coral Beach. At the reserve you'll dive to about 10 meters with an instructor, his or her arm reassuringly resting on your back, for about half an hour to forty minutes. After the initial panic it's easy as breathing! You can have your photo taken or even a video – useful for cynical friends and family back home who would never believe you plucked up the courage.

If you really don't want to dive, make sure you visit the UNDERWATER OBSERVATORY. Here you can see just what you're missing without getting wet. It's a very popular spot for tourists; everywhere around you you'll hear gasps of delight as more visitors stream into the circular aquarium of the observatory itself, built on the floor of the Red Sea. If you want to observe this silent world in peace, you'll have to get there first thing in the morning.

Another way to get a look at the fishy life of the coral reef is to take a trip in a GLASS-BOTTOMED BOAT. Somehow the name conjures up visions of romantic craft with transparent floors. Its not quite like that. The boats are usually rusty tubs with a narrow glass channel running through the middle of the boat. Passengers line up either side on bench seats and peer over. None the less, if you're not going to snorkel, dive or visit the observatory, this is better than nothing.

Just before the observatory, on the right, heading towards the Egyptian border, is the TEXAS RANCH. Built originally as a film set, it's now a stable with horses for hire. The ranch is a wild west town in miniature. There's a saloon bar, a sheriff's office, an undertaker, a dentist, a gunsmith, etc. If the whole set-up wasn't anachronistic enough, there's a Bedouin tent at the end of 'town' with camels to rent. Whatever you may think of the whole caboodle, there's not a child alive who wouldn't be utterly thrilled.

Eilat is situated on one of the principal migration routes for millions of birds winging their way along the Rift Valley from

A Bedouin, Eilat

Europe to Africa. Nearly 400 different species fly over, including gulls, terns, waders, pipits, warblers, buntings, eagles, storks and pelicans. There's a site specially earmarked for enthusiasts just a little east along the beach from the main hotel strip. There's also an information office which will provide you with detailed information and arrange hiking tours or visits to the nearby BIRD RINGING STATION.

If diving, snorkelling, riding or birdwatching doesn't appeal, you can windsurf (climatic conditions make Eilat a windsurfer's paradise), cycle, go deep-sea fishing, sail, water-ski, para-sail, go on a jeep or a camel safari, or just loll on the beach.

One or two shops and a few restaurants are closed on the Sabbath in Eilat, but generally speaking this is a town which would remind most truly Orthodox Jews of Sodom. There are plenty of restaurants and sidewalk cafes – many of them employing hawkers to persuade you to choose their establishment, open every day of the week. The food is generally uninspiring (there are exceptions and your best bet is to look for the places that do a regular, roaring trade) but you can find pretty well everything from hamburgers and falafel to pancakes, pasta, fish and chips and more ice-cream parlours than you can wave a cone at. At the 'gourmet' level the prices are obviously higher and the standards better; you'll find French, Chinese, Italian, Argentinian, specialist fish and 'international restaurants' and North African and Yemeni specialities.

There are pubs, bars, nightclubs and discos by the dozen, and although culture is a rare commodity here, there is a good MODERN ART MUSEUM, regular displays of folk dancing and a modern amphitheatre with the occasional concert. The Museum in the Israel Palace Hotel is worth a look – over 1,000 exquisitely handmade dolls tell the story of the Jewish people in a series of miniature sets.

Eilat certainly has its attractions, but stretching southwards behind is the NEGEV; miles of rocky, mountainous desert, painted lavishly in reds, dark browns, violets and gold and every hue in between. Only the occasional *wadi* or impossibly lush Kibbutz breaks the 'beginning of the world' atmosphere of the place.

Take the Tel Aviv road south for the HAI BAR NATURE RESERVE. The aim of the reserve is to breed and protect the wild animals mentioned in the Bible and to save many species from extinction. Their ultimate aim is to release the animals gradually back into the desert as stocks increase. It's not exactly a safari park, but it's a lovely place to spend a morning or afternoon. The reserve is traversed by 10 km of road; you

Desert palm grove, Eilat

musn't stray from this road or exceed the speed limits of 20 kph; the animals, which include ostriches, gazelles, ibex and rare white oryx, have strict right of way.

In the predators' centre at the southern end of the reserve you can see, safely enclosed, wolves, foxes, wild cats, leopards, hyenas, snakes, lizards and rodents.

You can buy a book from the friendly and informative staff at the entrance. It will tell you the full, interesting story of *Hai Bar* and give you details of all the animals in the sanctuary.

Before or after you visit the reserve take a look at the HAI BAR YOTVATA VISITORS' CENTRE. Using displays, photographs and an audio-visual presentation, the centre gives a fascinating insight into the desert; how man has adapted to living here over the ages, its flora, fauna, geology and archaeology.

TIMNA VALLEY is about 25 km outside Eilat on the same road as *Hai Bar*. Don't take the turning for the Timna Mines (closed down when the bottom fell out of the copper market) but turn west at the sign which says *'Biqe'at Timna'*.

Timna valley is a small but dramatically beautiful national park. If you've the time and energy and can stand the heat (take plenty of water) it's a paradise for hikers. For the less energetic, there's a road that runs to all the important sites. This area has been mined for copper on and off for over 6,000 years; evidence of early mining techniques, particularly Egyptian, is everywhere. The ticket office will give you a little leaflet with a map showing the roads, paths and observation points. The most interesting sights are SOLOMON'S PILLARS (nothing to do with Solomon, nor are they strictly speaking 'pillars') and the nearby Egyptian TEMPLE dedicated to the cow-goddess *Hathor* and built to service the mining community. Don't miss the Egyptian and Midianite ROCK DRAWINGS at the place marked in the leaflet map as the 'CHARIOTS'. You'll see why it's so called when you look at the drawings.

South of Solomon's Pillars is an ARTIFICIAL LAKE for swimming and a visitors' centre. You can buy cold drinks here and take a cool plunge. It positively heaves with visitors on the Sabbath holidays.

Leaving Timna and heading south for Eilat, if you haven't had enough of rock formations make a detour to the right off the main road for the impressive sandstone PILLARS OF AMRAM, about 12 km before Eilat. There's a wonderful view from the OBSERVATORY.

Eilat is a jumping off point for the SINAI DESERT as well as for buses to Cairo. The main destination in the Sinai is ST CATHERINE'S MONASTERY. One- and two-day excursions are offered (you can't take a hire car into the Sinai so you are stuck with an organised tour or taking the unreliable and infrequent bus over the border). Don't be tempted to take the one-day tour. It leaves at the crack of dawn to allow for lengthy formalities at both the Israeli and Egyptian borders. Having got through all that (on and off buses like a fiddler's elbow) you set off for the spectacular drive, about 4 hours or so, through the desert with an undignified and rapid tour of the monastery before a picnic lunch and the long haul back to go through the border formalities all over again. It's a long day and the object of the whole exercise – to see the monastery – becomes the most insignificant part of the whole trip. Take the two-day trip and stay overnight near the monastery; the tour companies make all the arrangements, but don't expect luxury accommodation.

The border at TABA is a few minutes down the road past the Underwater Observatory. Taba is no-man's land, currently claimed by both Israel and Egypt, and the subject of international arbitration in Geneva. It's a short stretch of beach with a big Israeli-built and Israeli-run five star hotel slap in the middle. For some odd reason the beach here is more 'liberal' than any of the others, with all sorts of exuberant goings on and states of undress.

It's not within the scope of this book to talk about the Sinai in any detail. It is after all Egyptian territory and would require a full section on its own to do it justice; it's over three times the size of Israel. None the less, St Catherine's is a popular excursion for tourists and pilgrims alike, so we feel it's well worth some space.

After you leave the tedious border formalities behind, your journey will carry you some way down the Sinai/Red Sea coast. The scenery here and inland is spectacular and the journey passes quickly with your nose pressed constantly to the window. Look out for CORAL ISLAND with the ruins of its CRUSADER CASTLE; day trips by boat can be taken from Eilat to the island, but, at the time of writing, you could only swim and dive around the island itself and not actually visit the castle. Check with the tourist office when you get to Eilat. Circumstances change with the temperature of relations between Israel and Egypt.

Continuing on the coastal road, look out for the palm-fringed inlet known locally as the FJORD. In spite of the inviting blue water, apparently it's not safe to swim here; the lack of movement of the water has led to stagnation. You'll pass by a series of small towns along the coast, their development as tourist resorts halted when the Egyptians took back the Sinai; there's no evidence currently that the Egyptians have any immediate intentions of carrying on the work. NUWEIBA is the first. An unprepossessing place, it does have a good beach and there are diving and snorkelling facilities. You'll turn inland here for St Catherine's

In the 4th C, Catherine, an Egyptian aristocrat, was tortured and eventually beheaded for her Christian beliefs. Her body was 'transported by angels' to the highest mountain in the Sinai where it was discovered by a monk who had dreamed that he would find a great treasure at the summit. The awesome monastery which commemorates her name is set at the foot of the 7,500 ft high Mount Sinai – perhaps one of the 'holiest' mountains in the world. Millions of Moslems, Christians and Jews believe that this is the place where God handed over the ten commandments to Moses. Don't attempt to climb unless you go early in the morning. It'll take you about two and a half hours, if you are averagely fit, to get to the top, and another hour and a half to get down. You don't want to risk this in the midday desert sun. Take plenty of water. At the summit there is only a small chapel and a breathtaking view.

There is some confusion as to who were the true founders of the monastery, but many believe that it was probably the omnipresent and unflagging churchbuilder, St Helena. The impressive fortifications you see today were added two centuries later by Justinian to help protect the community of Greek Orthodox monks. There is still a community here, although their number has dwindled to fifteen. A tour of the monastery includes a look at the CHAPEL OF THE BURNING BUSH. It is in typical Greek Orthodox style and heavily decorated with lamps, gilt, huge sombre paintings and icons. The monks keep a watchful eye on visitors and photography is forbidden. The monastery boasts one of the finest religious libraries in the world; second only, some scholars claim, to the Vatican library. Unfortunately, this part of the complex is not open to tourists although a good selection of ancient manuscripts and icons is on display outside the entrance to the chapel. After the chapel you will undoubtedly be shown the 'BURNING BUSH'. This will stretch your credibility somewhat – if you look closely at the bush and you know your flora, you'll see it's a raspberry plant. Well, why not?

Before you leave the complex, those with a taste for the macabre should visit the CHARNEL HOUSE. Here you will find the bones of the monks that have died at the monastery over the decades; skulls in one pile, leg bones in another and so on. In the centre of the crypt sits the dressed skeleton of St Stephen. If this all seems rather barbaric just ponder on how difficult it would be to carry out traditional burials in the rock hard ground of the Sinai.

Leaving the Charnel House, avoid the loos unless you're desperate; they are unspeakable. On your way out there's a little SOUVENIR SHOP and at the bottom of the track leading up to the monastery you can buy drinks and snacks and more souvenirs from the Bedouin shacks.

Incidentally, the Bedouins you see here are rather special. They are believed to be descended from Christian slaves, brought here by Justinian to build the monastery/fortress, who became Moslems over the centuries. They are of the *Jebeliah* tribe and are fiercely proud of their special position as guardians and servants of the tiny monastic community.

If you plan to visit the monastery, please remember it is a very holy place. If you aren't dressed in a seemly fashion the Bedouins will give you an all enveloping robe.

WARNING! In Eilat and in the Negev and Sinai Deserts the dry heat can dehydrate you very quickly without your even noticing it. Even if you don't feel thirsty **you must** drink copious quantities of water or other soft drinks. The hospital in Eilat has to cope with hundreds of tourists each year who ignore the warnings. So be warned, keep your head covered, wear good quality sunglasses and when snorkelling or swimming for any length of time, especially in the middle of the day, wear a T-shirt. There are more cases of sunstroke and ruined holidays here than you could possibly imagine.

C·H·A·P·T·E·R·8
General Information

Accommodation

Quite a few of the world's big international chains are represented in Jerusalem, Tel Aviv and Eilat, all of them offering accommodation in the luxury bracket with prices to match. Israel's own hotel group – the Dan – has excellent hotels in all the main areas as well as the magnificent King David in Jerusalem and the only hotel at Caesarea. Israel have cornered the market in luxury hotels in Eilat with the huge and impressive King Solomon's Palace as their flagship.

There are plenty of hotels in the three and four star bracket. They are variable and won't always live up to their grading in international terms. It's best to ask to see the accommodation before you commit yourself, especially outside Jerusalem, Tel Aviv and Eilat, where there is less choice and the facilities, might not meet your expectations.

The Ministry of Tourism accredits some 300 hotels in all categories, and a copy of their listings can be obtained from main tourist offices. The high, mid and low season rates are a little confusing and are different all over the country. Eilat, for instance, being a winter resort generally has lower prices in the summer months. The same applies for the Dead Sea area. Jerusalem is high season during the spring and summer and during all the many and varied religious festivals. Tel Aviv and Haifa follow much the same pattern as Jerusalem.

There are 31 youth hostels operated by the Israel Youth

Hostels Association and you can obtain a list of these from the Israel Government Tourist Office in London.

Both pilgrims and tourists can take advantage of the simple accommodation offered by Christian Hospices. The prices are reasonable but be aware that during peak pilgrimage periods (i.e. Easter and Christmas) there is unlikely to be any room for anyone who hasn't booked well in advance. A list of what is on offer can be obtained from the Israel Government Tourist Office or by writing to the Israel Pilgrimage Committee, PO Box 1018, Jerusalem 91009.

Campers, both those with their own tents and those wishing to rent tents, caravans, cabins, can get information on the sites available from the Israel Camping Union, PO Box 53, Nahariyya 22100. If you decide to pitch your tent outside of official camp-sites, be careful that you've not chosen a stretch of beach near a security zone. You could get a very rude awakening.

You can also stay at Kibbutz guest houses. These are graded into three and four star categories with prices to match. But it's an interesting experience and although they are usually quite separate from the Kibbutz itself, they do offer the chance to talk to kibbutzniks and get an insight into their way of life. You can get more information about Kibbutz guest houses through the Israeli Government Tourist Office or by writing to The Kibbutz Inn and Guest House Association, 90 Ben-Yehuda Street, PO Box 3193, Tel Aviv 63437.

Practical Tips

Unofficial Guides

You'll find them everywhere but particularly in Jerusalem. You will often find one who is genuinely knowledgeable, but most of the time their English will be little more than pidgin, and their knowledge scanty and often wholly inaccurate. They can be very persistent and will attach themselves to you with the least sign of encouragement, and then demand payment after the 'tour' is over. If you do decide to accept an offer, make sure you agree payment beforehand. *You* will have to bring the subject of payment up as most will offer to guide you in such a way that it will appear like a friendly local who just wants to help out.

Jerusalem Taxi Drivers

There are many places the world over where taxi drivers can be a problem. Jerusalem takes the biscuit. You *must insist* that they turn their meters on before you start off. Almost all will try and persuade you that they will give you a 'special price'. They certainly will. It will probably be near double what you would normally pay on the meter. If they refuse to put the meter on, get out of the cab and find another one.

Opening and Closing Times

There are three sabbaths. Friday for the Moslems, Saturday for the Jews and Sunday for the Christians. It can be infuriating if you are short of time and are trying to pack in as much as possible in some sort of logical order, only to arrive somewhere on your tightly planned itinerary to find that it's closed. Plan your itineraries with this in mind and check with the tourist offices and the Christian Information Centre near the Jaffa Gate in Jerusalem, for up-to-date information on what is open and when.

Ben Gurion Airport

There are few travellers who would complain about tight security. After all it is there for their own protection. But Ben Gurion Airport in high season is a chaotic nightmare, and if you are one of the unlucky travellers selected by the security guards for a regular going-over, you are going to have to grit your teeth and hold on to your temper. On the whole tourists, especially those travelling with groups, are not subjected to more than a baggage search, but independent travellers, particularly those who have been in the country for longer than two or three weeks, are often submitted to numerous searches and a real grilling. If you fall into this category make sure you keep receipts from hotels you have stayed in, cars you have hired, etc. and can give a fairly detailed account of where you have been and what you have seen. Also, be warned: if you are carrying gift wrapped packages you will almost certainly have to open them.

CLIMATE

With Israel's varied topography – deserts, mountains, flat coastal plains, and of course the deep Rift Valley – it comes as no surprise to hear that the climate varies just as much. Jerusalem itself is one of those blessed spots of the world, whose summers are cooled by gentle breezes despite constant sunshine, while the winters are mild with just an occasional dusting of snow. Rain falls only in the winter months.

GENERAL INFORMATION

As you drop down from the heights of Jerusalem, into the Rift Valley at Jericho, the summer heat hits you like an open furnace; it would be unbearable were it not so dry. In winter, Jericho and elsewhere in the valley are pleasantly warm, and it never rains.

Galilee too has its own low spot; the Sea of Galilee is 2m below sea level, and in summer this can get very hot. The best time to visit Galilee is in the spring months, before the fierce summer sun has had time to scorch the colour from the hills.

And then there's Eilat, at the southern tip of the country, which has a climate all of its own. Eilat has long been known as a 'winter sun' resort – even in January and February the temperature never drops below 70°F (21°C), and in summer the dry heat is very intense – frequently in the 100s in July and August. Of course it never rains here either.

RELIGIOUS FESTIVALS

As you can probably imagine there are plenty of these! We'll start with the Jewish Holy Days. The Hebrew Calendar, unlike the Gregorian, but in common with the Moslem calender, is subject to the movement of the moon. Therefore the festivals fall on different dates each year. The following is a general guideline as to when they fall and what each festival represents:

Rosh–Hashana and *Yom Kippur* (September/October)

'In the seventh month, on the first day of the month, you shall observe a day of solemn rest, a memorial proclaimed with a blast of trumpets, a holy convocation. You shall do no laborious work; and you shall present an offering by fire to the Lord' (Leviticus 23:23–5).

This is the Jewish equivalent of the New Year and ushers in ten days of penitence – a time for the faithful to repent their sins and to return to God in thanksgiving – leading up to *Yom Kippur* (Day of Atonement). Israel comes to a standstill on *Yom Kippur*, so be warned and make sure you sort out where you are going to eat in advance or make arrangements with your hotel.

Succoth and *Simchat Torah* (September/October)

Hard on the heels of *Yom Kippur* comes *Succoth* or the Feast of Tabernacles. *Succoth* is a kind of harvest festival and some

Israelis build a 'booth' (*Succoth* means booth or tabernacle) in their gardens or on their terraces to remind them of the rude shelters that their forefathers lived in during their years in the wilderness. Here they take their meals, and sometimes even live, with their family, for the week of the festival. The eighth day of *Succoth* is *Simchat Torah* – the Glorification of the Torah. In the synagogues the reading of the Pentateuch, the five books of the Old Testament that make up the Torah (Law), reaches a conclusion with a reading from Deuteronomy and then returns to the beginning, with readings from Genesis symbolising the eternity of God's law. Although this is a religious festival there is much dancing and singing and merrymaking in the streets – particularly in Jerusalem and Tel Aviv.

Hanukkah – Festival of Lights (November/December)

This festival celebrates a victory for freedom of worship. During the 2nd and 3rd C BC the Greeks were increasingly influencing the lives of many Jews. They were fascinated by the Greek customs and the Greek way of life and gradually, as they started to embrace Hellenism wholeheartedly, they began to ignore the observances called for in the Torah. But a minority of Jews clung steadfastly to their religious observances. When Antiochus IV, head of the vast Graeco-Syrian Empire, came to power in the 2nd C BC, he attempted, with considerable support from the Hellenised Jews, to force the minority to give up their religion, making such traditions as circumcision, keeping of the Sabbath and reading of the Old Testament punishable by death. To make things even worse he desecrated the Temple and re-dedicated it to Zeus, encouraging the sacrifice of swine on the Temple's hallowed altars. At this final and intolerable indignity the Jews revolted. After an heroic struggle the Temple was eventually retaken, cleansed and rededicated. When they first entered the Temple they found that the *menorah* (candelabrum) had been so seriously damaged that they were forced to fashion a makeshift *menorah* out of their spears. They also found that there was only enough oil to burn for one day. Miraculously, the oil lasted for eight days and Hanukkah also celebrates this miracle in the lighting of one branch of the *menorah* for each day that it so miraculously burned some 2,200 years ago.

This is a joyful festival – the nearest equivalent to the Christian Christmas, and celebrated by young and old with gifts and special foods.

GENERAL INFORMATION

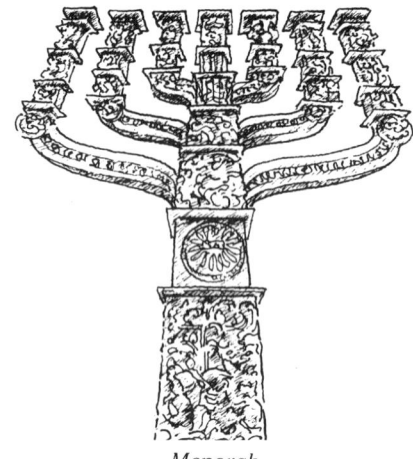

Menorah

Purim – Festival of Lots (February/March)

This religous feast celebrates a story that is recounted in the Book of Esther. In ancient Persia the Chancellor of King Ahasuerus, Haman, had taken a vicious dislike to the Jews living in Persia, and plotted to turn the King against them and destroy them. But the King's wife, Esther, and her uncle, Mordechai, foiled the plot and saved the Jews. The feast gets its name from the lots the wicked Haman cast to decide which day he would choose to destroy the Jews. It is a joyful affair, celebrating the Jews' lucky escape, and is marked with much dancing, feasting and drinking.

Pesach – Passover (March/April)

This is the most important and oldest festival in the Jewish calendar. Long before the Jews went to Egypt, this time of year was marked by a spring festival celebration. But, since the return from Egypt the festival has evolved into a celebration of the Jewish flight from Egyptian slavery. It is very much a family festival. Just before the festival begins Jewish homes are searched and any traces of leavened bread or yeast thrown out. Only unleavened bread is eaten, symbolising the haste with which the Jews left Egypt – there was no time for the bread to be left to rise before being put in the oven. The festivities are marked by special rituals within the home. On the eve of *Pesach, Seder* (the Passover meal) is eaten: on the table there will be bitter herbs representing the bitter lot of the Jews in Egypt as well as a mixture of nuts and apples to represent the mortar used by the Jewish slaves to meet the never ending demands of the Pharaohs for more and more building. The youngest child in the household is required to ask of his father a series of questions designed to prompt a reading of the story of the Egyptian Exodus.

Shavuoth – Festival of Weeks (May/June)

Five days after Passover is *Shavuoth*. Originally a celebration of the wheat harvest, this festival now commemorates the giving of the Law to Moses on Mount Sinai.

Tisha b'Av (July/August)

This is a fast day. It commemorates the destruction of the first and the second Temples.

As far as the Christian community is concerned all the main festivals are celebrated, but with the different sects celebrating the same festival on different dates with the exception of the Catholics and the Protestants.

Moslem holy days follow a lunar calendar as well. The following are the main festivals and holy days:

'id al-Azha – The Great Feast

This feast, held in the twelfth lunar month, commemorates Abraham's near sacrifice of his son – believed by the Arabs to be Ishmael. The feast is celebrated with the sacrifice of a goat, a cow or a camel, and the division of the meat into three parts for the subsequent feast – one for the family, one for relatives and friends, and the third for the poor.

Ramadan

All Moslems fast – abstaining from food, drink and sexual intercourse – during the daylight hours of the entire 29 days of the month of *Ramadan*. This celebrates the period when Mohammed first received his revelations from God. Every evening, after sunset, the end of the day's fast is celebrated with glee and gusto.

'id al-Fitr – Ending of the Fast

This joyous feast is celebrated at the end of *Ramadan*, and can last as long as three days, spent in prayer, feasting, family outings and the giving of alms to the needy.

Muharram – New Year

This is celebrated on the first days of the Islamic first month.

Mawlid an-Nabi – The Prophet's Birthday

Celebrated on the twelfth of the third month, this festival takes the form of prayers, poetry readings and processions.

FOOD AND DRINK

Although most of the Jews in Israel today were born there, a high proportion of their parents were immigrants. Since they came from countries as diverse as the Soviet Union, Poland, Morocco, Yemen, Germany, Hungary, India, etc. it's hardly surprising that there is no definitive Israeli cuisine, but rather a melting pot of culinary ideas that have little more than a general adherence to kosher rules and basic ingredients in common.

What is *Kosher*? The basic principle is that there must be a complete separation between meat and milk. Hence you won't get creamy sauces on your steak in a French-style restaurant nor will you be offered milk in your coffee after a meat meal. You'll get eggs and cheese together but don't expect a slice of cheese on your hamburger. A high proportion of Israeli restaurants and hotels are kosher although you'll find some in Tel Aviv and Eilat and elsewhere that don't adhere to the law of *kashrut*.

What is generally universal, especially in the large hotels, is the famous Israeli breakfast. Its reputation as a gargantuan feast is well deserved. You may well find huge buffet tables groaning with cheeses, salads, pickled fish, eggs, fresh and stewed fruits, cereals, yoghurts, fruit juices and all manner of breads. It's generally a good policy to stoke up on all this, as it's often included in the price, and then snack throughout the day until a main meal in the evening.

You can eat pizza (generally rather poor), pasta, hamburgers. You can make your cholesterol level soar with all manner of creamy cakes and pastries. You can eat rich savoury or sweet stuffed pancakes, chicken soup and *borscht*, stuffed chicken, potato latkes, smoke fish, chili con carne, all manner of salads, ghoulash and just about everything else you can think of. Virtually every type of fruit is available from exotic mangos, persimmons and papayas, through apples, strawberries, dates, oranges and grapes.

There is, of course, the typical middle-eastern food offered by the Arab population; always a good bet from sunset on

Friday to sunset on Saturday in Jerusalem and some of the more conservative Israeli towns, where getting a meal on the Sabbath can be difficult.

You'll find *humus*, a paste made from ground chickpeas and olive oil, and *tahina*, ground sesame seeds with oil, of varying quality served everywhere. Delicious varieties of garlicky eggplant salad and purée are popular staples. Look out for stuffed peppers, tomatoes and aubergines. There are plenty of kebab-style meats; lamb, beef, liver, chicken and turkey, no pork though; it is forbidden to both Moslems and Jews. Fish and shellfish can be found; the latter is also forbidden to Jews but you can buy it for a price. You can round the whole feast off with a variety of sticky honey and pistachio sweetmeats, guaranteed to satisfy even the most incurably sweet tooth. By the way, don't judge Arab eateries by their lack of glossy presentation. They may look like an unprepossessing levantine version of a transport café, but the food is often first class and reasonably priced.

There is one food that seems to cross all divides – the ubiquitous *felafel*. Arabs eat it, Israelis eat it – the well-to-do and the not-so-well-to-do – nuns and priests eat it and tourists, especially the budget variety, fall upon it with glee! It's cheap, quite healthy for a 'fast food' and when it's good (crisp, fresh salad, freshly cooked ground chickpea balls, thick sesame or chilli sauce) it's delicious. *Felafel* is served in a pouch of pitta bread. Go easy with the sauce. The chilli variety varies tremendously in its fiery qualities and if you put too much on, the bottom falls out of the pouch when you take your first awkward bite.

Fresh juices are one of the great joys in Israel. You can buy freshly squeezed citrus and vegetable juices everywhere, as well as all the usual thirst quenchers such as coke, orangeade, etc. The water is supposedly safe to drink, but it's advisable not to give your stomach too much of a jolt, so stick to bottled water, available everywhere. Both larger style beer and 'dark' beer is sold, and Israeli wines are really quite good, ranging through all tastes from very dry to sweet and sticky. Note that in some of the smaller Arab restaurants you won't be able to buy alcohol.

KIBBUTZIM AND MOSHAVIM

'To everyone according to his needs and from everyone according to his abilities.'

In the late 19th C pogroms in Russia provoked a wave of Jewish immigration to Palestine. To start with, these new arrivals settled in villages known as *moshavot,* set up and funded to a great extent by Edmund de Rothschild. At the turn of the century the pogroms in Russia became even more brutal and a second wave of Jewish immigrants arrived. These immigrants were fired with a revolutionary spirit, firm in the belief that socialism was the only way forward, and determined to apply their ideals to reclaiming the land of Palestine and building an egalitarian society firmly rooted in the soil of their forefathers. Some settled in the suburbs of Jaffa, on the land that was eventually to become Tel Aviv, but many formed themselves into collectives (Kibbutzim) and settled down to farm land purchased for them by the Jewish National Fund.

The problems they faced were huge. Many had no experience whatsoever of agriculture. Resources were scarce and the land they were able to settle on was often barren and lifeless, or even malarial swamp. All of them were subject to frequent Arab raids.

The Kibbutz movement has undergone a considerable evolution since its beginning in the early 20th C. Today many Kibbutzim have diversified into manufacturing, tourism and catering, to supplement their traditional agricultural base. Individual members will usually own their personal possessions – clothes, radios, televisions, etc. – and children will now often live with their parents rather than being brought up by experts in a part of the Kibbutz specially set aside for them. But the basic principles are essentially the same. The Kibbutz is a secular community in which everything is communally administered and owned. The members of Kibbutzim have all their needs – housing, food, education, health – taken care of, but are expected to work in the community for free. The Kibbutz is completely democratic. There is complete social and economic equality and there are weekly meetings for all the community to take democratic decisions on everything that affects Kibbutz life.

Kibbutzniks represent only about 3 per cent of all Israelis and their numbers are diminishing. But the settlements make a huge contribution to the Israeli economy and produce over a third of all the food in the country. They are also remarkably influential for such a small group, with around 10 per cent of members of the Israeli Parliament coming from their ranks. They are in the forefront of the development of high technology in the country and are in demand all over the Third World for their knowledge and expertise in the field of agriculture.

In their early years, many of Israel's great leaders were committed Kibbutzniks; from their ranks came women and men who formed the élite of Israel's fighting force in the years of conflict with the Arabs. This is an organisation whose incredible determination has wrought an agricultural miracle in a barren land and who seem set to continue to make a contribution to their country wholly out of proportion to their size for many years to come.

Moshav-Shitufi is a variation on the same theme. Essentially each family runs its own household but ownership of the land and the buildings is communal, and work is shared by the community. *Moshavim* are agricultural villages that share the cost of farming equipment and marketing their produce, but the members own their own land and the houses they live in.

Language

Since the Babylonians led the Jews into captivity, and later the Romans banished them from their beloved Jerusalem, the Jewish people have spread through almost every land in the world, from Europe to the Americas, throughout the Soviet Union, Africa, India and Australasia – there was even a large community of Jews in China. Over the centuries they assimilated much of the culture of the lands where they lived.

In the last 200 years, Jews have 'returned' from almost all of these lands, bringing diverse traditions and languages with them. At first this was an administrative nightmare for the new state of Israel, but gradually this colourful Babel has been replaced with the dream of the early Zionists – a new Hebrew. 100 years ago, Hebrew did not exist as a colloquial language; it was an ancient and holy tongue reserved for the synagogue and the *yeshiva*. Many orthodox Jews will not speak the modern Hebrew, as they consider it a defilement of the holy language of the Bible. Of course the language has been adapted for the demands of the 20th C, with such borrowings as *tractor, telefon, sigara.* Today this adaptation of ancient Hebrew is spoken by over 8 million people.

Hebrew is the official language of Israel, but of course a large proportion of the inhabitants speak Arabic. The two languages are 'brothers' in the Semitic family of languages, just as the two peoples are both Semitic (descended from Shem, the son of Noah). Thus if you can speak one of these languages, you're a long way towards being able to get by in the other.

But the visitor to Israel who speaks neither Arabic nor Hebrew will have no trouble in being understood, or finding people to talk to; English is commonly spoken amongst the young, and most of the immigrants welcome any opportunity to speak the language of their native country.

Shopping

If you come back from Jerusalem without a souvenir, then the wily merchants of the Old City *souk* must be losing their touch after hundreds of years of refined expertise at parting tourists from their shekels! Here you will find semi-precious stones, leather bags, shoes, slippers and jackets, embroidered cotton shirts and skirts, hand-blown glass, carved wooden boxes inlaid with mother-of-pearl, oriental carpets and all manner of religious figures and scenes carved out of olive wood, with a few 'home sweet home' plaques thrown in for good measure. A great proportion is junk but there are good buys to be found. Take your time and compare prices. You must haggle and don't be pressurised to buy in the first shop. When you do make up your mind, assume a disinterested stance, decide on the price you want to pay, offer about 20 per cent less and don't go any higher than your original decision. Some shopkeepers just won't budge. If you don't think the item's worth it, move on. You're quite likely to find the identical thing round the next corner.

There are of course plenty of other opportunities to shop, apart from Jerusalem's colourful bazaar. Look out for shops with the sign 'Listed by the Ministry of Tourism'. Here the prices won't be particularly low, bargaining is not the order of the day, but the goods on offer – sculptures, embroidery, pottery, religious artefacts – will be of a high quality.

Israel is also a good place to buy diamonds; especially in Haifa and Netanya. Surprisingly enough, you'll also find good furs.

Transport

Israel is a most conveniently compact country for the tourist. From Jerusalem to the Sea of Galilee is only a couple of hours in a bus or car – and that's a journey effectively from the centre of the country to the very north. Distances between major towns and sites of interest are surprisingly short.

The whole country is well served by the Israeli bus company, 'EGGED'. They run regular buses all over the country from Jerusalem's West Bus Station, as well as being the major tour operator. Their buses are well maintained, comfortable and often air-conditioned in the summer.

From the East Bus Station in Jerusalem, run the Arab buses.

GENERAL INFORMATION

These are mostly battered Mercedes serving the West Bank. These buses are not air-conditioned, and they're not as comfortable as the Egged buses, but it's a lively and jolly way to travel – and very much cheaper too.

There are not many railways in Israel; there's a fine scenic railway between Jerusalem and Tel Aviv, and that connects to a line that runs the length of the coast, but trains are slow and irregular, and nobody uses them. The buses are much more efficient. The Jerusalem train is a most enjoyable ride though, if you're not in a hurry.

Hitch-hiking is fairly easy in Israel, although the issue is always complicated by dozens of soldiers at every junction; they always get priority.

Given the difficulty of timing one's arrival at sites to coincide with their opening times, and the various sabbaths, CAR-HIRE is the best way to get around if you can stretch to it. The roads throughout the country are good, and this way you can please yourself. All the major towns have dozens of car-hire companies; the local ones tend to be cheaper.

Israel's tiny size doesn't really justify an extensive internal air network, but there is one domestic airline – 'Arkia'. Arkia flies from Jerusalem, Tel Aviv and Haifa to Eilat.

B·I·B·L·I·O·G·R·A·P·H·Y

This list is of course a drop in the ocean, given the enormous number of books that have been written on the Holy Land and all that has happened there. So this is just a random selection from some of the books that may increase the pleasure of your visit.

Antony Bridge, *The Crusades.* The best book on the subject I have read; knowledgeably written, giving all the details and background. Essential for an understanding of this cataclysmic episode of history.

Malcolm Billings, *The Cross and the Crescent.* Good well researched, wide period, easy, illustrated.

Stephen Runciman, *The Crusades.* The definitive work in 3 volumes.

Miron Grindea (ed.), *Jerusalem; the Holy City in Literature* (London: Kahn and Averill, 1968). An inspiring survey of the work of the many poets and writers inspired by Jerusalem – adds colour and vitality; also has an excellent history.

Evelyn Waugh, *Helena* (London: Chapman and Hall, 1960). A novel constructed around St Helena, the mother of Emperor Constantine, and discoverer of the True Cross. Elegant, readable, colourful and informative.

BIBLIOGRAPHY

George Turner, *Historical Geography of the Holy Land* (Michigan: Baker, 1983). Historical and geographical overview of the land and the peoples – profusely illustrated – useful but a little dull.

Hollis/Brownrigg, *Holy Places* (New York : Praeger, 1969). An excellent potted history of Jerusalem, the Holy Land and the various casts of characters, plus well informed historical and archaeological surveys of all the important monuments, sites and places. A few hours with your nose stuck in this well illustrated book will make a journey to Israel much more rewarding.

H.V. Morton, *In the Steps of the Master.* You can do no better than to share your journey to Israel with this great traveller. History, geography, religion and general observations written with wit and understanding.

Paul Johnson, *History of the Jews.* Hard going for casual holiday reading, but for an understanding of the Jews and the trials that have beset them, this is second to none.

Colin Thubron, *Jerusalem* (London: Century Hutchinson, 1986). The musings of a literate and urbane observer on the Holy City and its history. A stimulating companion.

A.W. Kinglake, *Eothen* (London: Century Hutchinson). Witty account of a journey through the near east by a 17th C traveller.

Rev J.E. Hanauer, *Folk-Lore of the Holy Land, Moslem, Christian and Jewish* (London: Sheldon Press, 1907). Words fail me in praising this book: bringing the place alive in a mystical sort of a way, it peoples the places you pass with spirits, *djinns,* goblins, wise peasants, interwoven with more familiar characters, thinly disguised by the purveyors of the tales. Your visit to the Holy Land would be the poorer without it.

Josephus, *The Jewish Wars.* Fairly dry old stuff, but it's good for an insight into this enigmatic character and the turbulent world of Roman Palestine.

John Drane, *The Old Testament Story.* (London: Lion Publishing, 1983). A companion to the Old Testament, smooths the way and brings to life the Bible stories. As a travelling companion in the Holy Land it is also invaluable as it explains much that happened, where and why. Highly recommended, erudite, thought-provoking and enlightening.

Solomon Nigosian, *Islam, the Way of Submission* (London: Crucible, 1987). A fine and simple exposition of the basic elements of Islam, written for those who are neither scholars nor theologians. Contributes greatly to an understanding of the subject.

Solomon Nigosian, *Judaism, The Way of Holiness* (London: Crucible, 1986). This does for Judaism what *The Way of Submission* does for Islam – highly recommended.

Access in Israel. This is a very useful little guide for the disabled planning to visit the Holy Land – available from Pauline Hephaistos Survey Projects, 39 Bradley Gardens, London W 13.

Index

Note: Main references are in **bold** type. Places of interest in Jerusalem are listed as sub-entries under JERUSALEM.

Abraham 6,7
Acre (Akko) **105**
Accommodation 189
Aelia Capitolina 14
Alexander the Great 10, 30
Aliyah, first 17
Al Jazzar Mosque 107
Allenby, General 18, 35, 38
Antiochus Epiphanes 11, 30
Assyrian Conquest 9
Arad **172**
Ark of the Covenant 8, 30
Ashkelon **126**
Avdat **189**

Babylon 10, 30
Baldwin 1 33
Balfour Declaration 18
Banyas **146**
Bar Kochba 14, 31
Bar'am **150**
Basilica of the Nativity 90
Beersheba **172**
Begin, Menachim 20, 23, 24
Ben Gurion 19, 174
Belvoir Crusader Castle **162**
Beth Hatefutsoth 124
Bethlehem **90**
Bet She'an **163**
Bet Shearim **161**
Burning Bush 188
British Mandate 18

Camp David 23, 181
Cana **158**
Capernaum **134**
Castle of Montfort 164
Cave of Elijah 110
Caeserea **113**
Churchill 19
Church of the Annunciation 152
Church of the Beatitudes 135
Church of St Catherine 92
Church of Jesus the Adolescent 157
Church of St Joseph 156

Church of Mary Magdalene 34
Church of St Peter 125
Church of the Redeemer 34
Climate 191
Constantine 14, 22
Convent of the Franciscan Sisters of Mary 157
Coral Beach 182, 187
Coral Island 187
Crusades 15, 33, 47, 105, 106, 115
Crusader City 107
Cyrus 10

Dan **145**
Dayan, General Moshe 22
Dead Sea **165**
Dead Sea Scrolls 166
Diaspora 10
Drink 196
Druze 111, 147

Ein Avdat **175**
Ein Bokek **171**
Ein Gedi **167**
En Gev **137**
En Hod **112**
En Qilt 97
Eilat **179**

First Revolt 13
Food 196

Galilee **129**
Gamla **139**
Golan Heights **137**
Great Mosque (Jamia el Kabir) 101
Great Synagogue 120
Grotto of the Nativity 91

Ha'Aretz Museum 123
Habima Theatre 122
Hadrian 14
Haganah 20, 35, 118, 121
Haganah Museum 121
Haifa **108**
Hai Bar Nature Reserve 184
Hammat Gader**140**

Haram el Khalil 95
Hasmonean Dynasty 12, 30
Hazor **143**
Hebron **94**
Helena Rubenstein Pavilion 122
Hellenism 11
Herodian 93
Herod's Winter Palace 99
Herzliya 117
History **5**
Holy Sepulchre 32
House of Simon the Tanner 126
Horns of Hattin 16, 159
Hula Valley **144**
Hurshat Tal 145

Independence Hall 122
Inn of the Good Samaritan 97
Islam 15, 32, 47
Irgun 20

Jaffa 117,**124**
Jericho **99**
Jeroboam 9
Joshua 7
JERUSALEM 27
 Absalom's Tomb 79
 Al Aqsa **57**
 Antonia Fortress 43, 60
 Armenian Catholic Church 44
 Armenian Quarter **65**
 Batei Mahse (Shelter House Square) 64
 Bazaar 53
 Bethany **74**
 Biblical Zoo 83
 Broad Wall 62
 Burnt House 62
 Calvary 46, 49
 Cardo 62
 Cathedral of St George 77
 Cathedral of St James 65, 66
 Cave of Gethsamene 74
 Cenacle 67, 68
 Chagall Windows 86

207

INDEX

Chapel of the Ascension 69
Chapel of Condemnation 43
Chapel of Flagellation 43
Chamber of the Holocaust 68
Christian Quarter **40**
Citadel of David 38
City of David **80**
Church of All Nations 72
Church of the Assumption 72
Church and Convent of the Ascension 69
Church of the Dormition 67
Church of the Holy Face of Veronica 44
Church of John the Baptist 86
Church of St John 53
Church of Mary Magdalene 70
Church of Mary and Martha 75
Church of Peter in Galicantu 67
Church of the Redeemer 53
Church of the Visitation 86
Convent of the Sisters of Sion 43
Damascus Gate 36
David's Tomb 67
Deir Es Sultan 52
Dome of the Ascension 57
Dome of the Chain 57
Dome of the Rock 55
Dominus Flevit 70
Dung Gate 39
East Jerusalem **76**
Ecce Homo Arch 43
Ein Kerem **85**
Et Tur 68
Gates **36**
Garden Tomb 77
Gethsemane 71
Golden Gate 40, 70
Greek Orthodox Partriarchate 53
Gihon Spring 79
Hadassah Hospital 86
Haram es Sharif 53
Hebrew University 75
Hezekiah's Tunnel **79**
History 29
Holy Land Hotel Model **85**
Holy Sepulchre 41, **44**

House of Simon the Leper 75
Hurva 63
Hurva Synagogue 63
Islamic Museum **58**
Israel Museum **83**
Jaffa Gate 37
Jewish Cemetry 70
Jewish Quarter **60**
Kidron Valley **78**, 70
King David Hotel **81**
Knesset **83**
Lithostratos 43
Madaba Map 62
Mea She'arim 82
Moneychangers 37
Mount of Olives **68**
Mount Scopus **75**
Mount Zion 67
Moslem Quarter **53**
Mosque of Omar **58**
Muristan 53
Nea Church 62, 64
Ninety Nine Bus 62, 64
Old Yishuv Court Museum 61
Partition 35
Parking 87
Pater Noster Church 69
Pool of Bethesda 42
Pool of Siloam 79, 80
Prison of Christ 43
Ramban Synagogue 63
Rockefeller Museum 76
Roman Courtyard 36
Rothschild House 64
Silwan 78
Sephardic Synagogues 63
St Mary's Well 86
St Anne's Church 42
Stations of the Cross
  Station I & II 43
  Stations III–IX 44
  Stations X–XIV 49
Struthion Pool 43
Son et Lumière 39
St Stephen's (Lion) Gate 40, 41
Temple **58**
Temple Mount 53, 54
Tomb of the Kings 76
Tomb of Lazarus 74
Tombs of the Prophets 70
Tomb of the Virgin Mary 72
Tourist Offices 86
Tourjeman Post Museum 78
Via Dolorosa 40, **41**
Walls **36**
Western Wall **58**

Warren's Shaft **80**
West Jerusalem **81**
Walking Tours 87
Yad Vashem **84**
Yemin Moshe **81**
YMCA 81
Jesus 13, 31
Jewish Brigade 19
Jordan Valley **161**
Joshua 7

Khorazin **136**
Kibbutzim 197
King David 8, 29
King Hezekiah 9
King Saul 8

Language 199
Lebanon 23
Lower Galilee **151**

Maccabean Revolt 11
Magdala 133
Mamelukes 16, 33
Mann Auditorium 122
Masada **168**
Megiddo **160**
Milk Grotto 92
Mitzpe Ramon **176**
Mohammed 15, 32
Mohammed Ali 34
Monastery of Mar Saba 98
Monastery of John the Baptist 100
Montfort **104**
Moshavim 197
Montefiore, Sir Moses 35
Moses 6, 7
Mount of the Beatitudes 135
Mount Carmel **108**
Mount Gerizim 101
Mount Hermon **148**
Mount Meron 150
Mount Tabor **159**
Museum of the Jewish Diaspora 124

Nablus (Shechem) **100**
Nahariya **104**
Nasser 22
Nazareth **151**
Netanya **116**
Negev (Northern & Central) **165**
Negev (Southern) **179**, 184
Neve Tzedek 119
Neve Zohar **171**
Nimrod Castle **147**

Oak of Mamre 96
Omar 15, 32
Ottomans 16, 34, 48

208

INDEX

Palace of Hisham 99
Palestinian Refugees 21
Palestinian Liberation
  Organisation 23
Partition Vote 20
Peres, Shimon 24
Persian Empire 10, 14
Philistines 7
Pillars of Amram 186
Plain of Sharon 113
Pompey 12, 30
Pontius Pilate 13
Practical Tips 190

Qazrin **138**
Qumran **166**

Ramallah 100
Rehoboam 9
Religious Festivals 192
River Jordan 192
Romans 12, 30
Roman City of Sebastia 102
Rosh Haniqra **103**, 108
Rosh Pinna **142**
Russian Orthodox Church 9

Sadat 23
Saladin 16, 33, 47
Samaritans 9
Saul 8
Sde Boker 174

Sea of Galilee **129**, 133
Sebastia 102
Selim 1 16
Seljuk Turks 15
Sennacherib 9
Septuagint 11
Shamir, Yitzak 24
Shalom Mayer Tower 119
Shepherds Fields 93
Shrine of Bab 109
Shrine of the Book 83
Shuq Ha' Carmel 120
Sinai 179, **186**
Sinai Campaign 22
Six Day War 22, 89
Sodom 171
Society for the Protection
  of Nature 98
Solomon 8, 30
Solomon's Pools **96**
State of Israel 21
St George's Monastery 98
Suez Crisis 22, 180
Suleyman the Magnificent
  16, 34
Sykes Picot Agreement 18
Szfat (Safed) **148**

Taba 186
Tabgha 133
Tel Aviv **117**
Tel of Ancient Jericho 100

Tel Aviv Museum 122
Tel Es Sultan 99
Tiberius **131**
Timna Valley 185
Tomb of Jethro 133
Tomb of Maimonides 132
Tombs of Rabbi Shimon
  and Rabbi Eleazar 150
Tombs of Rabbi Hillel and
  Shammai 150
Transport 200
Tribes of Israel 6
True Cross 14, 32, 46

Underwater Observatory
  182

Wad Hamam 133
Wadi Qilt 98
War of Independence 21,
  89
Well of Jacob 102
West Bank **89**
Wilderness of Judea **96**

Yemenite Quarter (Tel Aviv)
  120
Yom Kippur War 23

Zionism 18
Zippori **157**